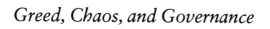

Greed, Chaos, and Governance

An elaboration and extension of themes developed in the
Rosenthal Lectures at Northwestern University Law School.

JERRY L. MASHAW

Greed, Chaos, and Governance

USING PUBLIC CHOICE TO IMPROVE PUBLIC LAW

Yale University Press
New Haven and London

Set in Sabon type by Keystone Typesetting, Inc., Orwigsburg, Pennsylvania.
Printed in the United States of America by BookCrafters, Inc., Chelsea, Michigan.

Mashaw, Jerry L.
    Greed, chaos, and governance : using public choice to improve
public law / Jerry L. Mashaw.
        p. cm.
    Includes bibliographical references and index.
    ISBN 0-300-06677-5 (cloth : alk. paper)
            0-300-07870-6 (pbk. : alk. paper)
        1. Legislation — United States.   2. Administrative procedure —
United States.   3. Social choice.   I. Title.
KF4930.M37   1997
342.73'066 — dc20
[347.30266]   96-22827
                    CIP

A catalogue record for this book is available from the British Library.

The paper in this book meets the guidelines for permanence and durability of the Committee on Production Guidelines for Book Longevity of the Council on Library Resources.

10 9 8 7 6 5 4 3 2

Contents

Preface

This book has had an absurdly long gestation. My interest in public choice ideas is traceable directly to James M. Buchanan and Gordon Tullock's classic, *The Calculus of Consent,* required reading at Henry Manne's first law and economics "summer camp for law professors" at Rochester in 1971. This led me to become a founding member of Pegasus, a public choice study group composed of lawyers and economists from the University of Virginia and Virginia Polytechnic Institute — Buchanan and Tullock among them. Our monthly meetings in the early 1970s alternated between Charlottesville and Blacksburg. Papers were read. Wine was drunk. Argument lasted deep into the night.

Similar fermentation was going on elsewhere. The few, lone public choice scholars of the late 1950s and 1960s were, by the end of the 1970s, a major intellectual movement with a national academic society and a respected journal. As I remember them, Public Choice Society meetings of that era had a slightly "mad scientist" quality. Bleary-eyed young practitioners were proving theorems on hotel scratchpads, while completed papers touted new public choice "results," presumptively applicable to virtually any collective human activity. Public choice's imperialistic claims were rewarded. The general importance of public choice ideas to the social sciences would soon be signaled by William Rikers's ascendancy to the presidency of the American Political

Science Association. Nobel Prizes in economics for George Stigler and James Buchanan were not far behind.

Legal academics, particularly those in and around law and economics, were excited by these ideas. But public choice proved difficult to domesticate. To be sure, some academic lawyers quickly applied the new learning to "explain" everything from the prosecutorial policies of the Federal Trade Commission to the reasons for the creation of an independent judiciary. But to most of us, the parsimonious constructs of the public choice fraternity seemed simultaneously tantalizing and treacherous. Tantalizing because of the prospect for saying something hard-edged about the dynamics of public institutions and public policy. Treacherous because the world looked so much more complex and various than the culturally and institutionally anemic actors that populated the public choice universe.

After a decade's dabbling at the edges of public choice and public law, I remained fascinated with the field. But I was equally frustrated by my inability to synthesize public choice ideas into usable knowledge at the level of either legal interpretation or institutional design. I was galvanized, nevertheless, to make a frontal attack on the problem by receipt of the Northwestern University Law School's invitation to give the Rosenthal Lectures in the winter of 1986. I proposed to provide that demanding audience with no less than an account of the meaning of public choice for public law, and, in accordance with the terms of the invitation, to convert the lectures into a book.

Although it has taken another decade to complete the project, the ideas developed and argued on those chilly days in Chicago in February 1986 still animate the chapters that follow. While I have broadened the inquiry, and I trust deepened it as well, my purpose has not changed, The attempt is to claim and hold an elusive middle ground between public choice theory's champions and its detractors — to demonstrate in a series of public law settings both the insights that spring from taking public choice ideas seriously and the necessity for maintaining a critical distance from theoretical enthusiasms that sometimes lack internal coherence, not to mention empirical support.

An intellectual odyssey of this length obviously is not taken alone. Indeed, by this point my debts to those who have stimulated, criticized, and sustained my efforts cannot all be recalled, much less acknowledged. Beyond the catalytic contribution of the Rosenthal lectureship, several crucial influences must be mentioned. My sometime colleague, and longtime friend, Warren Schwartz was there at the beginning and has nagged, cajoled, and inspired me ever since. Numerous colleagues at Yale — Bruce Ackerman, Akhil Amar, Jules Coleman, Michael Graetz, Al Klevorick, and Ted Marmor — have read and commented on various versions of these chapters. More important, they have provided a group of knowledgeable interlocutors for discussions of points both great and small.

Finally, I owe a major intellectual debt to a cadre of public choice scholars who have grappled in recent years with many of the same issues that I explore here — sometimes to opposite effect. Thinkers such as Matthew McCubbins, Roger Noll, Barry Weingast (McNollgast), John Ferejohn, Mo Fiorina, and Ken Shepsle have been a constant source of inspiration and provocation. As I hope to convince you in the pages that follow, they are about half right.

My thanks, once again, to my assistant, Patricia Page. Patti has typed so many versions of these pages that she can probably recite whole chapters from memory.

The Challenge of Positive Political Theory

Commenting on his portrait of Gertrude Stein, Pablo Picasso is reported to have said: "Everybody thinks she is not at all like her picture, but never mind, in the end she will manage to look just like it."

Picasso's statement may have been a product of his famous ego, but it contains an important insight. We are often the captives of our pictures of the world, and in the end, if the world does not look *just* like them, their influence on our perceptions is nevertheless profound.

The pictures that I want to discuss are not graphic representations but theories: verbal descriptions of how our political world is organized and how it works. They give us mental images of what to look for in political life and what to expect from it, in much the same way that Picasso's portrait leads us to expect, and perhaps to find, that Stein looks a certain way. My argument goes somewhat further than Picasso's, however. I want to argue that the influence of pictures or themes is not just on what we expect and what we see, but also on what we demand or affirm. Pictures lead not only to predictions but also to principles. Our vision of what *is* guides our approach to what *ought* to be.

This connection between "ises" and "oughts," between the "positive" or "descriptive" and the "normative" or "preferred," is both familiar and problematic. It is as familiar as the ancient fable of the fox and the "sour" grapes. If an end is unachievable, or believed to be beyond our reach, we tend to rationalize our disappointment by altering our view of its desirability. It is as contemporary as the hyperbolic charge by a former Bush administration official that "national health insurance would combine the frugality of military procurement with the empathy of an IRS audit." In short, any attempt to have what many Americans claim that they want would demonstrate that they do not actually want it. The general lesson from these old and recent examples seems clear. Our positive beliefs about what is, powerfully constrain and shape our normative beliefs about what is good or desirable.

Yet this familiar connection between ises and oughts is also problematic. Indeed, the use of reason to understand the nature of the world and to predict the likely effects of either individual or collective action is often sharply contrasted with the expression of either ethical commitments or personal preferences. On this view, positive theory is related to normative discourse in only instrumental terms. The definition of ends — what is good or what is right — comes first. An understanding of current reality and of the dynamics of change, that is, positive theory, then supplies only strategies for achieving the ends that have been specified. From this perspective tastes are rationally inexplicable ("chacun à son goût") and morality is a matter of faith. Neither is the domain of positive theory.

The contrast between these opposing views need not be quite so stark. The instrumental vision of positive theory may only represent a claim that scientific rationality should be the servant of some conception of the good or the right, not that there is no taste-shaping effect from our beliefs about the real or the possible. Such a position might be epitomized by the ironic comment, sometimes attributed to Frank Knight, "As an economist I cannot tell you whether you should adopt food price controls. I can tell you that, if you do, you should expect widespread hunger."

At one level, of course, Knight's pungent remark is a purely instrumental statement about institutional design. We may desperately want to lower food prices. But Knight reminds us that getting there from here may require a more circuitous route than direct regulation, that is, if we want to avoid some pretty harsh side effects. But the taste-shaping effect of the remark goes beyond the purely instrumental. In associating price controls with drastic shortages, Knight's aphorism may persuade us to be skeptical of any attempt by government to meddle with market prices. It might even cause us to associate all regulation of markets with the prospect of disaster. It is but a short hop from here to distrust of all government regulation and to an antigovernmental ideology that condemns any collective attempt to restrict individual economic activity however it might be implemented. On this view, reducing the size and scope of governmental action rapidly becomes an end in itself. Individual action becomes "good," governmental initiative "bad."

It is hardly likely, of course, that one jibe at price controls by an economics professor little known outside of elite academic circles will have a general taste-shaping effect. Nor would a quick glance at Picasso's portrait of Stein much influence our visions of its subject. Picasso's point, and mine, has to do with repeated exposure to representations or ideas, with a process of habituation or acculturation that is as subtle as it is profound.

Something like what I have in mind might emerge from another economically oriented example. For the economist, "economic man" is little more than a calculating machine attempting to become better off through rational consumer or producer behavior. This is, of course, merely a simplifying assumption. The economist claims to be able to predict market outcomes by assuming that people behave as if they were purely rational calculators of their own gains and losses from alternative courses of action. Yet, on first (and sometimes prolonged) exposure, many find the fundamental behavioral assumptions of micro-economics morally repugnant. This reaction, and it is often a strong one, seems to be based both on guilt and on fear. Guilt that we sometimes do behave as economic monsters, and fear that thinking about human behavior *as if* motivated solely by "rational self-interest" will have moral and political consequences. The unintentional side effect of micro-economic analysis may not only be to help us to rationalize our self-regard, but to suggest that the steely-eyed calculation of personal gains and losses is the decisional posture that we *should* cultivate in ourselves. To do otherwise is to be irrational — perhaps a dupe. To think like economic man is not only to lose one's guilt about selfish behavior, but to aspire to a life of pure self-interested calculation. Or so we may fear.

Perhaps enough has been said to get agreement on a weak form of my argument: it seems likely that there is at least some influence of facts or presumed facts on political values. But this brief exploration also suggests that the relationship between our ises and oughts is neither necessary nor straightforward.

One way of better understanding this claim is to explore some examples of how we have failed to keep our facts and values separate in American political life. Indeed, I am about to argue that the way we, as citizens, articulate and understand our most cherished political ideal, democratic governance, has been a product largely of our changing understandings of how human beings *do* behave within particular institutional settings, not changing ideas of the moral underpinnings of democracy itself. For this purpose we need to look at only two formative eras of American democratic ideology, the founding of the Republic and the Progressive–New Deal period. Our quest is to understand how the very idea of democracy has been shaped by the differing "political science" of each period. We will then fast-forward again to consider what I take to be the dominant vision of political life in late twentieth-century America. I characterize this vision, somewhat hyperbolically, as a world of greed and chaos, of private self-interest and public incoherence. It is this vision that provides the primary challenge for today's designers of public institutions. For it is a vision that makes all public action deeply suspect.

My basic claim is that this vision is already shaping our public life, both what we do and what we think to be right and good. Moreover, because the political values we affirm are powerfully tied to what we believe to be true about human nature and the dynamics of public institutions, a simple rejection of contemporary individualistic or market values in favor of alternative normative commitments, like equality or community, is not readily available to us. If we would reform or renew our democratic faith, we need a better understanding of what it is reasonable to expect from institutions of governance and how we might design them. The claim of positive political theory, or what is sometimes called "public choice theory," must be confronted on its own terms, its claim to truthful description, if it is to take its appropriate place in shaping our values and in helping us to better design our public institutions.

Federalist and New Deal Political Science

THE FEDERALISTS

One widely accepted view of our constitutional history is that the scheme of national government adopted in 1787 abandoned both the communal values of colonial America and the radical democratic values of the American Revolution in favor of institutions featuring the protection of propertied interests and rule by a "natural aristocracy." To read Madison's great statement of Federalist political science in *Federalist* 10[1] is to see the force of this interpretation, if not necessarily the conspiratorial connotations that some of its adherents find persuasive. For in *Federalist* 10 popular democracy's tendencies to instability, oppression, and ineffectualness are set forth as the major problems to be solved when constructing a government that can and will protect individual rights.

The structure of Madison's analysis, you may recall, is first to identify in human nature the causes of popular democracy's malaise and then to design a governmental scheme that avoids these pitfalls, while presumably retaining what is feasible of the democratic ideal. In Madison's account of popular democracy, the force of an inevitable factionalism, which leads to majoritarian tyranny, injustice, and the collapse of democratic legitimacy, would be reduced by the nation's large size, by the use of representative assemblies, and by internal checks and balances within the government. In short, the new American democracy would eschew what many thought democracy to be about—

local autonomy, direct citizen participation, and the sovereignty of popular majorities.

Just how much of the idea of popular democracy was being sacrificed by the Federalists' stratagems for inducing stability was, of course, the theme of many an anti-Federalist pamphlet. *Federalist* 10 responds to the charge that the Constitution is antidemocratic in two different ways, both of which rely on the positive theoretical presuppositions of Federalist political science. First, there is a basic argument from feasibility. Given the tendency of popular political action to degenerate into factional politics, a greater degree of either popular control or state sovereignty would be dysfunctional. The new government would be oppressive, ineffectual, or both. Second, there runs through the *Federalist* 10 analysis a subtle but clear difference between Federalist and anti-Federalist normative commitments — a difference which both reinforces and is reinforced by Federalist positive theory. Democratic self-determination emerges from Madison's analysis as only an instrumental end. The fundamental purpose of government is justice, the preservation of rights. If popular democracy tends toward oppression, ineffectualness, and instability, it is inadequate to the protection of rights and should be rejected.

To see how this view of the value of popular democracy was intimately related to the Federalist view of human nature, we need but contrast the views of the prominent anti-Federalists. For the anti-Federalists imagined a popular democracy that both teaches and is enriched by civic virtue. In this vision, it is through direct participation in governance that citizens achieve their highest ends. Nor is democratic participation here merely instrumental to the attainment of a separate good — civic virtue. The two goals are inseparable. Civic virtue is as necessary to democratic participation as democratic participation is to civic virtue. The anti-Federalists, therefore, charge (and there is much truth to the claim) that Federalists' fears about the likely outcomes of strong democracy have caused them to displace the only goal that makes self-government worth having — the cultivation of civic virtue in the citizenry. The Federalists' understanding of the possibilities of democratic self-rule have caused them to forget why the revolution was fought.

Moreover, having rejected what we might call "expressive democracy" in favor of "protective republicanism," the Federalists go further. *Federalist* 10 argues that the *permanent* interests of the community can only be *expressed* through representative assemblies composed of a natural aristocracy of merit. Popular democracy entails a sort of false consciousness in which men, driven by their passions and interests, fail to focus on the public good. Representatives, elected for their qualities of leadership and given an opportunity to deliberate at leisure, on the other hand, will be less likely to fall prey to the vice of faction. The representative assembly, properly checked and balanced, is thus not a pale substitute for the expression of the popular will, but rather is its true voice. In a remarkable transformation of values, rule by a "natural aristocracy" becomes the true democracy. "Justice," the maintenance of individual liberties and property rights, replaces civic virtue both as the product of and the necessary condition for democratic governance.

On this interpretation, *Federalist* 10 is a tour de force in the persuasive confusion of ises and oughts. Popular will is simultaneously suppressed and exalted by an argument that seems to proceed from merely the "facts" of human nature and the way it is shaped by institutional design.

PROGRESSIVES AND NEW DEALERS

Look ahead now a century and a quarter. If the triumph of Federalist political science was the legitimation of representative democracy as the true voice of the people, the triumph of Progressive and New Deal political science was the rationalization of the administrative state. The problem to be solved by these theorists was not the one Madison and his colleagues set for themselves, the protection of rights through a careful balancing and checking of majoritarian excesses. Indeed, the problem was almost the opposite. The theoretical task was to legitimate change in a society whose needs and demands were thwarted by vested interests. It was in part, of course, the legal protection of these interests through the elaboration of our Federalist Constitution that made them "vested." But the problem was not just in the courts.

Madison's representative assemblies had fallen into disrepute as well. Far from natural aristocracies of merit, by the turn of the twentieth century most legislative institutions were viewed as both corrupt and incompetent. They were also seen as conservative bottlenecks to the expression of the liberal public opinion that new techniques of sample polling revealed. "Progressive" political science was thus initially characterized by renewed enthusiasm for the anti-Federalists' basic ideas. Direct democracy in the form of the initiative and referendum was hailed as the institutional means for transforming the caretaker or guardian state into the positive or welfare state that the public demanded.

But the discovery that public opinion was more "advanced" than legislative action could not sustain a commitment to direct democracy in the face of other "facts." One cluster of facts resulted from the penetration of political science by social psychology. Psychological theory, and the empirical findings of social psychologists, increasingly featured irrational drives, passions, and prejudices as the mainsprings of human conduct. Moreover, individual irrationality seemed, if anything, to be magnified by group activity. This "crowd" or "herd" image of social groups hardly stimulated a sanguine view of the likely results of direct democracy. The social psychologists' dire visions also seemed to be borne out by events—the rise, and ultimately the "democratic" triumph, of fascism in Germany and in Italy.

Political theory thus seemed to produce an impasse. Public opinion demanded action to meet the social needs generated by industrialization and urbanization. Studies of the Congress and of the state legislatures suggested that a combination of features apparently endemic to American legislative assemblies—such as party corruption, committee power, and the seniority system—limited legislators' capacity to address a wide array of social ills either rationally or with dispatch. Representative democracy was not producing that attention to the general interests of the community that Federalist political science had predicted. Yet increased reliance on the momentum of popular democracy was obviously dangerous, for positive theory and current events portrayed voters as both apathetic and irresponsible. What forms of governance might be devised that could combine energy with intelligence, while maintaining the symbols of democratic control?

The answer seemed to be suggested by another emerging field of positive theory—management science. The industrial growth of the late nineteenth and early twentieth centuries had come to be understood as the joint product of technological and managerial innovation. The success of science combined with management bred an optimistic vision of "organized intelligence" as the cure for social ills. Indeed, a body of management theory was developing that seemed to promise success to any who would apply science, scientifically organized, to virtually any issue. While representative assemblies had failed to further Madison's "permanent interests of the community," those interests might yet be furthered by rational planning. Public administration thus was the key to meeting public demands while avoiding the dysfunctions of either popular or representative democracy.

The problem, of course, was what to do about "democracy" itself. Managerial government seemed at first blush quite different from, almost the opposite of, self-rule. And progressive political science was unlikely to persuade unless it could somehow explain that the new institutional arrangements it advocated need not abandon democratic ideals. The Progressives and New Dealers were as equal to this challenge as the Federalists had been. Moreover, their arguments bear a strong resemblance: Democracy was at base a system of governance so designed that the people got what they wanted. And what people most wanted, Progressive and New Deal theorists claimed, was "good government"—government that pursued the true long-term interests of the polity. Once it had been demonstrated that a government bound by antiquated notions of property rights and beholden to vicious party mechanisms for legislative policy choice could not provide good government, and that direct democracy led straight to irrational policy choice or authoritarianism, it was but a short step to the claim that managerial government was the government desired by the populace. The administrative state became the institutional means for achieving "rational democracy," that is, that system which gave the people the good government they demanded through "public opinion."

Note the degree to which the analyses of Federalist and New Deal political science coincide. Both are deeply suspicious of popular democracy and both fear it for much the same reason — the tendency of citizens' "passions" or "interests" to produce majoritarian tyranny. Twentieth-century political science merely added a psychological gloss and some more scientific observations of public attitudes to the eighteenth-century position. But late eighteenth- and early twentieth-century ideas of the appropriate role of the state and of particular governmental institutions were markedly different. Moreover, these normative positions were premised on fundamentally different images of how social organization was to be modeled, of how society, in fact, worked. These differences between Federalists and New Dealers once again dramatically illustrate the impact of positive theory on normative ideals.

In its simplest terms, the Federalist/New Deal dispute is a chicken-and-egg question concerning which came first, society or rights. In Federalist political science, individuals came endowed with natural rights. They entered into a social contract for governance primarily to secure the enjoyment of those rights. The preeminent task of statecraft thus was to design a mechanism that, through appropriate checks and balances, maintained social equilibrium and preserved the entitlements of the individual rightsholder.

Much of the energy of late nineteenth- and early twentieth-century political science was devoted to the empirical falsification of these basic Federalist premises. Comparative historical studies were done to demonstrate that there was and could be no agreement on any presocial set of natural rights — in short, that natural rights did not exist. Similar studies debunked the myth of the social contract. The growth of government everywhere was demonstrably by the evolution of traditional forms, rooted in particular cultural, geographic, and economic circumstances: rarely, if ever, by self-conscious acts of institution building in which citizens contracted for particular governmental forms.

The mechanistic Federalist imagery of checks, balances, and equipoise thus came to be viewed as historically or empirically naive. The reality of governance was not stasis but change; institutions did not operate according to mechanical laws, they evolved organically. As Woodrow Wilson put it in his classic, *Constitutional Government in the United States,*

Our statesmen of the generations quoted no one so often as Montesquieu, and they quoted him always as a scientific standard in the field of politics. Politics is turned into mechanics under his touch. The theory of gravitation is supreme.

The trouble with the theory is that government is not a machine, but a living thing. It falls, not under the theory of the universe, but under the theory of organic life. It is accountable to Darwin, not to Newton. It is modified by its environment, necessitated by its tasks, shaped to its functions by the sheer pressure of life. No living thing can have its organs offset against each other as checks, and live. On the contrary, its life is dependent upon their quick cooperation, their ready response to the commands of instinct or intelligence, their amicable community of purpose.[2]

These changed perceptions of social reality led to normative prescriptions radically different from those of the Federalists. If rights were not primary and government was not a contract, then the principal purpose of government could hardly be the protection of rights. Government was instead an organ for the accomplishment of social purposes. The "goodness" of a governmental institution was to be determined, therefore, not by its capacity to maintain the positions of the parties to a particular contractual bargain, but by its functional appropriateness in an ever-changing social context. Public welfare, not justice, should be the principal goal of government. The public good lay in the pursuit of public welfare.

This new vision of social life transformed not only ideas about the overall purposes of government but also the meaning attached to the fundamental normative building blocks of American constitutionalism. Listen, again, to Wilson on the idea of "freedom" or "liberty":

Political liberty consists in the best practicable adjustment between the power of the government and the privilege of the individual; and the freedom to alter the adjustment is as important as the adjustment itself for the ease and progress of affairs and the contentment of the citizen.

There are many analogies by which it is possible to illustrate the idea, if it needs illustration . . . . We speak of the "free" movement of the piston-rod in the perfectly made engine, and know of course that its freedom is proportioned to its perfect adjustment. The least lack of adjustment will heat it with friction and hold it stiff and unmanageable. There is nothing free in the sense of being unrestrained in a world of innumerable forces, and each force moves at its best when best adjusted to the forces about it. Spiritual things are not wholly comparable with material things, and political liberty is a thing of the spirits of men; but we speak of friction in things that affect our spirits, and do not feel that it is altogether a figure of speech. It is not forcing analogies, therefore, to say that it is the freest government in which there is the least friction,

—the least friction between the power of the government and the privilege of the individual. The adjustment may vary from generation to generation, but the principle never can. A constitutional government, being an instrument for the maintenance of liberty, is an instrumentality for the maintenance of a right adjustment, and must have a machinery of constant adaptation.[3]

Given this radical alteration in perspective, it is hardly surprising that the Federalists' governmental structure was found inadequate. In Wilson's analysis, only the rise of dominant political parties outside the constitutional scheme of government had made nationhood possible and had avoided the complete collapse of government for want of either energy or discipline. But surely American government could not rely forever on a nonpublic and often corrupt party structure to provide both the long-range planning and the disciplined implementation that twentieth-century social and economic life seemed to require. The Progressives and their New Deal heirs thus opted for an "apolitical" administrative state as the appropriate expression of the public will. Thus was our understanding of "democracy" and its possibilities transformed.

Contemporary Positive Theory

The positive political theory that seems most pervasive today is really a cluster of theories in a field often called the "theory of public choice." Practitioners of this arcane art combine highly abstract mathematical deduction with some of the basic behavioral assumptions of micro-economics to produce theories of the behavior of voters, of representative assemblies, of bureaucracies, and even of courts. Public choice theory thus seeks to explain, or at least to "model," "rational public choice" within the typical institutional environment of the modern welfare state.

Many aspects of public choice theory are often associated with three recent American Nobel laureates, Kenneth Arrow, James Buchanan, and George Stigler. Arrow and his successors have been concerned particularly with decisional outcomes under various voting rules. We will for convenience call their contributions "voting theory." Stigler, and others associated with his enterprise, have been much more interested in analyzing the likely legislative output of a pluralist, representative democracy. We will call this set of theories "interest group theory." Buchanan's writings straddle both domains and are broadly oriented to issues of institutional design. His is a set of concerns in "political economy" that resonates most strongly with the governmental theorists of the Federalist or the Progressive–New Deal periods. Buchanan's approach also connects him to another strong current in contemporary economics, game theory, or the study of how bargaining strategies, information, and institutional characteristics mold the outcomes of joint or collective decisionmaking. Others, William Niskanen and Mancur Olson prominent among them, have been concerned particularly with bureaucratic behavior and with the formation of political pressure groups.[4]

I should hasten to add that although I have attached these theories to prominent economists, the intellectual histories of the lines of thought we are exploring are long and thoroughly interdisciplinary. Arrow's contribution to voting theory owes much to the marquis de Condorcet, second secretary of the French Academy of Sciences, who was Madison's contemporary and whose work may have been known to the drafters of our Constitution. Moreover, although Arrow was an economist himself, his insights have been refined and elaborated as much by political scientists as by those finding their disciplinary homes in economics departments.

Similarly, Stigler's concern to understand the influence of interest groups on legislative outcomes was certainly shared by the author of Federalist 10, and Stigler's insights owe much to accounts by his contemporaries in political science. Indeed, while much of the more recent literature elaborating the interest group theory of legislation has been by economists, there is a rich parallel literature generated by political scientists working within both liberal and Marxist traditions.

Although the field we are now discussing covers a variety of interests and approaches, the one notion that unifies it is just this: We must always seek to understand political outcomes as a function of self-interested individual behaviors.[5] Voters, like consumers, try to choose what is best for them. Representatives, like business firms, try to supply what people want. There is demand and supply at work, a market for collective action. Like all markets, of course, the political market may have distortions. The signals from voters to representatives may be vague, conflicting, and poorly informed. The quality of the performance of representatives may be difficult to monitor. Collusion may lead to monopolistic or quasimonopolistic behavior. And so on. The basic idea, however, remains fixed. Politics can be understood by deploying the basic tools of economic analysis.

None of this is too surprising, of course. We hardly expect where people stand on political issues to be unconnected with their economic interests. And we are all familiar with ways in which markets may fail to supply the goods and services that we want. Much of welfare economics and public policy analysis is devoted to the question of how to regulate or structure markets to make them perform better — that is, to insure the maximum increase in public welfare. Market failure is to be expected in public policy markets too, and much institutional design work will surely consist in trying to correct these failures. That indeed is what Federalist and Progressive or New Deal political scientists considered to be their task. The striking thing about the public choice literature, however, is the degree of "government failure" it finds. Indeed, the message is generally not about the ameliorative steps needed to improve the political marketplace. It is instead a message about why political markets *cannot* work to satisfy the democratic wish, that is, to provide the people with the government that they want. Modern positive political theory provides a much bleaker picture of political life than virtually any of its influential predecessors. It suggests quite strongly that no appealing version of democracy is possible and that no possible version is very appealing. We begin with voting theory.

THE ARROW THEOREM AND VOTING THEORY

Much of what voting theorists do is wonderfully abstract and abstruse. Nevertheless, these axiomatically derived propositions challenge some of our most cherished beliefs. The central proof of axiomatic social choice theory, what is generally called the "Arrow Impossibility Theorem," suggests that majority-rule determination of social preferences must be either chaotic or illusory.

The Arrow Theorem generalizes an eighteenth-century proof called Condorcet's Paradox. Imagine for simplicity that three voters A, B and C are asked to vote on three policies X, Y, and Z. A prefers X to Y to Z; B prefers Y to Z to X; and C prefers Z to X to Y. These preference orderings can be depicted tabularly as follows:

Table 1.1. Condorcet's Voting Paradox

Voter	Preference Ordering (N)		
A	X	Y	Z
B	Y	Z	X
C	Z	X	Y

Obviously, no policy has a majority of first-place votes. Moreover, these preferences result in a "vicious" cycle when voted on in pairs. When X is paired against Y, X wins (A and C versus B). When X is paired against Z, Z wins (B and C versus A). When Z is paired against Y, Y wins (A and B versus C). That is, X beats Y, which beats Z, which beats X.

Ordinary voting routines simply will not choose a most preferred alternative. Indeed, the startling generality of Arrow's proof is that no voting rule which allows voters to express their true preference and which treats each preference as equally decisive can assure us that it will produce a single preferred choice for three or more voters who have at least three alternatives. In short, majority-rule systems may produce indeterminate, shifting, and therefore chaotic outcomes even if applied to small groups like committees, not to mention legislatures or the whole electorate.

As casual empiricists, we do not often observe the cycling phenomenon in operation. Elections routinely produce winners and representative assemblies make decisions that are not immediately undone by subsequent votes. Does this mean that the Arrow Theorem is either incorrect or irrelevant? Not at all. In fact, the absence of cycling gives the theory much of its normative interest. Stability can be achieved by relaxing any of the "conditions" that underlie the proof. We can give someone the power to constrain the alternatives or to determine the order of expressing preferences; we can give someone an extra vote; or we can allow false or strategic voting. But, of course, none of these choices is particularly attractive. Thus, the Arrow Theorem might be recharacterized as telling us that whenever we find stable choices, we cannot know that stability has not been bought at the price of unfairness in the underlying voting process. Our choice seems to be between incoherence (cycling) and some form of unfairness.

Most voting systems, whether governing elections or other types of choice, use some set of institutional devices to constrain choice, or else they explicitly abandon majority rule. In most elections, for example, we vote for one of two candidates and the winner is the candidate who obtains more than 50 percent of the votes cast. In multiple-candidate elections, various techniques may be used to produce a final majority. Run-off elections between the top two candidates are common. So is the electoral college winner-take-all system for American presidential elections—a system that not only produces a clear majority winner in the face of serious third-party candidates, but also sometimes permits a candidate to prevail without garnering a plurality of the popular vote.

But note what these devices say about majority-rule elections. Majoritarian elections dependent on getting the choices down to two. And who is elected depends critically on how the final list of two candidates is generated. It is, thus, intuitively obvious that if anyone had the authority to specify who the two candidates would be, they would thereby gain the power to determine who would be elected. It is just an extension of this obvious point to realize that it is the institutional machinery for setting the agenda, here a slate of candidates chosen by committees, conventions, caucuses, or primaries, that ultimately determines the outcome of the election. Or, to put the matter back in terms of our formal example, should X beat Y, we have no assurances that he or she would not have lost to Z, who would have been beaten by Y. The outcome may be as much a product of the order of voting, or some other aspect of agenda setting, as it is a product of the underlying preferences of the voters.

In some sense this result is quite familiar. We all have had the experience of seeing our favorite candidate disappear from the available choices before the general election, just as we have seen our favorite proposals disappear in committee or family discussions. We have also sometimes harbored the belief that our candidates or ideas could have beaten the ultimately victorious ones if they somehow could have been resuscitated before the final vote. (How did we end up at Disney World again when the original proposals had been Paris or the Bahamas?) But, of course, the election or committee rules (and often the unwritten rules of family discussion) prevented going back to the beginning and starting the whole process over. Recognition that the agenda matters — indeed, is crucial in majoritarian processes — also undergirds our common understanding that a legislative committee chair is a powerful position. And it fuels the fires of democratic unrest when we believe that the chair is "biased" or unrepresentative.

To be sure, agenda influence can be avoided, but usually at significant cost. Majority rule without a constrained agenda — that is, a binary choice — usually will produce no decision at all. So says the Arrow Theorem, and so says our ordinary experience as well. Unless the choices can be narrowed in some way, discussion will be endless. Possible candidates and possible policies are a dime a dozen, and there is an old rule of thumb in faculty politics that says that if three proposals can be got on the table, nothing will ever be done.

Majority rule itself can be abandoned in favor of plurality voting or proportional representation. In such systems decisions will be made no matter how many alternatives are presented. And they have the "democratic" advantage that everyone's candidate or proposal can be put before the voters. But proportional voting is useful only in elections, not in policy choices; and in elections it holds out the ever-present prospect of splintered and ineffectual governance. Plurality voting, by contrast, permits governance by a minority candidate or party, or selection of a minority-backed program; pluralities can pick "winners" who would have lost to one or many others in a head-to-head majority-rule vote. Hence democrats cling to majority rule notwithstanding the sense that the majority is not quite ruling.

The Arrow Impossibility Theorem has a somewhat ironic relationship to these common discontents with familiar majoritarian processes. It may in some way console us in relation to our particular disappointments with majoritarian outcomes. In the face of apparent unfairness or collective irrationality, it is some help to know that there is no majoritarian process that can assure both fair voting and preferred outcomes. But that "consoling" knowledge is itself profoundly unsettling. For it tells us that we may never be able to design institutions that will reflect majority sentiment, if by that we mean a governance structure that can flawlessly aggregate individual preferences into collective choices. Voting theory teaches that majoritarian democracy is a necessarily compromised process and that any institutional design chosen to promote democracy will have a problematic relationship to our normative aspirations.

INTEREST GROUP THEORIES OF LEGISLATION AND BUREAUCRACY

If the unhappy scenarios generated by voting theorists are troubling to committed democrats, public choice ideas on legislatures and bureaucracies are downright depressing. These theories add institutional detail to abstract voting theory. But unlike Federalist or Progressive political science, in which institutional design both corrected the faults of popular democracy and constrained assemblies or bureaucracies to act in the public interest, the new political science seems largely to explain only what forms of institutional unfairness and special interest oppression we have chosen. The basic story goes something like this:

Private groups prefer to have social resources shifted from the general public to their members. They are prepared to support (by votes and money) politicians who are willing to effect these wealth transfers. Politicians want to get reelected and are prepared to trade legislative action for support. Their problem is how to take money from the general public and give it to private groups without getting turned out by the voters at the next election.

The solution to this problem lies in rational voter apathy and the dynamics of group formation. In general, it does not pay voters to be informed or to vote. The probability that a particular vote will be decisive in electing a particular representative *and* will actually produce legislation that improves the voter's situation is absurdly small. After all, very few elections are decided by one vote and individual representatives have very limited capacity to deliver on their electoral promises, even if they want to do so. So why vote? The costs of voting — becoming informed, registering, going to the polls — overwhelm the expected value of its benefits. To be sure people do vote, at least some of the time, out of a sense of duty or for some other reason. But given the cost-benefit calculation we have just described, most voters are unlikely to spend as much time "shopping" for a congressperson as for a television set.

There are, however, ways to change this voting calculus. While individual voters may have a vanishingly small effect on the political process, groups count for more. Not only do groups have more votes with which to capture a potential representative's attention, they can wield significant power through collecting and dispensing funds, providing volunteer workers, and creating occasions for publicity (conventions, organizational newsletters, and so on). With these sorts of electoral favors to dispense, groups are more likely to influence electoral outcomes and to be able to see to it that electoral promises are followed by representational performances.

This idea of the group basis of politics has long been a staple of our understanding of American democracy. We often speak of our governance structure as a form of "pluralism" in which policy is the outcome of negotiation and competition among numerous political groupings. Often this description has benign or even positive connotations. The vision is of multiple clusters of citizens pursuing their various group interests through an open and competitive process. Presumably, through some combination of persuasion and accommodation, most people's interests can be served at least some of the time. The responsiveness of the system to multiple or pluralistic demands legitimates the process as, broadly speaking, majoritarian. Indeed, on some descriptions pluralism is so open and inclusive a process that it amounts almost to consensus governance. And if that were true, the core of the democratic vision would have been rescued. A model of pluralist bargaining even holds out the prospect of rescuing majority rule from the indeterminacy of agenda influence suggested by the Arrow Theorem. To see this, we must return for a moment to our formal representation of the voting paradox.

Suppose there were another set of alternative policies relating to a second public issue N_1, among which A, B, and C had the following preferences:

Table 1.2. A Variation on Condorcet's Paradox

Voter	Preference Ordering (N_1)		
A	X_1	Y_1	Z_1
B	Y_1	Z_1	X_1
C	Z_1	X_1	Y_1

Now suppose that A has a very strong preference for X over Y and Z, but a very weak preference for X_1 over Y_1 and Z_1. Conversely, B has a very weak preference for Y over Z and X, but a very strong preference for Y_1 over Z_1 and X_1. It would surely make sense for A and B to swap votes across issues N and N_1, with both voting for X and for Y_1. If they did, the voting paradox would disappear in favor of stable majorities on both issues. This result might also be considered satisfactory from a public-welfare perspective. A and B both increased their welfare (or, it is to be hoped, that of their constituents) by trading lesser-valued policies for greater-valued ones.

But alas, such vote trading ("logrolling") may as easily have unfortunate public-welfare effects. For once we allow intensity of preference to enter the picture, we can hardly forget about C. What if C's preferences for Z and Z_1 are much stronger than A and B's combined intensity for X and Y_1? If so, general welfare will have been reduced.

But not so fast. Pluralist heaven can be regained by adding yet another issue, N_2, and another and another. For if we allow trading across any number of issues, it should be possible for C's most intense preferences to be satisfied as well. By bargaining to vote sincerely on some issues and strategically on others, each voter or representative comes away with something. No group is left out, and because each vote trade results in a victory for the most intensely desired proposals, general welfare seems to be going up as well. Game theory — the consideration of how voters might behave strategically — has saved majoritarian democracy from both indeterminacy and disaster.

Yet, again, not so fast. Majority rule only requires that policies receive 51 percent of the votes to prevail. But the policies will bind everyone. Hence if a bare majority coalition can be built for a policy that gives the coalition members a surplus of benefits over their costs, it will be enacted even if the net costs to the minority indicate that the society as a whole loses. Indeed, constantly shifting coalitions can enact multiple programs each of which has a surplus of social costs over social benefits so long as in each instance the gains to the majority exceed their costs. Described in this way, vote trading creates its own paradox. By making incremental decisions that produce net benefits for the majority, voters or legislators could continually drive down social welfare. Disaster reemerges.

Real-world analogues for this hypothetical process are not hard to find. Vote trading on projects of intense local, but dubious national, value is the traditional logrolling that we have come to associate with "pork barrel" politics. And contemporary American voters have no need to be reminded how this process may distort national priorities and create national debt. For recent Congresses and presidents have been willing first to satisfy local demands that achieved majoritarian support and then *not* tax the general public to pay the bills. It is this latter propensity that Gramm-Rudman-Hollings budgetary ceilings and the budget reconciliation process seek to control. Moreover, a brief look at these budgetary techniques will set the stage for a different sort of critique of pluralism.

In principle, something like the current budget reconciliation process could ensure that the total legislative spending package in each legislative session is welfare-enhancing. For if all projects and all taxes to support them are voted on as a package, it should be hard to put together a majority for an omnibus bill that reduces overall social welfare. To see this, return again to vote trading among A, B, and C. Assume that X, Y, and Z represent local projects of interest to A, B, and C, respectively. The first thing to note here is that when X, Y, and Z are localized projects, they are not mutually exclusive policies. All can be chosen, and all probably will be. A, B, and C will all vote for each other's projects to prevent a bidding war among themselves in which A and B form a coalition which collapses when C makes B a better offer, which collapses when A makes C a better offer, and so on. Everybody will want to let everyone else into the coalition to avoid the risk of being the one left out in this vote-trading equivalent of musical chairs. Modern students of legislation call this the "norm of universalism."

Universalism also tends to be the norm in the face of a budget constraint. Assume for the sake of simplicity that only one project X or Y or Z could be built, given the budget ceiling. No one can get two voters for their local project because they will reap 100 percent of its gains while their coalition partner stands to pay one-third of its costs. A can enlist B's help only by offering to scale back X and support a similarly scaled back Y. But C can play this game too. The musical-votes game is back in high gear. To stop it, universalism must be the norm. Moreover, when the total package comes to be voted on, the total costs to each voter must not be greater than the total benefits received. If everyone votes for it, then the total benefits must exceed the total costs.

To be sure, universalism may break down. Voters or legislators may try to welch on deals or to move from coalition to coalition for strategic advantage. But if everyone's proposals must be voted on together in combination with a revenue package, cheaters are pretty easily detected and punished. The omnibus budget reconciliation process thus helps to reinforce universalism, which in turn promotes beneficial results. Indeed, there is massive evidence that universalism is the norm for legislative pork barrels both before and after the institutionalization of the budgetary reconciliation process.

Now we seem to be trapped in a contradiction. First, we argued that shifting coalitions might produce whopping overall social costs by approving projects having localized net benefits but national net costs. And we called on our common experience with pork barrel politics to buttress the case. But then we argued that universalism rather than shifting bare-majority coalitions are the norm and that this feature of logrolling would tend to produce omnibus legislation that is welfare-enhancing. Both arguments cannot be correct!

And they are not. According to interest group theory, the problem lies in our stylized version of pluralism. We have treated A, B, and C as voters who reap all the benefits and pay all the costs of their vote trading, or as representatives who internalize the costs and benefits for all of their constituents. And it is this latter assumption that is wildly off the mark. Representatives, at least from a rational choice perspective, will internalize the costs and benefits only of all *politically relevant* constituents, that is, those who are important to the representative's reelection. In a pluralist polity, that means all politically relevant groups. A look at the theory of interest group formation will reveal what is wrong with our conclusion that vote trading might both produce consensus and enhance welfare. Indeed, it will show us why pluralist politics may be simultaneously unfair and "inefficient."

The problem is this: While any group can play the pluralist game, not all groups can organize and operate effectively. Indeed, from a rational-actor perspective it may be surprising that any do. For no voter has any economically rational basis for supporting organizations that seek to obtain benefits for his or her group through political action. The voter benefits should the organization be successful whether or not he or she has contributed to the outcome. Legislation is usually a "pure public good" for persons falling within the benefited class; that is, those who produce the benefit cannot exclude others from enjoying it. If the Taxpayers Union reduces my taxes or the Sierra Club protects my nearby wilderness area, I benefit whether or not I contributed to these organizations' efforts. As a rational actor, I therefore have every incentive to "free ride" on the political efforts of others. And if most people behave in this way, many groups will not form and most others will be much weaker than they should be given the real underlying voter support for their activities.

Some groups, however, do form and become politically active. They somehow surmount the difficulties that incentives to free riding impose. This sometimes may occur because the group also produces "private goods" — information, valuable contacts, group discounts, and so on — that are unavailable to nonmembers. The "free ride" on the groups' political activities can be eliminated by tying the costs of that work to goods and services from which noncontributors can be excluded. The American Automobile Association and the American Association of Retired Persons, for example, are politically powerful organizations whose vast memberships may enroll primarily for the advantages of car towing, travel services, group discounts, and the like. These organizations certainly market memberships as if their consumable goods and services are sufficient to justify the membership fee. Their political activities may thus be a bonus, an embarrassment, or an irrelevance, depending on the preferences of particular members.

Other groups organize successfully because they have independent bases of solidarity (ethnic, professional, commercial, territorial) that make shirking — failing to provide a fair share of support — difficult and unrewarding. It is socially and/or economically costly to attempt to evade membership in many groups, ranging from the local neighborhood association to the American Hardware Association. This is not to say that groups relying purely on the "public spiritedness" or political convictions of their members never form and become politically active. The point is only that they are at a severe disadvantage. The groups that form, prosper, and wield significant political power are largely the traditional "special interests" that constantly seek legislative favor.

Almost by definition, of course, the general electorate is opposed to legislative programs desired by special interests — programs that the special interests promote precisely because they involve a transfer of wealth to them from the general electorate. But citizens in general are unorganized and uninformed. Their views are not politically salient. Indeed, on most issues most of the time, the general voter's views may be nonexistent. On a day-to-day basis, legislators can provide special interest programs in return for political support without fearing a substantial loss of standing with the general public. "Pluralism" on this account, therefore, is just a pleasant word for a continuing rip-off. All potential groups have access to the levers of power in our democratic polity, but only certain of them will amass sufficient financial or membership muscle to make those levers move anything. From a rational-choice perspective, therefore, legislation can be described theoretically in a very few words: It is a set of deals between legislators and private groups which make both better off, usually at the expense of the general public.

Hence, the "universalism" endemic to the legislative vote-trading game may well not protect the general public against deals that reduce overall public welfare. The costs and benefits of these trades can leave out of account the groups that do not form or that are too weak to be electorally relevant. Their disenfranchisement not only prejudices their interests, it limits the social welfare gains that might result from a true or universal pluralism. Pluralist politics is inefficient precisely because it is unfair.

Where Federalist political science saw the representative assembly as a means of escaping the passions and interests that plagued popular democracy, the contemporary theory of legislation sees instead a legislature maintained by factional deals. Nor do bicameralism, the separation of powers, or delegation to administrative agencies on the model of New Deal political science rescue the "permanent interests of the community" from the clutches of the interest groups. Bicameralism may make interest group influence somewhat more costly, but in the current theory of legislation the independent judiciary and bureaucratic implementation are said to reinforce, not limit, interest group power.

On this view, the judiciary provides the enforcement machinery needed to make legislative deals stable over time and, therefore, more valuable. And the courts get both their resources and their jurisdiction by legislative grant. Bureaus are conceptualized as being as susceptible to private interest influence as legislatures, and may assist the latter in obscuring the true nature of legislative action from the general public. By passing vague statutes that seem to be in the public interest, but then pressuring agencies to favor their supporters, legislators can have it both ways. They can take credit for good government while pandering to the special interests. Moreover, administrative institutions generate their own bureaucratic aims. They may function much like interest groups themselves by trading favors to powerful legislators (projects in the home district, help for a valued constituent) for aggrandizement of bureaucratic budgets or prerogatives.

The new "economic" or "rational-actor" models of positive political theory, combining voting and game theory with the interest group theory of legislation, do much to cement the claim of economics to constitute the "dismal science." Whereas Federalist and New Deal political science feared only those expressions of popular will unmediated by the rationalizing influence of either a representative assembly or an expert bureau, contemporary theorists despair of expressing the will or preferences of the people through any device whatever. For them, our public laws capture instead only a particular concatenation of private preferences made politically relevant by the dynamics of self-interested behavior on the part of voters and officials alike. The "public" in "public law" identifies only the nature of the power that is put in the service of private ends. Legislation elaborates norms without normativity; it expresses neither the passionate commitments nor the reasoned judgments of a political community.

The Potential Impact of Positive Political Theory

I shall return anon to a more detailed and critical examination of contemporary positive theory. For now I want merely to sketch some of the effects that this vision of collective reality might have on the development of American public institutions. Indeed, it would appear that public choice accounts of representative democracy have already had a major impact on institutional reform, both in the "activist" regulatory period of the late 1960s and early 1970s and in the deregulatory crusades of the more recent past.

OPTIMISTIC ACTIVISTS

Like their New Deal counterparts, the political activists of the 1960s viewed most social issues, whether civil rights, poverty, pollution, or product safety, as problems to be solved by the application of federal governmental power. They set about solving these problems by devising myriad new programs and new institutions at the national level. These activists were heavily influenced, however, by a post–New Deal intellectual climate. Critics on both the right and the left portrayed the pantheon of Progressive and New Deal agency heroes — the ICC, the FTC, the FCC, the FPC, and virtually all their alphabetic brethren — as stagnant bureaucracies that had failed to generate effective policy in their respective regulatory domains. The most prominent reason given for this regulatory lethargy was a variant of interest group theory, the "capture" of the old-line agencies by the groups that they had been designed to regulate. The Interstate Commerce Commission, created to regulate the railroads, had become instead a means for protecting them from trucking competition. The same story could be told of the Federal Communication Commission's solicitude for broadcasters faced by the new technology of cable, or for AT&T's long-distance telephone monopoly faced by competition from MCI and Sprint. The Federal Power Commission seemed largely in the business of keeping natural gas rates artificially high. The Federal Trade Commission, if it were doing anything, seemed only to be providing official auspices for the cartelization of trade practices in a wide variety of industries.

The 1960s activists were optimistic, however, that these dysfunctional bureaucratic behaviors could be reformed through institutional redesign. In the view of this activist political science, "capture" had been made possible by a combination of institutional design errors — vague legislative delegations, collegiate forms of administration, broad prosecutorial discretion, independence from executive direction, and inefficient case-by-case adjudicatory techniques. Hence they sought to assure that their new programs, run by new or redesigned agencies, would be different. Recognizing that interest groups were a standard feature of the political-regulatory scene, the 1960s institutional reformers attempted to even up the odds between the regulated "special interests" and the general public who were meant to be beneficiaries of the new health and safety regulation.

Agency mandates were to be made more specific; their power more concentrated in a single politically responsible administrator; their enforcement discretion more circumscribed by explicit directions and time limits; their decision processes more available to the participation of their putative beneficiaries. Perhaps most important, these new guardians of our health, safety, and welfare were expected to operate primarily through the establishment of mandatory general policy by rule. Policy was not to emerge from protracted, costly, and arcane adjudicatory proceedings where participation was limited, insiders held all the cards, and agencies that failed to do anything could hide behind "prosecutorial discretion." Instead, policy would be formulated in informal rule-making processes where participation was open to all. Agencies would have deadlines for the adoption of rules and public-interested citizens could sue them to force action if they failed to regulate in the public interest. Genuine openness and strict accountability would make these new forms of bureaucratic regulation express the public interest.[6]

ENTER PESSIMISM

Deregulatory reform movements from the mid-1970s to the present have also been informed by the interest group theory of politics. But whereas the reformers of the 1960s saw broadened interest group competition as the means for developing policy in the public interest, the new or positive political theory has been deeply skeptical that this competition will produce improvements in the general welfare. Rather than seeing the newly empowered consumers' or environmentalists' organizations as representatives of the public interest, critics have seen them as just new interest groups pursuing their own special ends. Study after study has purported to show that the regulatory efforts of the new agencies have produced modest improvements in the general welfare, while making massive redistributions of income from one group to another.[7] And some studies describe pernicious coalitions of traditional "special interest" and newer "public interest" groups which pursue converging organizational aims at the expense of both the public health and national economic growth. Thus, for example, have Appalachian soft coal interests joined with Western environmentalists to produce air quality regulation that dirties the air unnecessarily at enormous economic cost.[8]

This combination of positive theory and empirical evidence seems to have produced a quite remarkable change in general perceptions. The activist optimism of the 1960s has been replaced by a pessimism bordering on the cynical. Governmental efforts are viewed as inevitably flawed. The democratization of the regulatory process, far from solving the problems of regulatory capture, is now depicted as having merely provided a no-holds-barred domain for special interest pleading. Public policy reform from the Carter administration forward has been conceived of as a search for devices to prevent the implementation of costly regulatory policies and where possible to get the government out of the business of regulation. Institutional reform consists largely of the creation of roadblocks to regulatory initiative and in the withdrawal of both regulations and regulatory authority. All things "public" have become suspect. For some, the only public purpose worthy of respect seems to be the elimination of the public sector.

While not cast in the same technical jargon, the basic views of the public choice fraternity are replicated in popular discourse. The idea that politicians, administrators, "public interest groups," and the like are just "in it for themselves" has become a staple of political belief. Because of this shift, the question of how American government works and toward what ends is now contestable in more fundamental ways than it has been since the 1930s. At one level this is obvious. Since 1970, presidential election campaigns have tended to be waged not on issues of policy but on competing claims concerning who will be better at limiting public spending, reducing "the deficit," and downsizing the "bureaucracy." These campaigns have responded to a strong and growing sentiment in the populace that government is bloated, unresponsive, ineffectual — and often corrupt.

The political rhetoric of the late twentieth century has also been punctuated by a multitude of ideas for institutional redesign. Some are global, such as the continuing enthusiasm in some circles for a parliamentary-style government. Most are more modest — balanced budget amendments, term limitations, public financing of elections, and the like. And many — such as "sunset" laws, Office of Management and Budget regulatory review, regulatory negotiation — are invisible save to the cognoscenti, mostly in Washington and the academy.

Periods of disenchantment and reformative effort are hardly a novelty in American public life. Many such cycles, often followed by periods of "good feeling," at least quiescence, can be identified throughout our nation's history. The current situation, however, seems different. The "malaise" that affects us (to use Jimmy Carter's apt but, for him, politically unfortunate phrase) is not so much a response to a problem or set of problems as it is an attitude about problems and, in particular, the capacity of public institutions to respond to them. Indeed, if polling data are to be believed, a majority of Americans no longer think that government is even trying to pursue the "collective good" or the "public interest," however defined. Public sentiment is reformative, but in a different sense than it has been in the past. While making government better so that it can do more still animates some, reform has recently come to mean limiting the damage that public institutions can do or, if possible, dismantling them in favor of market solutions. Trust in the competence and good faith of public institutions seems to be receding with an ebb tide whose flow stubbornly refuses to cycle back toward confidence.

The challenge of public choice is thus clear. It asks us to reconsider the premises of the modern, activist administrative state. It seems to tell us that we made a wrong turn in the early decades of this century. We thought then that big government could ameliorate social ills without corrupting the very bases of American democracy. But we were wrong. Contemporary reanalysis of the mechanisms of collective choice by public choice theorists mocks our efforts at democratic governance. Majoritarianism is an illusion. Legislation and administrative regulation are little better than private contracts at public expense. We should therefore return to the principles of our Federalist forbearers. Better yet, to those of the anti-Federalists. The national government, all government, should be constrained radically. Our trust should be instead in the market, in voluntary associations, and in local, community-based governance. For only in these institutions are we likely to find either the integrity of arm's-length bargaining or the conditions for maintaining the altruistic public spirit necessary for the pursuit of truly collective aims.

A Response That Fails

It is time now to return to the theme with which this chapter began. For one response to the bleak vision of public choice theory is to urge its practitioners to abandon it. On this view, the question is not whether public choice descriptions of the effects of various institutional arrangements are true. It is instead whether these descriptions will destroy the possibility for democratic governance by destroying the public faith that is its prerequisite. This response to contemporary positive political science is inadequate, but it is far from silly. For it takes the question of the relationship between ises and oughts seriously.

Some democratic societies, after all, have had a particularly dim view of political theorizing that pointed repeatedly at democracy's defects. In Socrates' Athens, undermining public faith in democratic governance was sufficient to make out a capital case. And while a charge of corrupting the youth by teaching the ideas of public choice theory is unlikely today to result in the criminal trial of economists or political scientists, the power of positive theory to shape normative belief is no trivial matter, even to public choice theorists. Geoffrey Brennan and James Buchanan, for example, have felt obliged to defend public choice against Steven Kelman's charge that "cynical descriptive conclusions about behavior in government threaten to undermine the norm prescribing public spirit. The cynicism of journalists — and even the writings of professors — can decrease public spirit simply by describing what they claim to be its absence. Cynics are therefore in the business of making prophecies that threaten to become self-fulfilling. If the norm of public spirit dies, our society would look bleaker and our lives as individuals would be more impoverished. That is the tragedy of 'public choice.' "[9]

In answering Kelman, Brennan and Buchanan, to their great credit, explicitly eschewed all reliance on the "that's science" rationale for continuing to pursue the public choice scholarship for which Buchanan received the 1986 Nobel Prize in economics. They did not claim that the normative consequences of positive theory were of no concern to public choice practitioners. They responded instead: "Knowledge without hope, science without a conviction that it can lead to a better life—these are by no means unambiguously value-enhancing, and those who shatter illusions for the sheer pleasure of doing so are not so clearly to be applauded for their 'work.' "[10]

The defense they offered instead was both pragmatic and tentative. In Brennan and Buchanan's view, public choice can be justified only by its capacity to produce useful institutional reforms; reforms whose value to the community offset any deleterious effects that public choice talk might have on what Kelman calls the "public spirit." In the defenders' words:

> What is the appropriate model of man to be incorporated in the comparative analysis of alternative constitutional rules? In our response to this question, we follow the classical economists explicitly, and for precisely the reasons they stated. We model man as a wealth maximizer, not because this model is necessarily the most descriptive empirically, but because we seek a set of rules that will work well independently of the behavioral postulates introduced.
>
> From our perspective, then, we agree that there is cause for some concern with public choice interpreted as a predictive model of behavior in political roles. Where public choice is used to develop a predictive theory of political processes in a manner typical of "positive economics" — that is, with the focus solely on developing an empirically supportable theory of choice within rules, and with the ultimate normative purpose of constitutional design swept away in footnotes or neglected altogether—then the danger is that it will indeed breed the moral consequences previously discussed.[11]

The approach of Brennan and Buchanan is obviously plausible. They seem to be urging that we design institutions to protect us from self-interested political action, while recognizing that such activity may shape our attitudes toward governance. As designers, we should then compare the gains and losses from public choice–oriented institutional design with the gains and losses from institutional design premised on a rosier vision of human nature. But in a crucial sense the defense proffered by Brennan and Buchanan is ineffective, for it may have no points of tangency with Kelman's complaint.

Properly understood, Kelman's argument is that these are incommensurate worlds. The people who learn their politics from the design and operation of Brennan and Buchanan's defensive democratic institutions will become different people than the ones Kelman envisages. They will have different preferences and values. And they will design different institutions in pursuit of those values. There just is no Archimedean point from which to measure and compare the costs and benefits of these two worlds. Viewed in this way, not only are the prophecies of the public choice cynics self-fulfilling; the complaints of their neo-republican critics like Kelman are unanswerable. A continuous emphasis on designing public institutions and limiting public interventions to avoid the perils of self-interested behavior constructs a world in which the possibilities for nurturing the public spirit and extending its reach are sharply constrained. Civic republicanism will never have been given a trial.

This is not the end of the debate, however. Indeed, it is about here that things start to become interesting. For notice we now seem to have gotten past a major sticking point that has heretofore divided public choice practitioners and neo-republicans — the dispute about whether preferences should be imagined to be wholly exogenous to politics. Brennan, Buchanan, and Kelman all agree that citizens' preferences or values are in part a function of how they are governed or govern themselves, not something that is imported wholly from outside public life. Politics socializes us to a particular view of the world which, as I argued at the outset of this chapter, strongly influences our values and political commitments.

From this common ground, we can see also that the neo-republican critique of public choice is inadequate. It argues, at least implicitly, that, if we would but design our political institutions *as if* they were to be peopled by public-spirited rather than self-interested citizens, then those citizens would emerge. The argument is reminiscent of the anti-Federalists' argument for civic virtue's connection to institutions of popular democracy. And it is inadequate to defeat the public choice perspective for the same reasons that the anti-Federalists' arguments failed to triumph over Federalist political science.

For one thing, the notion of the "endogeneity" of political preferences seems to substitute one implausible view of human nature for another. Political socialization into virtuous or public-spirited habits and commitments cannot be the whole story of human preference formation. If it were, political conflict would disappear. Socialized by our joint participation in public affairs, we would ultimately all have the same values and preferences, all public choice would become consensual. In short, the so-called neo-republican vision of politics is but the flip side of the public choice vision. Where the latter sees atomized individuals relentlessly pursuing their own exogenously determined individual preferences, the former sees fully socialized altruists exercising civic virtue in the pursuit of community welfare.

One does not have to deny that some very strong forms of community exist to be very dubious that they often exist in contexts even remotely like the governance of a modern nation-state. We seem to lack the capacity for extended sympathy on a continuous basis beyond the family or perhaps the clan. At the very least, the sorry story of much of human history makes it extremely risky to rely on the public spirit as the lodestar of institutional design. And so we are left necessarily with the public choice theorists' puzzles about how best to aggregate refractory individual preferences, including the necessity of guarding against self-interested behavior.

Second, we do not really have much information about how to design institutions that take the taste-shaping aspects of public action seriously. We know very little about how institutional taste shaping works. Presumably, simply making people talk to each other until they all agree is not enough, unless we believe as well that all tastes shaped by dialogue are good ones. And if not, as is surely the case, under what conditions is such discussion likely to produce acceptable results? How would we design institutions to promote "appropriate" discussion leading toward "good" ends? Recognizing that consensus is often incomplete, what do we know about partially socialized tastes? Are they better than aggregated individualistic ones? Is it possible to work our way toward public-spirited governance by imagining that we are already there? Indeed, is this a status or condition that one can seek purposefully at all?[12]

These are very hard questions, and the answers are not obviously going to support the abandonment of public choice talk. After all, "strong consensus" can be just another term for "herd mentality." The practice of self-interested self-representation and arm's-length negotiation may be a prerequisite for a rationally autonomous and collectively civilized community. The strategic control of self-interest may be essential to both the achievement and the maintenance of a minimally rational and just polity.

These conundra suggest a simple conclusion: The necessary partiality and current vagueness of the idea that political institutions should be designed to promote the "public spirit" or civic virtue argue for the continued relevance and strategic utility of conventional public choice assumptions. A Kierkegaardian leap of faith into public-spiritedness may be a good strategy, but it may also be folly. We should want to be as good as we can, and we should attempt to avoid activities that make us underestimate our possibilities; but the task of reform almost certainly involves more than imagining a better world peopled by better selves.

Moreover, because ought implies can, it is impossible to disentangle the charge that public choice corrupts the public morals from the question of whether public choice theorists' exogenously formed and materially self-interested hypothesis about preferences provides a good explanation of what public action is like. If the public choice crowd has a good description of human behavior in political contexts, then it should give us *some* guidance on the question of what sorts of processes and institutions are possible for us and how to construct them. And if that theory provides good explanations of political behavior, particularly in institutional settings that currently emphasize republican virtues of persuasion, then it would hardly be immoral, even in the strategic sense of not promoting morality, to avoid shattering republican illusions. Exhorting people to be better than they possibly can be is the transmission of guilt, not moral education.

I am not here retreating from the view that Steven Kelman's critique of public choice is to a degree unanswerable. Analytic models do have normative consequences. And tests of public choice propositions can never demonstrate that an entirely new world is beyond our grasp. Indeed, such tests might buttress Kelman's position. For if public choice explanations are poor, they may reinforce the conviction that our imperfect political world can be made better—perhaps by focusing greater attention on the public spirit and on the institutions that nurture it. And if the predictions are sometimes good and sometimes bad, we might begin to understand better both how to achieve our ideals and the relationship between ideals and institutional arrangements. We cannot, by focusing on public morals, avoid the question of truth.

I want to argue, therefore, for a more complex understanding of Picasso's point concerning Stein's portrait. The artist's conviction that his painting would influence our perceptions was based on something more than an inflated estimation of the necessary influence of anything he painted. He was claiming instead that he had captured something fundamental about Stein in his likeness and that, on serious contemplation of the work, that fundamental element would overwhelm concerns about the details of the representation.

Contemporary positive political theory makes a similar claim. Its practitioners urge us to believe that they are onto something that lies at the heart of collective action—the pursuit of rational self-interest. Their claim is that if we will but grasp that fundamental idea, then we will not be misled by the contingencies of public interest rhetoric and democratic enthusiasm. We will instead see clearly what can be expected from various collective choice processes. And having seen what is true of all public institutions, we will be able to decide what form of government is best for us. But, like Picasso's claim for his portrait, public choice's vision of the necessary dynamics of governance may be false.

The Quest for Usable Knowledge

Are all those bad things that positive political theory is saying about our political life true? "No" would be a comforting answer. It might allow us to reimagine politics as the pursuit of principle and the public interest. It might suggest that we need not worry too much about the careful design of governmental institutions so long as we make sure that they are responsive to the people.

But surely this is a counsel of folly. Few human attempts at governance have been either unquestionably effective or enduring. It can hardly be the case that all unhappy instances have but a single lesson — that we have relied too little on governance through the "public spirit." Government should empower the citizenry, but it must also restrain it. We lack the hard-wired communitarian instincts of the social insects. All too often we do consider our own interests more important than, or perhaps synonymous with, the public interest. Our governmental institutions should attempt to instill more public spirit in us, to be sure. Yet governance arrangements that rely on the existence of that spirit, particularly its universality and durability under stress, are likely to fail.

In a sense, "yes" might be the second-best answer to the question of the truth of positive political theory's predictions about collective action. If we could be sure that institutions for collective action were almost certain to go wrong, particularly if they would only go wrong in systematic ways, our institutional design difficulties might be lessened. After all, we could then know that we did not have much to hope for from collective activity. We could set about to construct a minimalist state with extremely modest functions. We could not be sure, of course, that even those functions would be carried out effectively. But we could limit the damage by limiting government. With a vastly restricted jurisdiction, and checks and balances sufficient to prevent most governmental actions, we would have little to fear from government. Our difficulty instead would be how to deal with those social and economic problems that seem to have promoted the scope and direction of governance in modern nation-states.

Once again, it is hard to believe that this answer is acceptable. Even if we think that positive political theory is substantially correct, we seem, under modern social and economic conditions, to need somehow to organize a broad range of governmental activities. We are too interconnected, too interdependent, and too skeptical of the power of markets and voluntary associations to control their own external effects, to believe again in the "nightwatchman" state. Hence, even if positive political theory's dire predictions were basically sound, we would nonetheless be left with the need to attempt to maintain and construct some activist institutions. Moreover, as we shall see momentarily, positive political theory still has a lot of explaining to do. The theory is ambiguous and/or incoherent in some of its core approaches and findings. It may often predict the wrong outcome.

Alas for institutional designers, we seem to be in a third-best world. A confident yes or a confident no would overstate either the truth or the falsity of the findings of modern positive political theory. The job of this chapter, therefore, is to bring some of the claims of positive political theory more sharply into focus by analyzing the conceptual criticisms leveled against the theory and by assessing the theory's capacity to predict what really emerges from efforts at group formation, voting, and legislative and administrative action. We need to understand more about the limits and the strengths of a public choice orientation before proceeding to consider some important and enduring problems of institutional design to which the theory indeed has relevance. The idea is to attempt to grasp some middle way between a naive faith in the public interest and a cynical campaign to eliminate collective action wherever it rears its ugly head. We need to take up a more realistic posture which will allow us to use whatever truths modern public choice theory is telling us without succumbing to the excessively negative vision it so often supports.

Assessing Interest Group Theory

Remember for a moment what the economic theory of political behavior predicts. First, voters have no rational basis for engaging in political activity. They should be ignorant about politics, apathetic about political issues, and nonparticipants in political life. Second, because groups are difficult to form and hold together, we should expect that few groups will form to pursue the "public interest." Group cohesion is a function of small size and members' individual economic benefits from joining and supporting the group. It should be easy for the automobile manufacturers to act in concert to pursue their political interests, but hard for automobile consumers to do so.

Third, legislators are thought to respond essentially to group demands. The groups are the ones capable of supplying both the money and the votes needed to maintain legislators in office. Hence, we should expect to see the output of legislative assemblies sharply skewed in favor of those economic interests who form themselves effectively into political forces.

As I have said, all of this seems vaguely familiar. Voter turnout is low, at least in the United States, and there are constant complaints about the impact of one or another lobby on the shape of national legislation. How narrow interest groups got what they wanted in the legislative arena is the staple of investigative press reporting. And because in our checked and balanced government an interest group needs to control only one institution (the House, the Senate, or the presidency) to block legislation or to derail implementation in the bureaucracy or the courts, it seems quite reasonable to predict that even more public interest legislation may be blocked than private interest legislation is passed. We might further predict that, if passed, public interest legislation will be long on aspiration and short on effects.

Yet, this is not the whole story. A more balanced view requires two connected inquiries: The first explores the conceptual ambiguities and predictive anomalies that should temper our enthusiasm for drawing very general conclusions from public choice premises. The second reevaluates the utility of public choice ideas when deployed in a more tentative and discriminating fashion.

THE DEFECTS OF INTEREST GROUP THEORY

There are in fact a number of good reasons to reject some of the more general implications of the interest group theory of legislation. The first is that the theory makes obvious predictive errors. Interest group theories of regulation have had great difficulty, for example, accommodating the undeniable political movement toward deregulation. The existence and later development of a regulatory regime like that administered by the Civil Aeronautics Board fit happily within the basic capture theory of regulation. A small group of companies dominated a regulated industry, competed hardly at all on price, and prevented the certification of all new carriers on national routes for over thirty years. The result was high wages, high profits, and an easy life for the industry; high prices and limited choices for consumers. But then, strangely, the CAB and the Congress, who were supposed to be in the pockets of the special interests, shut the whole cozy system down. The result has been fierce competition, expanded service, new entrants, and dramatically lower airfares. Unorganized consumers have benefited while airline companies and air carrier labor unions have lost. How could this happen?[1]

Other familiar moves toward easing regulatory restrictions and opening up markets in transportation, banking, and elsewhere also provide counterexamples to interest group theory's predictions. Moreover, case studies of the processes by which various regulatory statutes were enacted during the 1970s have given little support to the interest group interpretation. The enactment of the Clean Air Act, for example, surely had interest group elements, but it seemed more fundamentally to be an aspect of what has been termed "entrepreneurial politics." Rather than waiting for some demand to emerge from organized interests, entrepreneurial politicians pursued issues of interest to a broader electorate and used the voters' positive responses to political advantage in seeking national office.[2] The interest group theorists seemed to have forgotten that political parties and aspiring presidents might simply bypass entrenched interests and go directly to the electorate.

Indeed, as one begins to look for them, more and more anomalies appear. As we just noted, the development of environmental legislation had interest group elements, but often the groups were "public interest" organizations. According to interest group theory, groups representing such diffuse interests as those "concerned about the environment" should never form, much less be effective. But for two decades the Sierra Club, the Environmental Defense Fund, the National Resources Defense Council, the National Wildlife Foundation, and a host of others have grown, prospered, and had influence.

Nor is environmentalism the only cause that has attracted effective champions for something other than the narrow self-interest of well-organized pressure groups. One could hardly accuse Ralph Nader of pursuing the interests of the automobile industry, as he and a band of epidemiologists and safety engineers, aided by a few entrepreneurial politicians, promoted the Motor Vehicle Safety Act.[3] And in some cases the unorganized and underrepresented seem to be protected without any visible group formation activities at all. The Gramm-Rudman-Hollings deficit reduction bill, for example, spares poverty programs from its budgetary doomsday machine. But as Robert Dole put it, "There is no poor-PAC." If statutes are the outcome of interest group pressure and bargaining with representatives, how are these results to be explained?

To some degree, deficiencies in the interest group theory's record of predictions might be explained away by broadening the theory's scope. The relevant "interest group" need not be an industry capturing rents. Wealth transfers created by statutes may run in several directions at once and provide benefits to a number of groups. If we consider the power and prestige of bureaucrats, the opportunities created for legislators to do special favors for regulated groups, the secondary benefit of changes in increased safety to insurance companies, the possible redistribution of resources regionally within the United States, and a host of other factors, we can find interest groups (or "latent" interest groups) who are being benefited by statutory change.

But this approach threatens to make public choice uninteresting as a predictive theory. Statutes always shift rights or expectations. After the fact, a benefited group can always be identified and, if we let bureaucrats and politicians serve as proxies for not-yet-formed groups, groups for whom they can later do favors, or with whom they can form coalitions, then the theory becomes both complete and tautological. Given the right hypotheses, everything can always be explained ex post. But interest group theory itself may give us very modest assistance in choosing the correct hypothesis concerning the political dynamics of particular issues ex ante. We have entered the realm of faith, leaving positive political theory with no claim to "scientific" explanation.

Nor is this the only difficulty. The components of the theory, which together define its causal dynamics, are often ambiguous. Consider the following questions:

When investigating the influence of interest groups on legislation, should we be looking for large or small groups? The theory really cannot say, because the currency of exchange is uncertain. Where representatives are being rewarded with money, most interest group theorists seem to believe that small size and large stakes in the outcome would be an advantage in forming, maintaining, and exerting interest group power. On the other hand, if votes are the medium of exchange, then groups of large size obviously have a significant advantage, even if their interests are not so intense. Should we imagine then that politicians will respond to large or to small groups? The answer seems to be to both. But if it is both, then the basic scenario of intense factions producing legislation that suits their interests at the expense of the general public begins to unravel. At best it must be significantly qualified by attention to a host of contingencies that bear on interest group power in particular contexts.

What about the technique of drafting legislation to effectuate interest group desires? Should we anticipate that statutes conferring benefits on private groups would be drafted in specific or in vague terms? Interest group theorists tell two different stories. Some imagine that interest group bargains will be set out in quite specific terms in order to assure that value is actually received by the interest group for its contribution of either monies or votes. Yet others predict that interest group legislation will be vague in form and contain broad delegations of authority to administrative personnel.[4] Presumably, in this later scenario future coalitions between regulated groups and administrative agencies will assure the returns from capture, while protecting legislative politicians from the assignment of responsibility for promoting a particular interest group's private ends.

Indeed, there is not even agreement on whether interest group competition in the political space ought to be viewed primarily as producing private goods at public expense or public goods that must of necessity be produced through collective action. At base this seems to be due to another ambiguity, differences in the models' specifications of who the bargainers are when interest groups seek or oppose legislation. Most interest group theorists seem to imagine a bargain between interest groups and legislators in which the legislators are induced to provide private goods at public expense in return for electoral support. But in other models representatives are mediators between or among interest groups in a market that demands and supplies an equilibrium level of public goods.[5] In these latter explanations, cheerful visions of pluralist compromise and the improvement of public welfare through politics reemerge as real possibilities.

Finally, the more depressing general predictions of interest group theory must be viewed with skepticism because of the implausibility of its account of both the electoral and the legislative processes. These two problems are rather different, but both are fundamental to a coherent story. You will remember that the basic interest group scenario is one in which intensely interested coalitions of voters procure legislation from representatives at the expense of the general population. The underlying mechanism depends upon the "rational apathy" of voters in general combined with close monitoring of representatives by interest groups. Logrolling in the legislative process also plays a prominent part.

Now, the shocking thing about voters is that they refuse to behave rationally. It is demonstrably not worth it for any voters to inform themselves on the issues, much less go to the polls and vote. Yet in election after election, millions turn out to engage in an activity that produces individually negative returns. This perverse behavior strongly suggests that calculations of personal self-interest, defined wholly in instrumental or economic terms, are not a dominant, perhaps not even an important, element in civic participation. But if this is true, then politicians cannot count on voters to be either uninformed or apathetic. Honoring the demands of "special interests" may not be costless.

It is also unclear what the mechanism is by which interest groups police the representatives that they support for failure to deliver on their promises. There are no transferable property rights in a representative's vote. Moreover, the ability of an interest group to punish a recalcitrant representative is sharply limited by the interest group's alternatives with respect to future trading partners. Collusion among representatives, not to mention their nonfungibility, makes the "market" for interest group influence highly imperfect. Representatives have significant opportunities to welch on deals and to rationalize that welching in terms of institutional obstacles to performance, or considerations of long-term interest in coalition building. And if the chair of the House Armed Services Committee welches on a deal, there is no alternative representative with whom to make a comparable bargain. Interest groups constantly have to deal with people who—at any one moment—have near monopoly power.

In short, there is an enormous amount of organizational slack in the linkage between interest groups and representatives. For all we know this slack may be allowing representatives to engage in consumption expenditures, including pursuit of the "public interest" as the representative understands it. After all, that is the perquisite uniquely available to public office holders. Indeed, one wonders why they have chosen to pursue the "public service," given its pattern of potential returns, unless they plan to obtain much of their satisfaction from seeking the good as they understand it. If interest groups are principals in the political process and representatives their agents, there seems to be a vast domain for "corruption" in the form of "voting one's conscience."

The little work that has been done on the principal-agent issue seems to validate what these speculations would predict. The narrow self-interest of the interest groups active in representatives' constituencies is not a very good predictor of their voting patterns. Prediction is much improved by adding in ideological variables which represent either legislator beliefs about what is good for the country or certain broad preferences based on general interests of constituents that are unrepresented by the activities of existing interest groups.[6]

None of this, of course, is to deny that interest group activity is massive and that the potential impact of faction on politics should be a cause for concern. The point is more modest. The interest group theory of legislation is often ambiguous and its predictions are beset by counterexamples. In some forms it is tautological and empty; in others it seems honored mostly in the breach. At least at the level of national politics, Madison's vision of the efficacy of the

Constitution's institutional structure to transform the raw material of the electorate's passions and interests into something approximating the public interest remains at least plausible. Perhaps civic virtue, the public spirit, and pursuit of the public interest are not dead.

INTEREST GROUP THEORY RECONSIDERED

The defects of interest group theory should not, however, be oversold. It is true that one observes outcomes that do not seem to fit well with the theory. Voters vote, legislation pursues things that seem to be in the general public interest, and politicians are even sometimes found to have character and conviction. But this does not make the interest group story untrue unless one imagines that it was meant to be *universally* true.

First, think about the notion that we do sometimes see legislation that pursues broad public interests rather than narrow special ones. Environmental legislation is often trotted out as a case in point. It surely is the case that environmental legislation, broadly considered, seems to pursue such a general interest that you would never imagine an effective group forming to promote protection of the environment. Indeed, since much environmental protection may be oriented at preserving the Earth for future generations, the beneficiaries of this legislation may be an interest group that could not possibly be organized to pursue its own self-interest.

The problem with taking too much comfort from this story is its incompleteness. First, we should probably turn a jaundiced eye on any claim that we can learn whether the public interest is alive and well or dead as a doornail from looking at the output of politics. That legislation has a particularly beneficial effect on a particular group or seems designed to benefit the general public tells us little about *why* the legislation was enacted. That we can provide a number of public interest stories as counterexamples to private interest predictions hardly means that legislative activity is generally public-interested. Indeed, a close look at virtually any individual piece of legislation will generate both a plausible private-interest and a plausible public-interest explanation.

Is occupational licensing a means of protecting consumers from fraud and incompetence, or a device for restricting competition and raising the earnings of licensees? Does Food and Drug Administration regulation of prescription pharmaceuticals protect the public from dangerous drugs? Or is it a hardy means for ensuring that only large producers will have the capacity to do drug development, thus limiting the supply and raising the prices of useful medications? Does Environmental Protection Agency regulation of sulfur dioxide in coal-fired electrical generating plants protect the public health? Or is it designed instead to curry favor with western real estate interests and protect the market for eastern high-sulfur coal?

In almost every case the answer is likely to be "both" or "all of the above." To be sure, some legislation is hard to explain as anything other than a reflection of majoritarian sentiments concerning what is good for the country. And a demonstration that legislation has big wealth-distribution effects; that it has large costs and few benefits; and that it was enacted through a process that was highly likely to have promoted nefarious forms of rent seeking by benefited groups, would provide a pretty strong indictment of that statute on public interest grounds. But the interesting question from the standpoint of institutional design is what we can know about how processes tend toward public interest results or what sorts of mechanisms might be useful in limiting private-interest wealth transfers. Positive political theory can assist in thinking through these issues so long as we do not demand that it provide definitive answers (and are not bamboozled by those who claim that it does).

Second, we should be wary of claims that anyone knows why legislators vote for legislation. There have now been a host of attempts to sort out the voting records of legislators, usually congressional representatives. The question generally asked is whether legislators vote the interests of the groups and constituents whose support they need for reelection, or instead vote their own views of good public policy. Analysts, indeed, have been extremely clever in attempts to determine and assess the mix of legislative motives that one finds in particular cases. While some of these studies are triumphs of scholarly energy and social science methodology, no one has yet been able to tell us more than that legislators seem to act out of some mix of personal ideology and reelection-oriented self-interest. This is not very big news. The problem is, of course, that it is very difficult to control for all the relevant variables — party membership, constituency characteristics, legislative position, campaign contributions, and personal ideology. These things are not only highly correlated one with another, researchers have no way of observing some of them directly.

Take, for example, studies that claim legislators vote their ideologies more than they vote the economic interests of their contributors or constituents. When such an empirical test is conducted, a legislator's "ideology" (view of the public interest) is constructed by looking at his or her voting records. Those records are then interpreted to place the legislator's views at some point on an issue-ideology scale — say, from liberal to conservative. The analyst then looks at whether this "liberal" or "conservative" votes the liberal or conservative line on specific issues that come before the Congress. If the ideological variable explains more votes than, say, the legislator's list of campaign contributors or the political coloration of the legislator's constituency, then it is concluded that this is a legislator voting his or her conscience.

The problem with this methodology is that the legislators' general patterns of voting, the ones that were used to locate them on the ideological scale, are being used to explain votes on particular issues. But if something that is not being or cannot be measured explains legislators' general voting patterns, then these things also explain the "ideology" that is being assigned to them by the ideological scale. When the legislators' positions on the ideological scale are then entered into the researchers' predictive model, legislators' "ideology" is being counted twice (or three or four times). About all that can be said is that models that contain both ideological and economic self-interest factors seem to outperform purely economic models in predicting the behavior of legislators.

The crucial point is this: Much of the social science research on voting behavior or interest group activity may be asking questions and giving answers at much too gross a scale. That there are public-interest-appearing outcomes in the world of practical politics and that legislators may vote their convictions or ideologies is cheerful news. But if we are asking that question simply about whole statutes, we may not be asking the relevant question. It is quite easy to concoct environmental legislation, for example, that is special interest in nature. But to see that it is, one must inspect the specifics of the legislation rather than focusing simply on the fact that a clean air act or a clean water bill got passed. God may be in the details, but special interest pleading may be there too. And it is devilishly hard to calculate whether the public interest benefits of doing something about environmental protection are overwhelmed by the costs of private-interest deals that are in the interstices of the legislation.

And what about those voters? Does it really mean that voters are altruistic in pursuing the public interest when they get out and vote? Actually, we know very little about why people vote, what motivated their votes when voting, and what, if any, connection there is between the motivations for voting itself and for voting in a particular way. Answers to these questions might even suggest that questions about whether legislators vote to help special interests or favored constituents, or instead vote their own convictions, are misguided. Moreover, these puzzles are important. If people vote for public-spirited reasons and, when voting, decide how to vote on the basis of their conception of the public interest, then reelection-oriented legislators, consulting only their own interest in retaining office, will nevertheless be compelled — obviously with some slack — to behave as if they were pursuing the public interest as perceived by their constituents. The basis for legislation would thus be ideology, but the ideology effectuated would be that of constituents, not legislators.

It probably serves no significant purpose, in this context, to pursue the issue of why voters vote. The more interesting question is why they vote as they do. Moreover, the debate about why voters vote is both inconclusive in itself and uninformative on the issue of primary interest. Empirical investigators have, therefore, by-passed the "why vote?" issue to pursue the "why vote that way?" question directly. In order to do so, they have constructed tests of whether voters vote their pocketbooks.

The results are to some degree contradictory. Studies looking at aggregate effects tend to confirm pocketbook voting. When economic conditions are bad or worsening, the "ins" are thrown out, and when they are improving, the "ins" are retained. By contrast, survey data has tended to show that while voting the *nation's* pocketbook, voters do not necessarily vote their *own*. Votes are better correlated with voters' perceptions of how the nation as a whole is doing economically than with how they are faring personally. A conventional social science interpretation of these results would be to believe the second set of individual-voter-level survey studies, that is, the "public interest" vision triumphs.[7] The problem with the aggregate-level studies' suggestion that voters were voting their pocketbooks is called the "ecological fallacy." Behavior found to characterize a population, at the population level, has been fallaciously assumed to characterize the behavior of individuals within the population. Because voters as a whole threw the ins out in bad times, it was assumed that the voters who did the throwing were themselves experiencing economic pain, when in fact they were just pursuing the general welfare of the country.

But social science is never so impressive as when demonstrating that we should not credit previous social science. On further careful exploration it turns out that voter surveys have not been constructed to isolate the effects of general economic conditions, rather than personal economic condition, on voter behavior. We cannot be certain that voters who look like they are pursuing the "public interest" because their votes do not fit their current pocketbooks are not voting on the basis of fears and hopes for their future pocketbooks. And because studies commit the "ecological fallacy" in looking over time at whether ins or outs get elected in good and hard times, they cannot disprove an altruistic or ideological explanation for individual voting.[8] On the basis of the best available information, we are left with something like complete agnosticism about the bases or motivations for voters' individual choices.

The Vices and Virtues of Voting Theory

The realism of voting theory must also be confronted. For, even if representatives are by and large attempting to pursue public values, voting theory suggests that they may be unable to do so. The usual escape route from this unhappy suggestion is down lines of argument tending to demonstrate the irrelevance of the Arrow Theorem to real-world concerns. But none of these is wholly persuasive.

One might claim, for example, that most theoretical work on preference aggregation fundamentally misconceives the process of public choice. For political choice is exercised in an environment of debate and deliberation which ultimately produces judgments about representatives or policies. Those judgments are shaped by the processes of political interaction; they are not wholly exogenous to it. Our old friends A, B, and C do not have to vote. They can talk it over instead. And after they do, they may find that K, not X, Y, or Z, is what should be done. To set up the issue of politics as how to start with raw preferences and aggregate them into a consistent social choice function is to pose a nonproblem whose nonsolution should not trouble us.

But, alas, this is less than a complete answer. For one thing, discussion may harden, not ameliorate, conflict. Moreover, while discussion may reveal that these voters are acting out of principle, not just preference, the aggregation problem that Arrow defines is not dependent upon any particular characterization of the psychological functions of the political participants. Whether one views tastes as shaped by factors endogenous to political choice or characterizes votes as considered judgments about the goodness of proposed candidates or policies, the Arrow Theorem holds so long as there are three alternatives and three voters. It is not just that using fair voting rules obscures the relationship of outcomes to underlying *preferences*. The lack of a fair means for consistent mapping from individuals to collectives infects all *choices*. And, because of its generality, Arrow's insight may have strong effects on appropriate institutional design.

Once again, we must take care not to confuse internal coherence with determinate consequences. The sturdiness of the Arrow results has been taken, for example, as a persuasive argument against populist or strongly democratic institutions. In *Liberalism Against Populism: A Confrontation Between the Theory of Democracy and the Theory of Social Choice,* William Riker argues that voting theory demonstrates the superiority of what he calls liberalism — essentially, representative democracy with specific guarantees of particular individual liberties — over populism or direct democracy.[9] His logic is straightforward: Populism is justified by an appeal to the fairness of majority-rule procedures that give each citizen an equal opportunity to express preferences and, therefore, presumably to determine collective decisions. However, because voting theory demonstrates that there is no necessary connection between the outcomes of majority-rule procedures and the underlying preferences of voters, the democratic control promised by populism is illusory.

Procedural fairness leads to meaninglessness, not to the expression of the will of the majority.

In Riker's view, liberalism is not subject to the same objection. The basic value of liberalism is the protection of individual interests. This can be accomplished through a system of specific guarantees combined with periodic opportunities to dismiss public decisionmakers. For even if dismissal or retention of public officeholders has no necessary relationship to the underlying preferences of the members of society, it will nevertheless prevent the maintenance of stable tyranny. Thus, in Riker's analysis, social choice theory demonstrates that while "expressive" democracy is impossible, "defensive" democracy can nevertheless be justified. In a significant sense Riker reaffirms the institutional arrangements of Federalist political science, although the claims that he makes for them are surely more modest than those we encounter in Federalist 10. There is no suggestion that the representative assembly represents the will of the people; only that since some public business must be done by some collective institution, about the best we can do is have a representative assembly that can be thrown out — combined with severe limitations on the degree to which individual interests can be set aside by government action.

But has Riker made out his basic claim? If liberalism (which he tends to equate with representative democracy subject to constitutional limitations) or representative democracy can be justified as instrumental to the preservation of individual rights, then why can populism not be justified as instrumental to the citizens' sense of self-worth or collective identification, or some other value? Riker seems to assume that the unavailability of a proceduralist justification for either liberalism or populism is a decisive criticism only against the latter. But Riker gives no rationale for his failure to explore the possible instrumental justifications for populism. Nor is it clear why the arbitrariness of outcomes in populist schemes is so troubling. After all, Riker views with equanimity a voting system for displacing officeholders that may operate about as rationally as a plague or a terrorist attack — or that may be under the control of some tyrannical, but clever, agenda manipulator. And he fails to consider the possibilities for combining populism with constitutional restraints on plebiscitary power or the invasion of individual liberties.

Moreover, as we saw in Chapter 1, the chaotic or arbitrary features of voting systems with no institutional mechanisms beyond majority rule are ameliorated by adding some institutional structure. The outcomes of a democratic political process are not meaningless. They just must be interpreted as a function *both* of the underlying voter preferences and of the institutional mechanisms for preference expression. Now to be sure, the idea that outcomes are *interpretable* in terms of some functional relationship between underlying preferences and existing institutional structures has little normative significance. We should still like to know what relationship the outcome has to underlying preferences or judgments and how the institutional structure shapes the outcome. For unless outcomes have some meaningful relationship to representatives' choices, or to an institutional structure for decisionmaking which can be justified on other grounds, we still seem to confront statute books that are full of nonrandom, but nevertheless arbitrary, statements.

The way out of this mess may be through more voting theory. For while voting theory says that anything is possible, it does not say that all things are equally possible. The likelihood that voting processes will produce chaotic results is directly related to the number of voters and the number of alternatives put before them. Institutional arrangements which constrain the number of decisionmakers and which reduce alternatives to a manageable number can produce coherent choice a very large proportion of the time. If we imagine, therefore, that the institutional structure of American government is one which delegates choice routinely to institutions such as congressional subcommittees or administrative agencies where small numbers and deliberation can produce coherence, there is no reason to imagine that the output of the public law process is chaotic. Meaning is to be found in the actions of those who exercise delegated power. Hence, we might better describe American governments not as representative democracy, but as a system of transitory institutional dictators. This may threaten the notion that statutes express the general will, but it does not challenge the meaningfulness of statutory language. Nor does "dictator" here have a particularly pejorative connotation. Our agenda setters and quasi-independent policy prescribers — presidents, congressional leaders and administrative agencies — are subject to multitudinous forms of public, political, and legal oversight.

Moreover, a related line of current research in voting theory has begun to explore the reasons for the observed coalescence of choice around a small number of alternatives. The basic logic of this position is straightforward: while the "anything is possible" proofs demonstrate that there are decision paths to any result, it is also demonstrable that widely preferred alternatives have many paths leading to them, while relatively nonpreferred alternatives have only a few. This suggests that repeated expressions of preference should demonstrate patterns coalescing on relatively preferred alternatives. There may still be cycles that are stopped only by some "arbitrary" feature of the institutional landscape, but those cycles are likely to be among alternatives all of which have significant support.

These preliminary explorations are of great potential significance.[10] Outcomes that persist seem to have some claim to be expressions of true underlying preferences. For the possibilities over time of changing both key institutional actors and the shape of decisional institutions suggest that the stable outcomes are not only artifacts of the institutional structure itself.

The Task Ahead

The perplexing truth about positive political theory is that we have an extremely poor understanding of when we should trust its predictions. The interest group branch, when interpreted broadly to include agency theory and game theory, has a marvelous capacity to generate hypotheses about why certain things happened or how certain institutional structures and procedures are to be explained. But the means thus far developed for testing these hypotheses are weak and the results variable. This branch of positive political theory has also come under withering attack for its use of untested and implausible behavioral assumptions and has been, quite properly, convicted of high crimes against social scientific method.[11]

Voting theory has different problems. Because it is largely axiomatic rather than empirical, its claim to truth rests on internal consistency rather than correspondence to reality. The basic theorems in this branch of public choice activity have thus stood up very well to repeated attempts to discredit them. The theoretical virtue of voting theory, however, is also a practical vice. It is nearly impossibly to move from axiomatic theory to real-world institutions. The real world of political choice is much too complex to be captured in a set of mathematically tractable axioms. Yet the great success of voting theorists in generating counterintuitive results from intuitively attractive axioms cautions against "seat of the pants" theorizing when mathematical modeling fails.

These admitted defects, however, are hardly enough to suggest that public choice analyses can be ignored as we attempt to understand and build better political institutions. Physics has no unified theory of how matter and energy behave, but it has provided sufficient insight to permit some pretty impressive feats of engineering. Positive political theory is hardly on as sound a footing as most physics appears to be, yet we would ignore its basic insights at our peril. A few simple examples should make the case.

Imagine yourself at a meeting of your faculty, department, board, or family. The chair, having heard some discussion, suggests that there seem to be three alternatives, A, B, and C, and that the thing to do is to vote. Will you ever again view the order or type of vote taken as an issue of little moment in determining what gets decided?

Or imagine yourself a member of your local zoning board, required to hold a public hearing on any proposed change in a zoning classification. After listening to whomever shows up to support or protest the change, are you likely to believe that you have heard the authentic voice of the people? Or will you temper that belief with a skeptical appreciation of why certain interests may be overrepresented, while other groups have failed to form or appear?

A public choice perspective on these matters may not tell you what to do. It does help you to articulate and think through dangers in collective decision-making that earlier were intuitively troubling, but not systematically understood. Indeed, you may now see potential trouble where your pre–public choice intuitions would have failed to sense a danger. Moreover, if you can simultaneously keep from being carried away by abstract theorizing while avoiding the rejection of all theory that provides no pat answers, you might even make some better-informed decisions about how to organize collective action. There are at least some tools here for analyzing claims that one or another position represents democratic process or the will of the people.

To some degree, of course, positive political theory also cannot be ignored because the political economists' theorizing too often aligns with our intuitive notions of how people behave and what motivates them. You do not need to read tomes on public choice to believe, with the League of Voters and Common Cause, that making voter registration easier (lowering its costs) would increase citizen participation in elections; or that limiting the need for special interest money in political campaigns is likely to also limit the influence of special interests in politics. In both of these cases, conventional wisdom implicitly accepts a "self-interested rational actor" model of political behavior.

A public choice perspective on institutional design goes somewhat further, however, than these relatively easy cases. It takes the pursuit of self-interest to be the principal object of interest in thinking about political life and seeks to explicate systematically the ways in which political actors can behave strategically to achieve their ends. As I have said, I believe that public choice theorists often overestimate the degree to which economic self-interest dominates culture, ideology, moral and religious belief, or sheer altruism, and that their models are too simple and too static to capture the dynamics of political life. Yet the invitation to think systematically and strategically about the pursuit of self-interest within political institutions yields insights that go beyond simple intuition, conventional wisdom, or "common sense."

Consider an issue that is being discussed as these lines are written — "soft money" campaign finance reform. The problem as generally stated is this: Many avenues of influence through campaign contributions have been clogged by regulatory proscriptions. One main artery, however, has been left open: donations to state political parties. Thus, huge contributions can be, and are, channeled through state party machinery in an attempt to seek influence. The money is "soft" because it is not directed specifically to one candidate. But the perception is that it warps the political process nevertheless. Hence the campaign to regulate soft money.

Superficially this sounds like a good idea. But a public choice approach invites a further analysis that may render it problematic. Begin with the public choice proposition that politics *inherently* involves groups seeking gains for themselves by making deals with politicians. Political institutions can channel and direct the means by which these transactions are carried out, but they cannot change the fundamental nature of the game. The question then is what forms of channeling or steering are likely to be useful in limiting straightforward seizures of public power by private interests.

Arguably, soft money contributions are, from this perspective, a good device for limiting special deals and increasing democratic accountability. Why? The analysis is straightforward. The legislature is highly unlikely to cut itself off from all means of receiving private support in political campaigns. The real question, therefore, is whether we want individual legislators to have major political obligations directly to contributors or only indirectly through a party machinery that can discipline them — by withholding funds — if they fail to support the party's program, at least most of the time. It is hardly obvious that the former structure of political obligations dominates the latter. Indeed, many now believe that one of the major failings of late twentieth-century American democracy is the decline of party authority. Not only has the rise of the politician as independent entrepreneur produced a "gridlocked" legislative process with extraordinary levels of special interest access, it has made it impossible for citizens to hold parties responsible for proposing and producing coherent programs in pursuit of public ends.

Channeling contributions such that they empower parties thus begins to look attractive. Moreover, individual legislators beholden to party leaders for campaign support would have strong incentives not only to accept party discipline, but to struggle to ensure that the party's program was attractive to the general public. They would also have every reason to attempt to make good on the party's promises. For if they did not, the voters presumably would throw them out at the next election.

To put the matter in terms of recent political struggles, the exploitation of soft money "loopholes" was instrumental in the Republican takeover of the Congress engineered by Newt Gingerich in the 1994 elections. Moreover, we are currently witnessing a higher degree of party specification of its legislative program and of party discipline in voting for it than at any time perhaps since Sam Rayburn and Lyndon Johnson ruled the Democratic congressional roost (under very different electoral and internal congressional rules). Republicans are about the business of keeping their promises — an act of political responsibility for which the voters may, of course, turn them out in 1996. The point, however, is not that soft money financing necessarily produces good or popular policy. The claim is that it may increase both responsibility and accountability. Indeed, as a device for increasing accountability and responsibility, soft money begins to look so good that, rather than ruling it out, we might be well advised to make it the exclusive means for financing election campaigns.

Now to be sure, this argument glosses over many problems and requires much more extended analysis. Discipline and corrupt parties can be a democratic disease as well as a facilitator of representative democracy. The point the soft money example illustrates, however, is important. Taking public choice ideas seriously can lead to some interesting insights and potentially innovative reforms. Systematic thinking about how to restructure a political process that cannot eliminate the pursuit of individual self-interest, and that also has complex and nonobvious interactions, seems necessary. Public choice approaches thus promise to provide an apparently skeptical analysis of reform ideas and conventional practices that we tend to believe to be beneficial, but which may, on reflection, be quite problematic.

It is this sort of instruction that we will seek to derive from public choice ideas as we look in subsequent chapters at some perennial issues in the design of American public institutions: What should be the role of bureaucratic decisionmaking in shaping public policy? What role should the judiciary play in invalidating allegedly unreasonable legislation? How does the separation of powers advantage or disadvantage particular governmental institutions? Even a cautious use of public choice notions often produces unconventional answers to conventional questions.

For example, contrary to existing doctrine, and to the views of most constitutional lawyers, I conclude that the Supreme Court's wholesale retreat from "rationality" review in the 1930s was a mistake. I will argue in Chapter 3 that this retreat is more apparent than real, is potentially more dangerous when done behind the smokescreen of alternative doctrines rather than candidly, and denies litigants both the protection of important rights and legitimate explanation of why their interests should be subordinated to collective purposes. Most important from the perspective of public choice's potential contribution to public law, I will argue that insights from interest group theory can provide important process criteria for the exercise of rationality review that will make the "countermajoritarian difficulty" — the substitution of the "legal" reasonableness judgment of unelected judges for the "political" reasonableness judgment of elected legislators — much less distressing. "Democracy" should not be a constitutional trump suit where democracy demonstrably fails.

Chapter 4 carries forward this contrarian agenda in two ways. First, I will analyze prior efforts to mine public choice approaches — particularly interest group theory — for usable guides to the interpretation of statutes. My conclusion is that, while this is the arena in which prior public law analysts have most often found public choice ideas useful, the value of a public choice approach to interpretation has been vastly oversold. Nevertheless, I discern some gold and silver mixed in with the fools' gold and quicksilver notions that have trumpeted public choice analysis as the rosetta stone of statutory interpretation.

The important thing that public choice analysis allows us to see is just how powerful interpretation is, given our particular constitutional system. Several connected, counterintuitive, and hence unconventional ideas surface from this exploration. First, judicial "misconstruction" of a statute may make it impossible in a large class of cases for the legislature to overturn the policy imposed by the judiciary. And in virtually all cases it will prevent the legislature from reenacting the original legislative policy. Second, because this is true, statutory interpretation is often more strongly countermajoritarian than judicial review. Finally, it follows from the above propositions that the canon of statutory construction which cautions courts to construe statutes to avoid constitutional issues may, in a large class of cases, create precisely the disrespect for majoritarian processes that the canon is meant to avoid.

Chapters 5 through 8 will explore the contributions of public choice to our understanding of the structure and functioning of the modern administrative state. Notwithstanding the ubiquitousness of "capture" stories, Chapter 5 is deeply skeptical of public choice claims that administrative process can be explained as the means by which Congress establishes monitoring devices for the benefit of dominant political interests. The public choice story surely contains important cautionary tales for lawyers fixated on administrative process as a set of structures and decision techniques designed to insure fairness and the rule of law. But, as a way of understanding how American administrative law took its current form, the public choice account is internally inconsistent and radically incomplete.

Chapter 6 is similarly skeptical of public choice attacks on the modern practice of delegating broad policy choice to administrators. Here, of course, public choice practitioners join hands with other legal and political theorists who bemoan these delegations as constructing a governance regime that is characterized by the exercise of "power without responsibility."[12] Contrary to this increasingly conventional view, I argue that a careful public choice analysis reveals that broad delegations to administrators might easily support both democratic accountability and majority rule.

Chapters 7 and 8 further analyze the idea of administrative accountability using a game theoretic account of judicial review and of political oversight of rulemaking. In Chapter 7 I will argue that the legal culture's insistence on pre-enforcement review of regulations has seriously undermined both governmental capacities and the rule of law. Chapter 8 develops reasons to believe that, contrary to the views of most commentators, the Supreme Court's Constitution-based rejection of the "legislative veto" of administrative rule making has seriously skewed the political control of agency action in favor of the executive branch. This imbalance fuels a series of dysfunctional legislative practices, including overly specific statutory drafting and the provision of pre-enforcement judicial review of virtually all rule making.

I hold these often controversial and sometimes contrarian views because I have attempted to take public choice seriously. But not too seriously. When public choice analysts argue that "agency theory" explains the structure of administrative law, or that legislative interpretation should be approached as if the court were interpreting a fully specified private contract, I find their evidence unconvincing and their arguments incoherent. I will sometimes argue that public choice's reach has vastly exceeded its grasp, but at other times that its insights have not been pursued far enough or in a sufficiently systematic fashion. This is not a book simply of praise or of condemnation. It is instead an attempt to grapple with some enduring issues of governmental structure and public law from the perspective of an unconventional discipline. It is also an attempt to maintain a critical distance from disciplinary enthusiasm that can easily translate into grotesque descriptions of public life and unwise approaches to institutional and legal reform.

3

Public Choice and Rationality Review

For nearly two hundred years American lawyers, judges, and legal academics have been looking for a fully persuasive theory that would justify the judicial invalidation of statutes because they fail to satisfy the judiciary's understanding of what the Constitution requires. To many outside the legal profession, this must seem an extremely curious enterprise. For one thing, federal judges have been exercising the power to declare statutes unconstitutional since the early nineteenth century. For another, over these two centuries the Supreme Court has invalidated less than one congressional statute per year. Moreover, in most cases the ruling of unconstitutionality affected only some, often correctable, provision of the statute, and interfered only modestly with Congress's power to work its will. In short, the practice is well established and has little practical impact.

Seen from this perspective, the centrality of the question of the legitimacy of judicial review in constitutional law scholarship seems like a throwback to medieval scholasticism. Argument about the number of angels who can dance on the head of a pin seems at least as diverting and important as arguments about the circumstances under which the courts of the United States are justified in overruling the considered judgments of the Congress of the United States, or of the legislatures of the fifty states.

Yet to view the matter in this way is quite wrong. Indeed, it is almost exactly backwards. The importance of judicial review in American legal, constitutional, and political life is not to be measured by statutes struck down and binding limitations imposed upon our elected legislatures. The practical importance of judicial review should be understood instead in terms of the legitimating force that it gives to laws sustained or never attacked. In a polity where constitutionalism is often viewed as a form of civic religion, that some laws *can* be unconstitutional sanctifies those that are not. Americans believe that they live "under law" in part because all law can be rendered problematic by constitutional challenge.

Equally important, judicial review highlights the tension between the American commitment to majority rule (democracy) and a simultaneous commitment to individual freedom (liberalism). Judicial review is thus a sort of constitutional glue that must be sparingly applied. For without judicial review's binding (pun intended) force, it would be difficult to organize the ongoing conversation about what sort of governance *is* constitutional in these United States. And without that conversation, it would be impossible to preserve the idea of constitutionalism itself.

Judicial review comes, however, in a number of different forms and in more or less controversial formulations. This chapter will focus on a particular, long-contested arena where judicial invalidation seems to present the greatest challenge to majority rule. The question is whether, when, and through what methodology a court is justified in striking down a statute simply because it is "arbitrary" in the sense of "irrational" or "unreasonable." For it is here that public choice theory promises to provide the greatest payoff as it seeks to explain the degree to which rationality (in the weak sense of "transitivity" or lack of cycling) can be expected and focuses on the potential divergence between legislative outputs and the pursuit of the common good because of interest group pressures.

Although public choice theory cannot answer the perennial and much vexed normative question of the appropriate forms and scope of judicial review, it may be able to give us some insights into how legislatures might function and malfunction. And, if so, it can also suggest where we might most want to see an active monitoring of legislative action for constitutional legitimacy. In so doing, public choice might even show us that some of our conventional views about these matters are not entirely sound.

Both in this chapter on rationality review and in the next on the legislative process and statutory interpretation, I hope to show that we do indeed have something to learn from the basic ideas of the public choice theorists. But in each case that "something to learn" should not be confused with notions such as "ideas to adopt," or even "arguments to use," in constitutional analysis.

Perspectives from the public choice tool kit are useful in thinking about constitutional doctrine. But each must be labeled "Handle with care."

Rationality Review: An Overview of the Legal Landscape

Rationality review — or, perhaps better put, the review of legislation for "reasonableness" — is at once a constitutional necessity, a political impossibility, and a conceptual muddle.

The constitutional necessity for some form of reasonableness check on legislative activity is embedded in our general commitment to the protection of individual liberty and in the idea of a government of limited powers. According to both the Fifth and the Fourteenth Amendments, no person is to be deprived of life, liberty, or property by the national or any state government without due process of law. And although this text is so vague as to be nearly vacuous, its very capaciousness has permitted American litigants and American courts to ask a fundamental question about any legislation that injures individual or group interests: What plausible exercise of governmental power justifies this injury? Unless a story can be told about how the legislation furthers some public interest that is also within the legislature's authority to pursue, the legislation is arbitrary and a violation of due process of law.

As constitutional lawyers might put it, all legislation must embody reasonable legislative means in the pursuit of some constitutionally acceptable legislative purpose. This promise of nonarbitrariness helps make acceptable the inevitable sacrifice of private interests in the pursuit of collective ends. Therein lies the constitutional necessity of a review for nonarbitrariness.

But, as a constitutional doctrine, the judiciary has found rationality review to be so unruly as to be very nearly politically unmanageable. As a historical matter, we need only recall the well-worn story of the Old Court and the New Deal. As government recognized new needs and new activities that fit uneasily into our nineteenth-century understandings of permissible governmental ends and means, the Supreme Court invoked "substantive due process" (the nonarbitrariness constraint) to thwart the desires of both state and federal legislatures. But the Court's resistance to the activist state in the name of liberty became politically unacceptable. Under Franklin Roosevelt's credible threat to have the Congress raise the number of Supreme Court justices from nine to fifteen, the Court engaged in the famous "switch in time that saved nine." In essence, the Court retained the power to review legislation for reasonableness, but created an almost irrebuttable presumption that whatever the legislature did was, from some perspective, reasonable.

This solution was both intellectually coherent and politically prudent. For once the Court recognized that state legislatures had (under their "police power") the legitimate authority to protect the public's "health, welfare, and morals," and gave a similarly expansive reading to the commerce and general welfare clauses of the federal Constitution, there was little place for a court to stand in labeling the legislature's goals or its means of achieving them unreasonable. The line between a politically sensible thing to do and a constitutionally reasonable action was so nearly invisible that it could not be drawn with persuasiveness, much less precision, in judicial opinions. The legitimacy of rationality review evaporated along with the capacity to distinguish constitutional legality from political judgment. The symbolic threat of rationality review remained. But in reality rationality review became a "formal" doctrine of modest — almost nonexistent — application. Indeed, constitutional politics aside, commentators have pointed out with great cogency that the whole idea of rationality review is something of a conceptual muddle. If the constitutional complaint is about the *goal* that the legislature pursued in enacting the legislation, then the real issue is whether the legislature has the power to pursue that particular goal. "Rationality" in the sense of a good fit between means and ends is not the point.

Policing the *means* legislatures employ to carry out their purposes faces even more daunting intellectual hurdles. Indeed, any attempt to monitor the "instrumental rationality" of legislative *means* rather than *ends* encounters a paradox. On the one hand, it is unlikely that the legislatures have unitary goals when enacting legislation. And because multiple goals will always be at crosspurposes some of the time, the means for achieving one of several purposes almost certainly will not seem rational from the perspective of some other purpose. Statutes are political compromises, not exercises in abstract policy analysis. Looked at hard enough, they will always contain "irrationalities."

On the other hand, the whole project of trying to understand legislative purposes and to check the "fit" of means to ends can just as easily lead to the conclusion that no statute could ever be irrational. True legislative purposes can only be understood by looking at a statute whole — at its goals, the means for implementing those goals, and the resources appropriated for the task. Indeed, it is hardly too much to say that statutory purposes only take on meaning through implementation.

But if this is true, then what the legislature intended to do is best understood by looking at what it did, ends and means combined. It thus follows that the means chosen are always perfectly fitted to the ends that are being pursued. If those ends are legitimate, the statute is acceptable. The notion of reviewing statutes to determine whether they have chosen reasonable means for the promotion of acceptable goals has once again collapsed into a simple question of the government's authority to do what it did.

Reviewing legislation as an act of instrumental rationality thus seems doomed. A hard look that artificially separates ends from means is likely to find ubiquitous irrationality and invalidate virtually every statute in sight. A sympathetic interpretation of legislation as a political compromise in which purpose cannot be discerned when divorced from implementation, will never find an unreasonable piece of legislation.

Given this devastating political, historical, and intellectual critique of rationality review, one might think that we would simply chuck it in the ashbin of failed constitutional ideas and get on with the business of governance. But that is not American constitutional history.

In part, the idea persists because in some areas of our constitutional life we have found it necessary to apply a much more stringent test of means/ends rationality to legislation. Where the goal sought by the legislature is usually constitutionally prohibited — say, the limitation of freedom of speech — but sometimes justifiable — committing treason by transmitting state secrets to an enemy is, after all, speech — we have greater confidence in the appropriateness of a much stricter rationality test. Here, according to existing constitutional doctrine, the state must have an extremely strong reason or "high public purpose" for invading an otherwise prohibited domain and must demonstrate that it has used means that are the "least restrictive possible" to achieve the necessary goal.

But note that this so called "strict scrutiny" rationality test is playing a quite different role than we imagined for rationality review in our prior discussion. Rather than imposing a general limitation on broadly conferred governmental powers, rationality review is in the speech case a means of waiving, in a limited class of cases, a restriction on government action designed to preserve individual liberty. Courts exercising "strict scrutiny" over certain types of legislation are applying a test of political necessity in the context of constitutional limitations on government which are expected to receive judicial protection — but which, if absolute, might destroy the state entirely. In this context, therefore, the necessity for some sort of means-ends inquiry seems patent. The political warrant of the Court both in reviewing state action and in applying such a "rationality test" is much more secure.

As a consequence, the Supreme Court has tended to sort rationality questions into two bins. In one bin are those statutes which have to do with general issues of social and economic regulation. To those it applies a general rationality test that is so undemanding as to be virtually nonexistent. In the other bin are protected civil liberties. These liberties are trumps in a contest with governmental authority unless the government satisfies the demanding rationality test often formulated as the pursuit "of a fundamental state interest" through "carefully tailored" and "least restrictive" statutory means. Indeed, once the Court sorts the case into one or another constitutional bin, the outcome is virtually foreordained. Statutes allocated to bin one are constitutional, those allocated to bin number two are unconstitutional, save in exceptional circumstances.

Yet the question of how to approach judicial review for "reasonableness" will not go away. It remains interesting precisely because this tidy bipolar structure constantly threatens to collapse. Clever lawyers, for example, constantly invite the courts to engage in "strict scrutiny" in cases where legislation only tangentially affects protected individual freedoms. And they entice them further into the rationality-review thicket by suggesting that the "two-tier" approach is itself unreasonable. Surely many claims fall in a middle ground. They seek protection for constitutionally important interests that are not yet "core" liberties. Or they present the interests of what the Court calls "discrete and insular minorities" who may be especially disadvantaged in majoritarian politics. In such cases some "intermediate" form of means-ends scrutiny seems required either to protect liberty or to enhance democracy. Thus the battle continues over the reasonableness of reasonableness review. Indeed, our inability to settle the issue once and for all may have much to do with some of the basic notions of public choice theory.

A Public Choice View of the Constitutional Terrain

Let us abandon for the moment the ways that constitutional lawyers and legal theorists look at rationality review. What might public choice have to say about the matter? Reverting for a moment to Condorcet's voting paradox or the Arrow Theorem, we might immediately become suspicious of the democratic legitimacy of many legislative outcomes. After all, if statutes are artifacts of the structuring of the agenda, perhaps even of its control by certain powerful legislative actors or institutions, what claim does legislation have to represent the "will of the people?" It may not even represent the will of the legislature.

The tale is sadder yet if looked at through the lens of "interest group theory." Because all potential groups do not form, and those that do have significant extra power in the legislative process, it is all too plausible to imagine that much legislation is the result of interest group control over the institutional actors who have the capacity to set legislative agendas.

In short, public choice theory seems to give us two ways of thinking about legislation. On the one hand, it may have emerged by mere chance — an artifact of the legislative organization and voting rules which are probably too complex, their effects too mysterious, for them to be fully understood, controlled, or manipulated by anyone. This approach gives legislation essentially the same democratic legitimacy as selecting statutes by lottery. On the other hand, if institutional rules and positions permit people to change the lottery into purposive action, those same rules and institutions suggest the ever-present possibility that "special interests" will have captured the machinery of governance and turned it to their own ends. As I said earlier, the explanation for much legislative output might be characterized by one of two words: greed or chaos. If that were the case, then it would surely be in our interests as citizens to try to breathe some life back into the requirement that legislation be "nonarbitrary."

A Real-World Example

To make the discussion more concrete, consider these ideas in the context of a particular case. *New Motor Vehicle Board of California v. Orrin W. Fox Co.*[1] involved a California statute that required approval from the state's New Motor Vehicle Board for the opening or relocation of a retail automobile dealership within the market area (314 square miles) of any existing dealership carrying the same make of car. Under the statute, objection by an existing dealer resulted in notice to the proposed dealership that its plans must be held in abeyance pending a hearing in which the objectors would attempt to establish "good cause" for not creating an additional franchise in that market area. The objectors bore the burden of proof at the hearing, but they had only to say "I protest" in order to secure the notice of hearing that would maintain the status quo.

Fox, one of the plaintiffs, demonstrated at trial that the principal use of the statute was to delay the opening of new dealerships. Of 117 protests filed with the board, only one had been sustained at hearing and two-thirds had been withdrawn. Nevertheless, the existing dealer's objection was sufficient to defer Fox's opening for at least fifteen months — more than a complete model year — and one of the plaintiffs had had its relocation completely stymied when delay forced it to default on its lease.

Plaintiffs attacked the statute on several grounds. Their principal argument was that the automatic deferral of their proposed action by the filing of a protest deprived them of due process of law. In their view, the board's failure at this stage to inquire into at least the plausibility of the protest and its prospects for ultimate success denied them the individualized judgment prior to the exercise of state power that is required by the Constitution. This procedural due process argument was combined with an argument characterizing the "empty protest" mechanism as a standardless delegation of state power to private citizens. Plaintiffs further argued that, by giving effect to private attempts to restrain trade, the California statute conflicted with the Sherman Antitrust Act.

Justice Brennan, writing for the majority, made short work of these arguments. In his view, the procedural due process claim was really a disguised substantive due process argument. The Court was being asked to determine the reasonableness of the statute. Because the legislation gave the board no discretion in scheduling a hearing, it was the statute that delayed plaintiffs' activities and not a summary administrative order. Viewed as an attack on the statute, the question was whether the plaintiffs had some right to be free from state economic regulation that was expressly identified by the legislature as protecting the "general economy of the state and the public welfare." Quoting the language of *Ferguson v. Skrupa* that "[l]egislative bodies have broad scope to experiment with economic problems,"[2] the Court answered with the usual resounding no.

Once the basic claim had been thus characterized, the delegation and antitrust questions were easy. Otherwise valid state regulation is not invalid merely because it employs private enforcement or has anticompetitive effects. A contrary holding on these two issues would lead, respectively, to the absurd conclusions that most schemes of state private law were unconstitutional and that states had virtually no power to engage in economic regulation.

Note the legal sophistication of Fox's attorneys. They never mentioned rationality review or substantive due process in their arguments. And they surely did not argue that the state of California could engage in economic regulation only if it had a significant state interest and used the least restrictive means possible to pursue those interests. Fox's attorneys clearly were concerned with the "arbitrariness" and "special interest" character of the legislation, but they were busy trying to smuggle these arguments into the case through the use of other doctrinal categories, such as the arbitrariness of the *procedure* or the standardless delegation of state power to private parties.

The *Fox* majority was not taken in. They quickly transformed the procedural due process claim into its substantive analogue and recognized the other claims for what they were, an attempt to limit the regulatory power of the state of California as to both means (the use of competitors as complainants) and ends (intervention in the resale automobile market). Recast in that way, Fox got the usual post–New Deal answer to a complaint about arguably useless and/or pernicious state regulation: "Next case, please!"

Consider how easily a straightforward characterization of the plaintiffs' complaint, however, maps onto the interest group theory branch of public choice analysis. The Fox dealership and its cohorts (and, to be fair Justice Stevens in dissent) see private parties making use of state power to harass competitors. They want to know what justifies this disadvantage. Potential competitors are told, in effect, that their private interest must yield to the public interest. But given the now conventional approach to rationality review, the public interest is not to be discussed with any seriousness. If the state intones certain buzzwords like "overreaching" or "ruinous competition" — or even "protection of the public" — the discussion is over.

Although we shall return in a more systematic way to what might be "discussable" in such cases, we should note that the *Fox* plaintiffs had some prima facie plausible rebuttals to the state's buzzwords. Ostensibly, the California scheme is meant to protect two groups: franchisees from overreaching by manufacturers, and the public generally from the shoddy service that might attend "ruinous competition."

But California already had other legislation that directly served both of those ends. Automobile dealers were licensed, and to obtain those licenses they were required to meet qualifications designed to assure adequate and responsible service. There was also direct policing of the form and execution of franchise agreements. Given these regulations, the *Fox* plaintiffs might sensibly have wondered what the territorial-limits statute added to consumer protection or franchising equity.

Is a licensing scheme *without* competition better for consumers than a licensing scheme *with* competition? How do you persuade potential franchisees to put up a hundred thousand dollars or more of their own money to join manufacturers in a plot to "overfranchise" an area to the detriment of the public and all franchise holders? What does the manufacturer say to induce this lemming-like behavior? "How would you like to get involved in some ruinous competition (in which you will probably be bankrupted) under the sponsorship of a manufacturer who uses multiple franchising to gouge the franchisees who survive?"

But if the public interest gains seem ephemeral, the private damages are real. People do not become automobile dealers, or much of anything else, by random choice of occupation. They do so because they have personal histories that fit them for the position — or at least seem to fit them better for that than for the alternatives. We needn't tell poignant tales of working one's way up from mechanic or clerk or salesman to branching out on one's own, to recognize that to thwart ambition is often to preclude the application of expertise garnered, perhaps "hard-won," over a substantial portion of a working life.[3]

The unhappy systemic effect of the individual harm is, of course, the increasingly frequent blocking of the avenues of opportunity and self-realization that make bearable the constant need to accommodate our personal desires to the rights of others in a world of scarce resources.

But none of this is talked about in *Fox*. The plaintiffs, no fools, were not about to frame their attack in terms of the rationality of the statute. A strategy was developed that avoided the substantive jugular and instead hacked away at the capillaries — delegation, procedure, antitrust. The Court's consistent refusal to consider substantive-rationality attacks on "economic" regulation, of course, invites this strategy. The majority's recharacterization of the claim in jugular terms thus must have been a shock. It also meant that the case was decided on a theory that was never argued — indeed, is generally considered to be "nonarguable." Perhaps for this reason, the substantive question is treated in its most general form as a claim to freedom from state regulation — a sure loser.

But the general power of the state to regulate is obviously not what the plaintiffs in *Fox* wanted to talk about. They wanted to talk about their serious and substantial interest in carrying on their occupations, about the opportunities the statute provides for potentially crippling harassment from competitors, and about the extremely modest public gains that flow from the legislation. In short, they thought this legislation arbitrary and, hence, unconstitutional. Why not let them argue that?

Historically, we have already answered that question. The Supreme Court gave up on direct rationality review of state legislation soon after the famous case of *Lochner v. New York*.[4] In that case the Court overturned a New York statute regulating the hours of work of bakers on the grounds that New York had not demonstrated any particular reasons for interfering with the usual power of bakers, and others, to contract about the terms of their service. But, as Justice Holmes pointed out in his *Lochner* dissent, the requirement that the state demonstrate sufficient state purposes, appropriately pursued, in order to justify its regulation gave "freedom of contract" an unexamined and powerful constitutional status. In Justice Holmes's famous phrase, "the Constitution does not enact Mr. Herbert Spencer's Social Statics."[5] In short, Holmes was attacking the majority because it was giving either laissez-faire economics or Darwinian sociology a privileged position in constitutional analysis.

Unfortunately, the current posture of the Court with respect to rationality review has a similar defect. From the perspective of public choice, it can easily be viewed as giving a similarly privileged position to the view that "democracy works" or that legislation "reflects the general will" — at least within the domain of what the court calls "social and economic legislation."

By refusing to review the substance of state economic legislation, the Court asserts the preeminence of the democratic political process. As fundamental values go, democracy is of course pretty unobjectionable. The point is that it is not *always* unobjectionable, nor does the category "social and economic legislation" identify a domain within which objections to democracy do not operate.

All of this may be obvious. The institution of judicial review, after all, presupposes that democratic judgment as expressed through state legislation is not always accorded constitutional supremacy. It is commonplace that the "founding fathers" did not wholly trust legislatures.[6] And the drafters of the Civil War amendments particularly distrusted state legislatures. As someone (only mock-humorously) once suggested, "At Appomattox General Lee surrendered to John Marshall."

But as we noted earlier, it is not only constitutional history that dampens our enthusiasm for democracy. The unhappy fact is that if by "democracy" we mean "majority rule," and if we expect majority rule to produce what a majority really wants, then we know that democracy cannot work flawlessly even in theory. When one adds to these difficulties the obvious impediments to the expression of true majority sentiment that inhere in mediate or representative democracy,[7] plus the predictable outcomes of coalition formation with logrolling,[8] it seems peculiar to draft a constitution that wraps legislative outputs in a legally impervious mantle called "democracy" or "majoritarianism."

Theoretical imperfections do not, of course, exhaust our concerns with the use of democracy cum majoritarianism cum state legislative action as an unexamined major premise in constitutional adjudication. We also know something about state legislatures as real-world institutions. Perhaps no governmental institution is held in as little esteem as our state legislatures. Cataloguing their weaknesses has provided professional employment for generations of political scientists.[9] And telling tales of their inanities, irregularities, and outright dishonesty is a favorite indoor sport for those "in the know" about the state legislative process.

It seems reasonable to conclude that the reverse-*Lochner,* no-review policy of the Supreme Court stands indicted on very much the same grounds that Holmes criticized *Lochner* itself. It does not seriously address the question of why democracy should be given conclusive weight where "economic" or "social" questions are involved. Indeed, this posture produces one of the results that most outrages the critics of Lochneresque review: a constitutional axiom that flies in the face of social reality. That state legislation always represents the will of the people seems at least as laughable as the proposition that sweatshop working conditions *always* represented the contractual will of bakers.

Tricks and Dodges and Judicial (Non)Restraint

The Supreme Court is not entirely oblivious to these arguments. While it says that state, social, and economic legislation will not be reviewed, it does in fact review it. The problem is that the review tends to occur either in some disguised form of procedural review or via some connected, and otherwise protected, substantive value. In either guise the review is misdirected and therefore potentially irrational.

In a way, the suggestion that the Court seriously reviews and invalidates social and economic regulation is too easy.[10] What could be more obvious than that de jure segregation of the races was regulation both social and economic; that invalidation of a prohibition on providing counseling as to means of contraception thwarted a social policy; or that state laws precluding advertising of the prices of pharmaceuticals implemented state economic policy?[11] Nor is there any reason in either the text of the Constitution or the importance of the interest to individual human beings to treat all straightforward questions of access to economic opportunity as systematically different from those same questions when presented as issues of racial discrimination, marital privacy, or speech. The Constitution, after all, does not say that segregation is unequal, that advertising is speech (or that "Congress" also means "state"), or that marital privacy has any constitutional status at all. Moreover, it is difficult to imagine the citizen who would not trade some tiny smidgen of speech, privacy, or racial equality for some large portion of personally relevant economic opportunity.

But that argument is too easy, and it leads in the wrong direction. All of these examples of review of social or economic legislation are not simply examples of Supreme Court error. Rather, the cases mostly demonstrate that intervention by the Court into the realm of social and economic regulation is inevitable — even when some previously determined or newly constructed fundamental value is not at issue — and that that intervention is only made less coherent, and ultimately less sensible, by denying what is going on.

Consider, for example, the famous pharmaceuticals advertising case *Virginia State Board of Pharmacy v. Virginia Citizens Consumer Council, Inc.*[12] The anticompetitive effects of the prohibition on price advertising of pharmaceuticals was clear. What was less clear was the effect of advertising on the integrity of the process of dispensing drugs. But does anyone seriously believe that that question gets easier by framing the issue as a question of free speech? As we saw from our brief discussion of the strict-scrutiny rationality test, the infusion of the speech idea only reverses the presumption. This provides a different rule of decision, but no additional clarity concerning the issue that is central to rational decisionmaking. Moreover, it can make constitutional doctrine subject to bizarre forms of litigant "gaming." Would we, for example, really want the Court to think carefully about a regulation affecting *advertising* by car dealers within another's "territory," but not about a regulation affecting the location of a competitive business within that territory? If so, Fox's complaint should have emphasized that the regulation suppressed putting up the sign that would have identified his firm to potential customers.

Thus it comes ineluctably to pass that in the next case (or the next, or the next) the Court perceives the ghost of Lochneresque review lurking behind the free speech claim. And at that point, seeking somehow to preserve the anti-*Lochner* principle — that is, that it is not about to second-guess legislative policy judgments — the Court must take evasive action. One possibility is to modify free speech doctrine so that commercial speech does not get a strong presumption of protection. Another is to identify some state regulatory purposes that will get special consideration. A third is to compartmentalize commercial speech into important and unimportant commercial speech. In fact, in the case that revealed the ghost at the banquet table, the Court took *all* these routes at once.[13] (Ghosts are scary.) But the irony is that these devices do not exorcise substantive review, they invite it. The Court must ask what the state's purposes are, how the regulation effects those purposes, what the uses are of the speech that is being suppressed, how alternative regulation might accommodate all the values involved, and so on.

Now, as the next section will make clear, anyone coming to this discussion with modest exposure to public choice notions of the many ways that the legislative process can produce grotesque statutes should not object to consideration of those questions in appropriate ways and in appropriate contexts. But here the Court is being led into the substantive review thicket on a peculiar pretext — that it must do so to protect speech, speech that (given the Court's limited approach to review of commercial speech) it must not view as fundamentally related to the core purposes of the First Amendment. If the Court is to review the rationality of some state economic and social regulation seriously, surely there are better criteria of selection than the tangential involvement of a nonfundamental free speech claim.

Observation of later cases tends to reinforce the suspicion that the analysis of "commercial speech" claims might be improved were the specter of the speech issue excised from the proceedings. When the Court tells us, for example, that advertising drug prices is to be distinguished from trade-name advertising of optical services because drug price advertising involves health and is therefore inherently more valuable speech, my respect for the tradition of judicial reason giving is being stretched very thin.

Nor are the commercial speech cases even the best examples of rationality review combined with reason giving bordering on the lunatic. As the previous discussion of *Fox* reveals, translation of substantive claims into procedural ones is an obviously attractive device for inducing review. *Fox* got caught with its substantive claim showing — or perhaps we should say that for some reason the Court was willing to look through the procedural veil to see the substantive rationality issue. But this is not always true. Sometimes the Court is blinded by a process claim that is transparent to everyone else.

The "irrebuttable presumption" cases of the early 1970s are classics of this genre. What was painfully clear in cases like *Bell v. Burson* and *Stanley v. Illinois* was that the legislation involved was overly general.[14] All drivers who are involved in accidents but have no insurance (*Bell*) are not dangerous or irresponsible. All unwed fathers (*Stanley*) are not poor parents. But the attack in these cases was not directly on the rationality of the substantive legislation. Rather, the plaintiffs demanded hearings. Their argument was that the statutory rules "decided" individual cases on the basis of irrebuttable factual presumptions, thereby denying the plaintiffs *procedural* due process of law — to wit, an opportunity to establish that the facts were different in their cases. The Supreme Court agreed. It ordered that the plaintiffs be given hearings. Later, in the same line of cases, the Court enunciated the rule that irrebuttable statutory presumptions could not be used to decide particular cases unless they were "necessarily" and "universally" true.[15]

There are two major problems with this approach. First, the cases make hash of the prior procedural due process jurisprudence. It had been (indeed still is) thought obvious that there was no need for a hearing where there was nothing to talk about.[16] And since the driver in *Bell* and the father in *Stanley* admitted that they fell squarely within the legislative disqualifications, "hearing" talk seems misplaced — substance and procedure had been conflated. But unlike its posture in *Fox*, the Court refused to recognize the conflation.

Analytic confusion might, of course, have no disastrous consequences. But in this instance it does. The irrebuttable presumption doctrine has a voracious appetite for statutes. Left long at large, it will gnaw its way through substantial portions of the codes of the fifty states and the U.S. Code as well.[17] If the validity of some of our most ubiquitous legal rules — the fifty-five-mile-per-hour speed limit, twenty-one years as the age of majority, statutes of limitations, formal requirements for testamentary disposition, for example — is to be tested by asking whether the general principle or purpose that underlies the rule (safety, knowing consent, and so on) is furthered *in every instance* of its application, then rules are no longer possible.

Because such a state of affairs is insupportable, we need some way of avoiding this particular proceduralist perspective. But in the irrebuttable presumption cases the Court does not (and indeed cannot) tell us when an attack on legislative overgenerality should be perceived for what it is — a substantive rationality claim that under current doctrine is a sure loser — and when it may be translated into a "right-to-hearing"/"irrebuttable presumption" claim that is a sure winner.[18] Confronted with an extremely important question (When is it permissible to generalize by rule rather than particularize by reference to a principle or standard?), the Court, having barred itself from considering the substantive rationality of legislative judgments, has nothing to say.

A final technique for inducing substantive review provides a nice counterpoint to the irrebuttable presumption cases. In this situation it is the movement from a rule to a standard with individualized decisionmaking that, at least in part, excites judicial interest. The case in point is *Gibson v. Berryhill,* another in the long and continuing line of challenges to state regulation of the practice of optometry — a line that in *Williamson v. Lee Optical Co.* seemed to provide the reductio ad absurdum that confirmed the total destruction of Lochneresque review.[19]

Berryhill involved action by the Alabama Board of Optometry to remove the licenses of optometrists who practiced in the optical departments of corporations or other business establishments. The charge was that such practice constituted unprofessional conduct — a charge that entitled the licensees to a hearing before the board. Interestingly, the statutes of Alabama had, until 1965, clearly conferred authority to practice in the challenged manner. In that year, however, the legislature rewrote the "optometry code," eliminating the clear contemplation of practice in corporations and other commercial establishments. The board immediately began proceedings to bar corporate practice under the general "unprofessional conduct" provision.

The plaintiffs sought to enjoin the board's action on the procedural ground that they could not get a fair hearing before the board. Their argument was that the board was composed entirely of self-employed optometrists, that lifting the licenses of the "commercial" optometrists would cut the number of optometrists in the state in half, and that the board was thus obviously financially interested in the proceedings. The district court found, as a fact, that the board was self-interested and granted the injunction. The Supreme Court affirmed on the facts, merely noting its prior cases holding that personal financial interest disqualified an adjudicator.[20]

Berryhill has several interesting aspects. First, we should note the Court's circumspection. It affirms a factual finding of financial self-interest. It does not approve a simple inference of self-interest from the existence of regulation of one competitor by another. The standard forms of professional licensing remain untouched. Second, the procedural posture of the case clearly suggests that had the Board of Optometry persuaded the legislature to eliminate "commercial" practice by statute, the plaintiffs would have been left without an argument. The chink in the armor of the no-substantive-review principle is thus small. The legislature must confer the power to suppress competition on a private group in a fashion that leaves open the question whether competition will indeed be suppressed, before this procedural approach has a fighting chance.

Yet, if we combine this technique with the others we have discussed—association of the claim with a recognized fundamental value and the irrebuttable presumption idea—it becomes clear that our old friend *Fox* had the makings of a case. Surely there is something to the notion that Fox's freedom of movement, not to mention its freedom of association and speech, were being impaired by the California scheme. Moreover, the failure of the New Motor Vehicle Board to exercise any discretion about the plausibility of a protest transferred a tactic for harassment, à la *Berryhill,* directly to Fox's competitors. Finally, the statute contains an "irrebuttable presumption" that any location or relocation that excites a protest is worth looking into via a hearing device with all its attendant delay—a presumption that the California board's experience hardly reveals to be universally true.

But I do not want to argue that the Court should have listened to Fox's claim more carefully because it could have been articulated in terms sometimes found persuasive in cases that might otherwise be recognized as requests for review of the substantive rationality of state economic and social legislation. These techniques are, after all, techniques of evasion. They misdirect analysis, and because they do, they may generate unwarranted judicial intrusion into state policymaking. The requirement that claims be presented obliquely, that review of substantive irrationality be under cover, that it be tied to the contingency of the form of the legal proscription or the tangential involvement of some otherwise protected interest, makes it as difficult for courts to be appropriately restrained as it is to be appropriately activist. The requirement that substantive rationality be officially ignored, in the face of plausible claims of irrational injury, may produce its own peculiarly irrational forms of judicial second-guessing of legislative policy choices.

Can Public Choice Get Us out of This Mess?

If the foregoing is at all persuasive, we should by now be agreed that the attempted wholesale retreat from review of economic and social legislation produces many ills. Lawyers might be persuaded at least that the judiciary's attempt at modesty and self-restraint has produced a relatively incoherent jurisprudence. From a public choice perspective, one would be more likely to focus on the bad sense of refusing to monitor seriously a form of collective action—legislation—that is predictably prone to bizarre or manipulated outcomes. Raising the flag of "democracy" and retreating from the field seems peculiarly myopic.

On the other hand, we may nevertheless suspect that as a comparative matter we get fewer perverse results with the Court's current posture than we would if it returned to the sort of review actually espoused in the *Lochner* case. Perhaps. But I am not convinced.

The underlying difficulties of the old economic substantive due process were twofold. First, the means-ends rationality approach invited oversimplification. As has been demonstrated with great clarity, there is in such review a substantial propensity to conflate complex purposes into unitary ends, and to reject as irrational means that merely reflect an appreciation of conflicting purposes.[21]

Second, at least as originally practiced, substantive due process review failed to appreciate (or rejected) the distributional purposes of legislation. That society might view bakers, or workers in general, as worthy of special contractual protections was not credited unless the Court could divine a special problem, a need, that justified deviation from the usual rules of contract. The Court sought a market failure justification where paternalism would have sufficed.

The question, then, is whether there is a role for judicial review when the full play of dominant and subsidiary legislative purposes, of allocational and distributional ends, is recognized. In my view there is. But in order to orient such review appropriately, we need to put it on a somewhat different footing: to recognize that the appropriate constitutional demand is not for "rational" or "efficient" legislation, but for legislation that is public-regarding—that can make a coherent and plausible claim to serve some public, rather than a merely private, interest.

That such a demand has support in the Constitution itself is relatively non-problematic. There is hardly an idea of greater moment in the whole of the constitutional structure than the notion that public legislation should provide for the *public* welfare. Indeed, the idea of legislative action for the public welfare, rather than for private or factional gain, is so pervasive with respect to the national government that it is difficult to locate it in any particular constitutional text. There is, of course, the preamble, which tells us something about how the rest of the document is to be interpreted. And it is commonplace that the general structure of checked and balanced powers was designed to avoid the evils of dominant factions that might use governmental institutions for their own ends. Legislators are also enjoined from concurrently holding other offices or from feathering a subsequent nest by increasing the pecuniary rewards. Surely these specific and structural features, plus the "tax and spend for the general welfare" clause, should be enough to convince anyone who found the initial statement of the proposition at all problematic.[22]

Moreover, it bears pointing out that these notions did not appear by magic in our eighteenth-century constitutional document. They are a part of an Enlightenment political science that is the precursor of modern public choice theory. Montesquieu, Madison, and Condorcet were contemporaries. And when Madison talks of the dangers of faction or of "ambition checking ambition," he speaks a language that is the inspiration for the modern public choice approach, as James Buchanan has explicitly acknowledged. Public choice ideas — particularly the ever-present threat of the use of public power for private ends — are foundational to our constitutional scheme.

"But what about the states?" you may say. The separation of powers principle and the general welfare clauses do not, strictly speaking, apply to them. And that statement is certainly correct, although I would hasten to add that the emasculation of the guarantee clause, the privileges and immunities clause, and the Ninth Amendment has something to do with its correctness. But we need not flay dead horses. No one, to my knowledge, has ever argued that state governmental powers can legitimately be exercised for private ends. The difficulty has been to sort out the public from the private, given the wide range of efficiency and equity concerns that might actuate public policy, and the multitude of implementation devices that just *might* further those policies in an uncertain social and economic environment. Of course, it is implicit in the constitutional scheme that legislation be public-regarding. But is that a justiciable standard for judicial review?

To put the matter in its usual institutional terms, if we would recognize "public-regardingness" as a principle of constitutional moment, to be enforced in part through judicial review, we must explain how to accommodate majority rule with public regardingness in realistic cases of legislative action. For the question whether the legislative action has a public purpose is always one that the legislature purports to have decided affirmatively. The state does not come into court admitting that it had no legitimate purpose. And at that point, a critic will suggest, we must presume either that the Court will seek to discover a "true" public- or private-regarding motive, or that it will decide whether the legislation's public benefit was worth the cost to the affected private interests. The first enters a fantasyland, probing the collective consciousness of the legislature, that the Court has hitherto wisely (for the most part) avoided;[23] the second usurps the policy function of the legislature.

I do not, of course, want to argue for full-scale judicial inquiry into legislative motive. On the other hand, a refusal to search for motivation should not encompass a willingness to accept insubstantial public purposes as substantial and validating. That the Court suspects fraud should not serve to protect ineptitude or corruption. The Court need not take up the awkward judicial posture of "bending over backwards" to avoid the suggestion that it is searching for motive.[24] On the other hand, I do, obviously, advocate judicial review of the adequacy of a statute's beneficial purposes when judged in the light of its harmful effects. Any citizen should be entitled to an explanation of why her private harm is at least arguably outweighed by some coherent and plausible conception of the public good.

Majorities, Minorities, and "Democratic" Oppression

Once again modern public choice ideas are supportive. For example, interest group theory suggests that the post-*Lochner* vision of "legitimate" judicial review is based on a mistaken — at least an impoverished — vision of political life.

Nonlawyers will perhaps be amused to know that the post-*Lochner* edifice of judicial review has been built almost wholly on a footnote in *United States v. Carolene Products, Inc.*[25] This famous footnote 4 sets forth, without supporting argument, the categories of legislation toward which courts should cast a suspicious eye and in relation to which arbitrariness review should retain some force. The most important of these categories is legislation affecting "discrete and insular minorities," that is, persons likely to have little influence, and therefore little opportunity to protect their interests, in the general political process.

But, as Bruce Ackerman has argued with great cogency, we have come to understand since the *Carolene Products* footnote that discreetness and insularity can confer political power as well as political impotence.[26] For discreetness and insularity may reduce the organizational costs of group formation and maintenance, focus political action on singular targets, and give intense but highly parochial preferences much greater salience in a pluralist polity than the unorganized interests of the majority of citizens.

This is obviously not to say that the *Carolene Products* warning concerning minority oppression by the majority is not a real concern. It is only to say that minority seizures of state power are an equally plausible ground for concern about the "democratic" pedigree of legislative actions. If judicial review is in part about assuring the nonarbitrariness of legislation, looking only at minority oppression as a signal of the need for serious analysis of legislative reasonableness is a remarkably underinclusive approach. We need not accept the jaundiced view of many in the public choice fraternity, who see private gain at public expense as the explanation for virtually any and all legislative actions. Rather, we can simply learn a more general lesson: The possibilities for "legislative failure" are ubiquitous and courts should be prepared to act on that knowledge. The question, of course, is how? And, how much?

Public Choice Lessons and Legal Limitations

My basic position — that rationality review is both inevitable and justifiable — is hardly noncontroversial. And I am somewhat discomfited by the realization that the most ardent support for increases in rationality review seems to come from those who are comfortable with nineteenth-century visions of property rights and perhaps sixteenth-century ideas of social relations.[27] Nevertheless, it is useful to look at the positions of both supporters and critics of rationality review, particularly those who use public choice ideas to assist them. In that process I hope to begin to demonstrate my sense of the way that public choice should be used — that is, without succumbing to extreme, private interest visions of the political process, or ritualistic invocation of theorems divorced from empirical investigation or normative argument.

For present purposes I will sort the positions to be discussed into three broad categories: "true believers," "proceduralists," and "conventionalists." True Believers view most statutes through Arrovian or interest group lenses. Whether they represent accidental artifacts of voting procedures or private interest deals, neither pedigree justifies much judicial deference to their "democratic" character. For these commentators aggressive judicial review, on virtually any ground, is justified to preserve individual liberty.

Proceduralists agree that much legislation is poorly crafted to secure public ends. But their remedy of choice is *procedural* review to assure better outcomes, rather than substantive review to strike down arbitrary legislation. Conventionalists either believe that legislative malfunctioning is overstated or are agnostic about its extent. As a comparative matter, however, they believe that rationality review is a cure that is worse than the disease.

In my view true believers overstate the "lessons" of public choice for our particular brand of constitutional democracy. Proceduralists and conventionalists, by contrast, should rethink their positions while taking public choice ideas more seriously.

TRUE BELIEVERS

William Riker has launched perhaps the most direct public choice attack on the meaningfulness of majority rule voting processes and on the claim of legislative majorities to represent the will of the people. For him the vagaries of voting processes — their tendency toward either cycling, randomness, or dicta-torship — render most legislation highly suspect. Because true democracy — "populism" in his terminology — is impossible, the preservation of liberty should have the highest priority. Thus, demanding that all legislation stand up to some strong form of the rational basis test would, in Riker's view, promote the public welfare.[28]

A similarly dismal view of legislation has been espoused by Judge Frank Easterbrook.[29] While echoing Riker's views based on Arrovian considera-tions, Easterbrook also imagines statutes to be mostly private interest "deals." From the first perspective he considers them uninterpretable; from the second, socially pernicious. In either event the judiciary seems to be justified in any attempt to limit statutes' domains and ameliorate their presumptive harm to the public welfare. Because Judge Easterbrook focuses his remedial strategies largely on a narrow construction of statutes rather than their invalidation, I will analyze his views more fully in Chapter 4. For now our attention will be devoted to Riker's claims.

One obvious criticism of Riker's approach was foreshadowed in the discus-sion of his views in Chapter 2. The institution-free populist democracy imag-ined by Riker may well be chaotic, but that is not the legislative process that we have. As noted previously, the introduction of institutional structure tends to dampen tendencies toward voting cycles. And even in their absence, rela-tively stable results may be obtained because more-preferred results are more likely to emerge than less-preferred ones. We just cannot be *certain* that some relatively idiosyncratic alternative will not emerge as the collective decision. In short, Riker is overreading the predictions of voting theory, both abstractly considered and as applied to our existing arrangements.

But there is a deeper problem with his approach. For Riker could respond that chaotic or random results are not his only indictment of the democratic process. Stability clearly exists much of the time, but it is bought at the price of dictatorship — at least oligopoly. For if institutional structures that limit alter-natives and channel voting opportunities are the mechanisms of stable legisla-tive choice, that just reveals that true majority rule does not describe the realities of the legislative process. Statutes may not be meaningless, but they have no truly democratic pedigree either. Courts should have no anxiety, therefore, about striking them down if they do not seem to pursue the public good.

While I am obviously sympathetic to Riker's view that the courts have gone too far in their attempts to avoid rationality review for fear of offending "democratic" ideals or "majority rule," I believe that he has somewhat mischaracterized the nature of the constitutional problem that rationality review confronts. Admitting that we have a highly compromised form of democracy — chock full of checks, balances, and veto points — in no way answers the questions of how vigorous courts should be in insisting on legislative reasonableness. For the question is not simply how democratic our democracy is, but what the constitutional order presumes to be the judgmental prerogatives of the legislative branch. Indeed, the other structural protections against legislative malfunctioning built into the system could be seen as implying a power of judicial nullification only in the clearest cases of a violation of constitutionally protected individual rights.

In short, while theorists like Riker and Easterbrook point to an obvious problem with a retreat from rationality review any time the words "counter-majoritarian difficulty" are intoned, their debunking moves too far in the opposite direction. For our constitutional order does not presume that legislative legitimacy flows from some simple-minded mapping of majoritarian preferences onto statutory commands. And, as our constitutional history demonstrates, it will not countenance significant judicial second-guessing of legislative policymaking simply because a populist pedigree has been shown to be absent — indeed impossible.

PROCEDURALISTS

A second set of reformers believe that the appropriate way to monitor legislative rationality is essentially procedural rather than substantive. These are indeed an important set of ideas and they have much affinity with the concerns of public choice theory. Their careful consideration might justify yet another book. For now we will consider only the issue of whether proceduralism dominates rationality review as a means for ensuring nonarbitrary legislation.

The most thoroughgoing constitutional proceduralist is Hans Linde.[30] Linde believes that the real job of the judiciary should be to police legislative procedure to assure that it is established in a way to produce reasonable results. Linde would require what he calls a "due process of lawmaking" which would transform legislatures into something like the original Progressive vision of the administrative agency. Legislatures would only act after holding hearings and finding facts; they would give ample opportunity for opposing points of view; and they would act through documents that explained the relationship between the facts as they had found them and the policies that they adopted.

Justice Linde's writings do not suggest that his proposals are informed by any of the ideas of the public choice fraternity and the many failings they ascribe to legislative processes. His are instead the practically informed views of an experienced state judge who has seen more than his share of the products of state legislative action. Hence, it is unlikely that Linde sees state legislatures as merely uninformed. His proceduralization of the legislative process is designed not only to inform but also to equalize access and to promote deliberation and openness.

The problem with the ideas as put forward by Linde, and by others of a more openly "civic republican" stripe, is a combination of impracticability and unpredictability. By impracticability I do not mean to suggest merely that the legislature is unlikely to get its work done — which it is not — while behaving like a quasijudicial tribunal. The suggestion instead is that this proposal fails to take proper account of the interest group theory of politics and of the extraordinary power that proceduralization gives to special interests. The American legislative process is nothing if not a system of checks and balances. And those who have studied the power of interest groups empirically find that they are most effective at blocking what they do not want, not at getting what they do want (and others wish not to give them).[31] Moreover, as virtually every lawyer knows in his or her bones, there is virtually no better way to stop all action than to require that decisionmaking be cast in the form of a judicial or quasijudicial proceeding. Laypersons can convince themselves of the same proposition by spending a few hours reading Charles Dickens's *Bleak House* or watching tapes of the O.J. Simpson trial. (The Dickens approach is strongly recommended.)

Now, to be sure, Linde does not propose that legislatures be required to act exactly like courts. They should be required to do so only to the extent necessary to make reasonable decisions. But it is quite unclear how that judgment is to be made, absent some determination of what a reasonable decision looks like. And if it is reasonableness that one is after, it would seem more sensible simply to ask the question straight out. Indeed, one would expect courts to be better at checking for arbitrariness in individual cases than at engineering legislative processes that produce reasonable outcomes. (There is, of course, also the minor textual quibble that the Constitution prescribes some legislative procedure and seems to confer the authority to develop the rest on the House and the Senate.)

Nonetheless, I believe that a proceduralist approach can be of value in policing for truly arbitrary exercises of legislative power. The key task for proceduralism, however, is not to devise reforms to make the legislature more rational. It should instead be to seek to understand how existing procedures, combined with self-interested group mobilization, can skew legislative action to the detriment of underrepresented interests. As I shall shortly argue, this public-choice–oriented brand of process-based analysis can suggest one of the "danger signals" that should activate a more searching judicial inquiry into the nonarbitrariness of legislation.

CONVENTIONALISTS

The conventionalists' concern with proposals for a reinvigorated rationality review is basically a concern about unmanageable judicial standards. Among those who are most conversant with the public choice literature, there is a particular concern that the judiciary will adopt a Riker-Easterbrook view of legislation and invalidate virtually every statute in sight.[32] Or, put more moderately, the concern is that the judiciary will invalidate every statute with which it disagrees, claiming either that it is the product of chaotic legislative processes that have no relationship to majoritarian preferences or that it is the product of private interest-group deals. Indeed, because every statute can be seen to benefit some groups more than others, the post hoc tendency to override legislation because of private interest benefits could be overwhelming.

Moreover, conventionalists argue, were judges to eschew post hoc theorizing about who *must* have instigated or "bought" a particular piece of legislation because of the ex post benefits, and look for the "real" participants in the legislative process, they probably would be unable to identify them. If courts believe in the quasiconspiratorial, interest-group-deal approach to legislation, they will hardly take comments spread on a public record in hearings, markups, and committee reports as truly indicative of where the special interests got their access and influence. That being the case, the judiciary will either never have enough evidence to indict the legislation as a special interest deal, or it might in a proceduralist turn require — implausibly and ineffectually — that no one speak to their congressperson except on the public record.

Even if one were to think that rationality review would not move rapidly to either of the extremes of irrelevance or impertinence just suggested, one might still be concerned that the judiciary would never be able to explain with any persuasiveness why it thought one or another piece of legislation was too unreasonable to be constitutional, while another almost equally screwy statute passed constitutional muster. The upshot would be a judiciary accused of being a simple Council of Revision and unable to defend itself convincingly against the charge.

In short, the conventionalists' critique of a reinvigorated attempt to police for rationality asks a conventional question: How is this to be accomplished while maintaining an appropriate respect for the policy functions of the legislature? How is it to avoid *Lochner*-ian excess without dissolving into the contemporary impotence of toothless rationality review, punctuated occasionally by eclectic and disguised interventionism?

Public Choice Danger Signals and Judicial Restraint

My answer is, "In the same muddled way that interests and claims are balanced in other areas of constitutional adjudication." The potential gains and losses are analyzed and the legislature's choice is validated unless its cost-benefit calculus is patently unreasonable.[33] Such balancing is never wholly convincing, and presumptions of validity decide most cases. But withholding a similar analysis from claims asserting unreasonable invasions of private interests in realms denominated "economic" or "social" can be justified only by opposing all "balancing" or by demonstrating the peculiarly unmanageable nature of balancing in the domain of economic and social policy.

To critics of all balancing as an adjudicatory technique,[34] I have little to offer. To be sure, they point to a discontinuity between pleading a constitutional law claim and deciding a constitutional law case. Pleading demands rights assertions, while decisionmaking seems only to balance interests.

But the solution to this "problem," if it is such, does not lie in the "rights analysis" direction. It is simply not possible to sustain a vision of a world in which constitutional (or other) rights ring out true and clear, unencumbered by contrary considerations of the conflicting "rights" of others. And it is the fundamentally compromised nature of social life that "balancing interests" both recognizes and confronts. An attempt to function solely at the level of rights, and without balancing, can result only in a submersion of substantive problem solving in formal categories and in the misdirections and hypocrisies of formal characterization that I have previously described.

Yet there is a subtler objection to interest balancing that may partially rehabilitate the notion that constitutional adjudication should proceed only on the basis of claims of right. It is the requirement that a right be asserted that potentially distinguishes judicial from legislative interest balancing. The assertion of a right provides a legitimate occasion for judicial review and, by restricting its domain, prevents the Court from becoming a simple Council of Revision. If no right to be free from economic and social regulation is being asserted, judicial review is simply a review of the wisdom (or lack thereof) of state or federal legislatures. Shouldn't anyone making such a claim be tossed out of court for simple failure to state a legally cognizable cause of action? Or, alternatively, wouldn't counting such claims as legal claims necessarily invade the appropriate domain of legislative policy choice?

My answer is no, but the question is a good one. It requires that I state the cause of action that I espouse with somewhat more precision and say something about the "facts" that would be relevant to its proof. If this can be done, there seems no reason to object to a demand for public-regarding legislation as raising an inherently unmanageable type of constitutional claim.

The claim is, in fact, relatively straightforward: It begins by alleging some cognizable harm — injury-in-fact, to use the vernacular of the standing cases. The further "elements" of the claim include the lack of a coherent and plausible public purpose, either on the face of the statute or when it is considered in operation (and in the context of other legal norms), and the absence of important circumstantial "process" guarantees on the "public spiritedness" of legislation that usually attend legislative action.

To fix these ideas somewhat more concretely, let us return to *Fox*. There, you will remember, the car dealers complained of lost profits from delay, and occasionally of total frustration of a proposed enterprise, with attendant out-of-pocket losses. Injury-in-fact seems clear enough.

THE ANALYSIS OF PUBLIC PURPOSE

The suggested requirements for a satisfactory public purpose are that it be "coherent and plausible." Of course, some purposes will be excluded by direct prohibitions. One could imagine the *Fox* statute as a redistributive scheme designed to insure quasimonopoly rents to automobile dealers. But that purpose is excluded by the antitrust laws. The question in a case like *Fox* would then be whether the consumer protection and dealer oppression purposes are coherent and plausible.

The consumer protection notion certainly verges on the incoherent. It is difficult to see how consumers in a rising marginal-cost industry would be made better off by reducing competition.[35] Moreover, the protection of consumers via the preexisting licensing scheme renders this purpose implausible. Protection of dealers from manufacturer overreaching seems, on the other hand, a coherent purpose. In many long-term contracts there may occur periods in which events make it possible for one of the parties to skew the advantages from continuing the arrangement strongly in its favor.[36] Where history, expertise, and market power suggest that one party will have a decided advantage in the initial structuring of the relationship, legislative constraints on the exercise of bargaining power may seem advisable.

But the plausibility of this purpose in the case of the *Fox* statute strains credulity. How could manufacturers entice new dealers to join them in coercing prior dealers when the predictable costs are bankruptcy? And given the unlikelihood of new dealers moving into saturated markets, how could manufacturers oppress dealers (whose franchises are already protected from arbitrary termination by other legislation) by backing unreasonable demands with threats of new competition?

The enforcement scheme in *Fox* is also peculiarly unsuitable to the purposes envisaged. Although consumers and oppressed dealers are the purported beneficiaries, there is no role for the former in enforcement and the state has no power to protect either on its own initiative. Moreover, the complaint procedure is set up in a fashion that maximizes the opportunities for harassment while sharply constraining the state's power to control pernicious uses of the system. It is not merely that one can imagine better ways of implementing the purported purposes of the legislation — it is hard to contrive worse schemes. And the historic output of the process confirms this a priori analysis. Whatever the legislature wanted to do, what it in fact did was provide a means for delaying, and perhaps thwarting, new competition.

I do not want to oversell this analysis. One can imagine that some peculiarity of the California market (the licensing scheme, perhaps) makes automobile dealers natural monopolies. It is conceivable that dealers give better service without competition. The legislature may have reason to mistrust agency enforcement discretion. Perhaps the manufacturers are capable of extortion via threats of ruinous franchising. Maybe the legislature just wants to limit the number of automobile franchises for aesthetic reasons. Or to produce a waiting period in which ill-considered franchising or relocation plans can be reconsidered. But these imaginings seem rather fanciful. In the absence of some demonstration to the contrary, why not describe the legislation in terms of its dominant effects: It permits existing dealers to delay and sometimes forestall potential entrants. And that is not a permissible public purpose.

Yet even with this lopsided "substantive" analysis, there is some discomfiture in arguing for invalidation. If the legislative scheme has merely turned out badly, why not return to the legislature and make the argument there? Legislative correction would solve the problem without either the unhappy confrontation of legislative and judicial power or the potential for dampening legislative willingness to experiment with new forms of economic regulation or redistribution. Indeed, because I believe these views to be basically sound, I would advocate invalidation only when the underlying structure of competition in the political marketplace suggests that self-correction is unlikely. In short, the search is not just for legislative error but for probable legislative failure.

THE "SPECIAL INTERESTS" PROBLEM

In some sense, all legislation is special interest legislation. We rely, therefore, on competition among special interests to limit simple transfers from the general public to particular persons or groups in circumstances that make the donees improbable subjects of general social concern.[37] Logrolling, disguised transfers, and outright corruption make the competitive democratic check an imperfect protection, but the structure of governmental institutions — bicameralism, executive vetoes, and judicial review — adds further insulation. Because the last check, judicial review, speaks with apparent finality and is less connected to electoral politics than other checks, the appropriate place of judicial review has always been considered a problem. Most would perhaps agree that judicial activism is most appropriate when other checks are inadequate. The question is what evidence of inadequacy should be required to actuate serious judicial review.

As we have noted, the conventional response is that of the *Carolene Products* footnote.[38] Courts should enforce direct prohibitions, should be alert to protect "discrete and insular minorities" from the effects of democracy combined with prejudice, and (perhaps) should also have a special role in maintaining the openness of democratic institutions. This description of an appropriate judicial role has a certain intuitive, as well as a historically validated, appeal. Indeed, to the extent that it focuses on defects in the democratic process and uses those defects as justifications for judicial intervention, it looks in the right direction. But there is a subsidiary theme in the *Carolene Products* footnote. It seems to distinguish the review it approves from the economic due process review which the remainder of the case disapproves on grounds of judicial competence. Yet the specific prohibitions of the Bill of Rights, and the ideas of minority status and the integrity of the democratic process, speak with greater clarity concerning important constitutional values only on superficial inquiry.[39] *Brown v. Board of Education* leads inevitably to *Regents of the University of California v. Bakke*.[40] One-man-one-vote turns out to be a gerrymanderer's delight, and freedom of speech doctrine approaches the principled clarity of the Internal Revenue Code.[41] There is no absolute value or procedural approach to the question of the appropriate role of judicial review that will save the courts from the hard questions of when legislative judgment is legitimate. The question of "legislative failure" should be confronted directly.

Consider again the *Fox* situation. Three groups are potentially harmed by the legislation in question: consumers, new car dealers, and manufacturers. The consumer is, of course, the "pitiful giant" of legislative processes. Numerically a majority — indeed, almost coextensive with "voters" — consumers are traditionally viewed as unorganized and, therefore, relatively powerless politically. Yet surely this overstates the weakness of consumer interests. Political entrepreneurship in electoral politics consists, at least in part, in seeking out unrepresented interests and representing them.[42] The potential for "Olson effects" cannot alone be the basis for declaring the political process inoperative, if democratic governance is to remain the dominant form of policy choice.

But in *Fox* the amorphousness of consumer interests is combined with a situation in which the more focused opponents of a simple transfer to existing car dealers are also powerless. The class of *potential* dealers may turn out to be substantial over time, but it is not likely to have many existing representatives at any time in particular. And the manufacturers are out-of-state corporations. This combination of factors makes it unlikely that effective political competition surrounded the passage of the statute or that the legislative process will be self-correcting. State representatives who hitch their political wagons to nonexistent and/or extraterritorial interests are not long for the constituent assembly.

I should hasten to add that I do not believe that only state legislation will fail serious inquiry into its reasonableness based on the sorts of criteria that I have suggested. My sense is that much of what goes on under the Agricultural Marketing Agreement Act of 1937, for example, could be considered the outcome of "public-spirited" legislation only by the politically myopic. Milk marketing orders are illustrative. Such orders are supposed to maintain the prices of whole milk and establish an orderly system for marketing milk products. The more general purpose, however, is to ensure that consumers will have available an adequate supply of whole milk and other milk products. The statute presumably was not passed simply to subsidize the dairy industry.

Yet that is how the system operates and apparently has been designed to operate. In *Block v. Community Nutrition Institute*,[43] consumers sought review of agricultural marketing orders that denied them access to a particular form of long-lived, reconstituted milk that has been on the grocery shelves of most other nations for decades. The Supreme Court, however, found that consumers had no standing to obtain judicial review of the marketing orders of the secretary of agriculture. Carefully perusing the statute, the Court determined that the Congress had explicitly excluded all consumer participation both in the process of developing milk marketing orders and in seeking a judicial determination of their validity. The Court concluded, therefore, that "[a]llowing consumers to sue the Secretary would severely disrupt this complex and delicate administrative scheme."[44]

The Court may well have been correct in its interpretation of the Agricultural Marketing Agreement Act. But the case would have looked very different had the arbitrariness or rationality of the scheme itself been put at issue. If consumers had offered the court the option either of inserting them into the scheme through participation in judicial review, or of declaring the scheme to be unreasonable in the light of its general purposes, the case might well have come out differently. But because under our current jurisprudence the invalidation alternative seems foreclosed, the Court was not even asked to assess the reasonableness of consumer protection excluding all consumer participation.

It may be objected, of course, that I have misread the underlying purpose of the Agricultural Marketing Agreement Act. Perhaps it is a sufficient public purpose to establish an "orderly system" for marketing agricultural products. Nevertheless, being able to put that question to a court would frame a serious issue for discussion: Can "orderliness" be given enough content — enough plausibility and coherence as a public purpose — to sustain this exercise of congressional power? And, of course, relevant to that inquiry would be the question of why orderly marketing is better accomplished without taking the interest of consumers into account. Perhaps, the statute would be sustained. But at least cogent questions would have been asked about whether the statute merely created a framework for the private use of public power.

Again, note that the claim is modest. I do not advocate overturning legislation on "process" grounds (because relevant political competitors are arguably excluded) when coherent and plausible public purposes are served by legislation. Nor should a court ignore actual political competition, however implausible its occurrence may seem a priori. Ideologies may substitute for interest groups or provide proxies who "represent" them. "Public-regardingness" turns, thus, on a combination of substantive and process concerns. I would have the courts look for a combination of substantive and decision-process "danger signals" that together would suggest that legislation is essentially private-regarding — that it benefits some group in ways that cannot convincingly be explained in terms of a broad range of possible public purposes, or in terms of a well-functioning democratic process. Methodologically, the argument is for viewing both the Constitution and constitutional cases whole; for taking seriously, to paraphrase Justice Frankfurter, the complicated as well as the simple-minded ways in which legislation fails its most basic function — to pursue the public welfare.

This suggestion, of course, raises as many questions as it answers. It launches the Court into areas of judicial review that it has attempted to avoid. To be sure, it has not avoided them, but it has avoided many of the hard questions that straightforward review entails; questions that cannot be resolved on the high ground of neutral principles, whatever the level of judicial craftsmanship. Many questions — such as what counts as a public purpose, how burdens of proof should be allocated, what "failings" of representative democracy are inconsistent with a well-functioning legislative system, how broad or narrow the constitutional remands from the courts to the legislature should be, what level of public purpose spread on the legislative record or embodied in the statutory form will sustain legislation in the face of effects demonstrably unrelated to the achievement of those public ends — remain to be addressed.

These are the perennial issues of judicial review in other areas. They must be addressed, as elsewhere, in context. And I cannot here speculate on how the Court will resolve the question of the constitutionality of the myriad statutory schemes that might be presented to it. The basic point, however, bears repeating. The Constitution presumes that private activity will be constrained only to promote public purposes. The recognition, first, that there is a wide range of such purposes, and second, that democratic, collective choice may pursue any or all of them in a complex and eclectic body of statutes, in no way reduces the force of the basic principle. Citizens have a constitutional right to demand that public law be public-regarding. Otherwise, their private harms are constitutionally inexplicable.

By their relentless focus on institutional failures and self-interested behaviors, modern public choice analysts have sounded an alarm about legislative action that reinforces the constitutional vision of the framers, but perhaps extends its reach. Modern constitutional doctrine has been loathe to respond to the public choice challenge lest the courts once again stumble into a political conflagration. But this fate is unnecessary. Constitutional law can heed the warnings of public choice without adjudicating on the basis of some of its practitioners' theoretical constructs or vivid imaginations. Law, after all, can still demand that facts be supplied in support of theory, and it can resolve uncertainty on the basis of institutional comity. Judicial restraint demands neither abdication nor deception. Nor does it demand that courts ignore ideas that James Madison and his colleagues would have found congenial.

4

Legislatures, Deals, and Statutory Interpretation

The United States is often referred to as a "common law" country. Although trivially true as a means for distinguishing the legal traditions of England and its former colonies from the civil law culture of the remainder of Europe, the notion that twentieth-century American law is primarily common law is preposterous. Americans remain preoccupied with the drama of cases, but at or just below the surface of nearly all legal decisionmaking lies a statute, perhaps a whole constellation of them.

This is peculiarly true in the public law realm — the domain of relationships among governments and between the government and private parties. Save for that limited number of official actions that can be predicated directly on the Constitution, all official authorization derives ultimately from statute. And just as officials can do only what statutes authorize them to do, citizens (or other private parties) are bound by public obligations only if a statute so prescribes. To talk about the powers, immunities, obligations, or privileges of the government in relation to its citizenry, or vice versa, is to talk about the meaning of the statutes that structure those relations. Statutory interpretation is not just an important part of public law, it is the very essence of public law decisionmaking, and much of private law decisionmaking as well.

The ubiquity, nay the necessity, of continuous statutory interpretation notwithstanding, the question of *how* statutes should be interpreted is only episodically controversial. Strident controversy erupted in the late nineteenth and early twentieth centuries as practitioners and judges recognized that statues were supplanting much of the common law that governed private affairs. Reactionary lawyers and judges attempted to beat back the power of state and federal legislators by deploying legislation-limiting "canons of construction," such as the hoary maxim that "statutes in derogation of the common law must be strictly construed." Controversy reemerged around the New Deal in a slightly different form: the question then was how to integrate a major new interpreter, the federal administrative agency, into the hierarchy of interpretative authority that predated the rise of the administrative state. In both of these cases, controversy over the methodology of statutory interpretation signaled a major shift in the constitutional order and raised important questions about the authority and legitimacy of new forms of lawgiving.

In the 1990s statutory interpretation has once again taken center stage in academic debates and, to a lesser degree, in judicial and political dialogue. But why this should be so is not entirely clear. In part, the fixation on interpretative methodology may be a spillover from intellectual currents outside of the law. The "interpretive turn" has had a more than three-decade run in literary and social theory. The message there is that interpretation is everything—an idea both banal and revolutionary. Banal, because who could have doubted it? Meaning can hardly emerge unmediated by human agency, that is, without the engagement of a human actor with a text. Revolutionary, because the notion implies that everything is *just* interpretation. All texts are radically incomplete. They can and do have multiple meanings for multiple readers and multiple contexts. Meaning is up for grabs. It can be asserted, debated, critiqued, and elaborated; but it cannot be "found."

For law, this latter vision is profoundly unsettling. After all, the application of law relies on the authority of the text. If the text literally can mean anything, then the law is simply whatever the interpreter says it is. The legitimacy of the application of law will thus have to depend on some agreed methodology for giving meaning to legal texts. Otherwise, we are simply at the mercy of the preferences or political ideology of the official interpreters. In such a world, democratic control of lawgiving and "government under law" might be only comforting myths, not everyday realities. Or so some critical theorists claim.

Obviously, this intellectual challenge to the legitimacy of legal decisionmaking might itself be enough to energize debate about interpretive methodology. The idea of legitimacy becomes precisely the idea of legitimate interpretation. We may invoke the text, but authority must flow from some agreed upon means of reading and applying it.

Yet, the spillover of hermeneutics into legal theory is not a wholly satisfying explanation for contemporary interest in interpretive method. Interpretive theory is about what to do when meaning is in doubt—what default rules or background understandings take over when terms are ambiguous or vague. And when interpretive theory itself becomes problematic, this seems to signal that, once again, the very nature of the public legal order has become controversial. Anxiety about how one ought to approach the task of interpretation emerges when political debate has gone beyond the realm of policy struggle to engage fundamental questions about the legitimate role of the state.

Recall the sketch of the development of public law ideas in Chapter 1. The Progressive and New Deal reforms of the first half of this century were undertaken in the name of the "public interest." Moreover, this elite ideology was widely understood and believed. Industrialization and urbanization had created a vibrant and productive society, but one that now revealed new risks that demanded collective action. Whether the issue was unfair trade practices, monopolization, securities speculation, or labor relations, private contracting in the market had failed to provide necessary guarantees of fair dealing and economic security. The government was called upon to regulate and restructure these private institutions, to "socialize" them in ways that promoted the general welfare.

Public law thus was seen as pragmatic and purposive. Many interpretive problems arose in the administration of the plethora of Progressive and New Deal statutes, but the political zeitgeist seemed to promote an optimistic vision of how interpretation should proceed. The task was merely to understand the general reform purpose that motivated the statute and to give effect to that purpose as individual instances for its application arose. This often meant supporting the efforts of specialized agencies whose "expertise" gave authority to their interpretive practices. In other cases it involved extending the statute's reach to "unprovided for cases" that nevertheless fell within the statutes' general purposes. In yet others, courts were called upon to develop procedural, evidentiary, or remedial principles that would further the implementation of the legislators' purposes.

Sometime in the 1960s this optimistic vision began to unravel. The New Deal agencies began to be seen as stodgy bureaucracies that served the economic interests of their "regulated" constituencies. Under the dual onslaughts of the Vietnam debacle and the Nixon presidency, faith in the public-spiritedness of federal governmental activity diminished. Government became suspect; both its motives and its competence were called into question.

To be sure, the decline in confidence in government did not occur all at once. Nineteen-sixties' activists were optimistic that the difficulties with New Deal arrangements could be surmounted through institutional reform. But this optimism did not hold. In the 1990s governmental efforts tend to be viewed as inevitably flawed. Public policy reform is directed almost exclusively at limiting direct government expenditure and preventing the implementation of costly regulatory policies. Institutional reform consists largely of privatization, desolution, and downsizing — and of creating roadblocks to regulatory initiative.

While this shift in public perceptions of the likely effects of state action can easily be oversold, the new vision of governmental limitations promotes a parallel shift in the understanding of the way public law should be read. Contrast, for example, the interpretive mind-sets suggested, respectively, by New Deal optimism and 1990s pessimism.

The New Dealer, convinced of the purposive and public-interested nature of public action, would be attracted by the approach to legal interpretation made famous by the Hart and Sachs legal process materials of 1958. The interpreter should imagine that the designers of any public law statute were "reasonable people pursuing reasonable purposes reasonably." A number of mental attitudes seem to follow from this basic posture. First, statutes should be interpreted as if they are understandable and coherent. They, after all, represent the application of organized intelligence to human affairs. Second, the purposes that are being served should have widespread normative appeal. Governmental action in a democracy is responsive to public demands for the solution of pressing public problems. Third, in cases of doubt, or when confronting the proverbial unprovided for case, a construction should be put on the statute that promotes its underlying purposes.

In particular, those purposes should also be consulted when courts address procedural, evidentiary, or remedial questions within a statute's general domain. Although such issues often are given inadequate attention in legislation, their resolution may dramatically influence the efficacy of particular statutory schemes as well as the overall coherence of the public legal order. Interpretation, thus, should be approached as facilitating the pursuit of the public interest in a constantly evolving polity.

The basic interpretive mind-set induced by contemporary skepticism of governmental interventions obviously would be quite different. Courts should perhaps wonder whether statutes *have* public purposes, much less whether they have been understandably or coherently expressed in the statutory language that has emerged from the legislative process. In our most despairing moments, we might imagine statutes as constituting simply the vector sum of organized political forces mediated by a legislative process designed primarily to promote the reelection of existing officeholders. There is no reason to believe that these expressions represent either rational instrumental choices or broadly acceptable value judgments. A court, or any interpreter, confronting such a statute will surely be puzzled about how to proceed. At best it may be engaged in the enforcement of a compromise among contending special interests. At worst it may be implementing legal rules whose only coherent explanation is the political advantage provided to legislators.

This jaundiced view of the political world is surely sufficient to create a crisis for "purposivist" statutory interpretation. In this description, law is not the expression of underlying communal purposes or broadly acceptable social norms. It is rather an artifact of institutional processes combined with self-interested political mobilization. This is law as will, not law as reason. Thus, it might seem the height of folly to imagine interpretation as a process of deducing interpretive conclusions from underlying purposes. Indeed, where legislation is the result of political compromise and/or complex and mysterious institutional processes, there is no reason to believe that the various sections of a statute should even hang together in a reasonable or coherent fashion.

At the very least, an interpreter imbued with this vision of legislation should not be expected to extend the reach of statutes by filling in gaps or applying them in situations not clearly addressed. Procedural, evidentiary, and remedial developments similarly should be constrained. For these traditional avenues of expansion through implementation cannot be motivated by statutory purpose unless a purpose is perceived.

To put the matter succinctly, a statutory interpreter uncertain of the purposiveness or even the coherence of legislative utterances is in a pickle. And, seeking to preserve the authority of law, such an interpreter might be led to focus more and more on the literal or "plain meaning" of words and the formal legitimacy of legislative pronouncements. Our contemporary interpreter would perhaps be sensitive to restricting the domain of statutes to those areas precisely covered by its language. For, in this new political world, construction cannot confidently extend the domain of a statute in a purposive fashion.

To some degree these tendencies are observable in federal public law jurisprudence. Many commentators have found the Burger and Rehnquist Supreme Courts, for example, much more formalist, literalist, and positivist than their immediate predecessors.[1] We need not here pursue the details of illustrative cases. The general pattern emerges both from constitutional arenas such as interpretations of the Due Process Clause or of the separation of powers,[2] and also from a more literalist approach to statutory construction. Such tendencies are particularly evident in areas such as "standing" doctrine (who can sue to test the legality of official action), or the issue of whether federal statutes create "implied rights of action" for their beneficiaries.[3] The Court has become increasingly reluctant to construe statutes to broaden beneficiary rights. For to do so broadens the range of application of the statute in ways that often could be supported only by a "purposivist" approach — one that naively accepts the "public-spiritedness" and "remedial" character of legislation.

Indeed, in domains long subject to federal common law development, such as the abatement of navigational nuisances and the control of interstate pollution, the Supreme Court now finds that comprehensive statutory schemes not only provide no rights of action not explicitly conferred, but also preclude the further development of federal common law.[4] If statutes are unprincipled compromises, this may make perfect sense. The underlying theory of common law development, principled elaboration, would conflict with the new understanding of how the "democratic will" is expressed in statutes. To turn an old maxim on its head, common law principles are to be strictly construed because principled elaboration is in derogation of positive statutory command.

Enter Public Choice Theory — Stage Right

The Supreme Court's perceptible shift in interpretive methodology has thus followed and combined with other broad intellectual currents to provoke a renewed debate about how statutes should be read. Moreover, public choice ideas seem to have a peculiar affinity with the political zeitgeist that I have identified as underlying the contemporary methodological malaise. For at a theoretical level public choice theory gives voice to parallel ideas about public processes. The voting theory strand of public choice seems to reinforce the notion that collective action may be either uninterpretable in terms of underlying human purposes, or the artifact of agenda manipulation within the public choice process. Interest group theory reinforces the notion of legislation as private interest "deals" — narrowly tailored compromises that neither create nor express public values.

It is not surprising, therefore, that some have attempted to justify new interpretive methods in terms of public choice findings. Indeed, public choice ideas have been used both to justify interpretive methodologies and to explain interpretive behavior. Many of these efforts are more notable for their ambition than for their accomplishment. But this hardly distinguishes public choice efforts from other attempts at a grand theory of interpretation. My interest is not so much in whether to praise or condemn these attempts as to mine them for bits and pieces of usable knowledge in the unending quest for an acceptable and practicable method to construe and apply statutory language.

The discussion that follows will be divided into three general parts, corresponding to the three strains of public choice theory identified earlier: voting theory, game theory, and interest group theory. In all three of these areas, public choice practitioners have made contributions to our understanding. In particular, the public choice perspective has focused attention on the creators of legislative texts. It asks hard questions about who is speaking when statutes are enacted, how that speech is accomplished, and how attention to these "who" and "how" questions might affect interpretative method. Moreover, when it looks at interpreters, public choice views them as plural rather than singular and as having mixed motives. Interpreters may act as "faithful agents" of the legislature or promote policy preferences of their own. In both ways, public choice adds a more sophisticated perspective to standard legal analysis, which tends to be riveted on the judiciary and to speak of "the legislature" as if its capacity for collective expression of singular intent was nonproblematic.

On the other hand, as a guide to interpretive method, public choice theory has a singular weakness: A theory of legal interpretation is inherently normative. Hence, while public choice theory may help us understand why public institutions behave as they do, as a positive theory it can supply us directly with no normative foundation upon which to assess the appropriateness of those actions. But, as I noted in Chapter 1, public choice practitioners, like the rest of us, often have difficulty separating their ises from their oughts. Some become so convinced of the inevitability of the world they describe that they take it to be normatively appropriate as well as empirically true. Others see that inevitability as constraining what is possible and, therefore, what can realistically be affirmed as desirable. In yet other cases, normative premises are imported into the discussion with no attempt to ground them in any persuasive normative vision. Here, as elsewhere, attention to the use of public choice ideas must be concerned both with descriptive accuracy and with movements from descriptive hypotheses to prescriptive conclusions.

But these ruminations get somewhat ahead of the story. Let us take each domain of public choice theory in turn and examine its potential to inform legal interpretive methodology. Because interest group theory has been used most often in this regard, we will begin there.

The Myriad Uses of Interest Group Perspectives

Recall the basic dynamics of the interest group perspective. Groups, not individuals, are the primary units of political action. Using both votes and dollars, they seek favors from legislators who, whatever else they may want, want to be reelected. But because of public goods problems, not all groups form or are similarly well endowed to participate in legislative bargaining.

From this perspective, legislation that would benefit everyone (or most citizens) by a small amount is particularly unlikely to have a group representative. Or, to put the matter another way, the statutes that are most likely to be directed at enhancing the general public welfare are the least likely to have organized and energetic lobbyists pushing their adoption.

As I noted earlier, Bruce Ackerman uses this approach as a way of critiquing the Supreme Court's concern to protect the interests of "discrete and insular minorities" from mistreatment at the hands of the legislature. For, from an interest group perspective, it may well be "diffuse and dispersed majorities" that are most disadvantaged in the legislative process. At the level of statutory interpretation, the belief that interest group theory accurately describes the legislative process has led several authors to view virtually all legislative products as containing narrow bargains among influential actors who have finally settled on a "contract" expressed as legislation. We will call this the "deals" approach to legislative interpretation.

Judge Frank Easterbrook is perhaps the leading proponent of this view.[5] Easterbrook seems to believe that the most cynical versions of interest group theory provide a good description of the nature of most public law statutes. Moreover, he would make that description the predicate for the judicial construction of public law. Using the deals metaphor for all it is worth, Easterbrook contends that statutory construction is nothing more than the enforcement of arm's-length bargains. He concludes, therefore, that statutes should be construed to cover only those domains of human conduct explicitly treated by the statutory language. In the deals vernacular, statutes should be limited to providing interested parties with "exactly what they bargained for." For Easterbrook, "strict construction" is the appropriate methodology to be applied to modern public law statutes.

Although Easterbrook's deals framework has been influential in later discussions of statutory interpretation, that influence is puzzling. For one thing, Easterbrook seems confused about the implications of his own approach. The standard form of interest group theory imagines that bargains are struck between interest groups and reelection-oriented legislators. It is this trading of votes or money for private goods (in the form of legislation) that suggests that such statutes are contrary to the general welfare. Easterbrook, by contrast, seems to imagine that legislative deals are between or among interest groups, with legislators acting merely as the mediators who formalize the bargain. But if that is true, then he is using a model that has been developed more rigorously by Gary Becker.[6] And Becker's model predicts that such "bargains" will *enhance* general welfare.

The basic intuition underlying Becker's analysis is straight out of Adam

Smith. If one believes that private contracting among individuals and firms is socially beneficial (the invisible hand), to put those contracts in legislative rather than contractual language is a mere formal change that should not alter the aggregate welfare affects. Given the model he employs, Easterbrook needs to explain why he believes that legislative "deals" are pernicious, and to justify his desire to have these deals strictly construed.

Perhaps Easterbrook has simply been mesmerized by his contract analogy. But here again a puzzle arises: Easterbrook says that statutes should be construed like contracts. He then asserts that contracts are strictly construed. But this massively misstates standard contract doctrine. Only certain types of contracts are strictly construed, and then for particular policy reasons. In other cases courts are concerned to give full effect to the intentions of the parties: They constantly supply "unprovided for" terms and conditions that they believe to be generally beneficial. Indeed, the contemporary vision of contracts as mostly "relational," or long-term, suggests that the job of judicial construction is one of managing ongoing relationships. The idea is that contract interpreters should strive to achieve the underlying purposes of the association brought about by the contract. For it is the realization of these joint programs that enhances public welfare.

In short, the contract metaphor simply will not bear the weight that Easterbrook imposes upon it. Calling statutes "deals" could as easily lead us back to "purposivism" as toward "strict construction." Hence, he must have some other normative vision of why interest-group–generated legislation is bad. But that normative vision is never revealed. The one thing that seems clear is that Easterbrook is very skeptical that public interest goals are a prominent feature of the statutory landscape. Statutes that either limit entry into markets, provide subsidies for private activities, or entail any limitations on private contracting are for him presumptively a species of special interest legislation. Judged by these criteria, of course, a very large proportion of public law statutes would seem to be a special interest variety.

John Macey reveals much the same positive perspective as Easterbrook.[7] He views most statutes as the product of special interest deals. However, he develops a quite different judicial approach to interpretation. Whereas Easterbrook counsels judges to take a narrow and literal approach to statutes, Macey argues for a very activist form of judicial intervention. Macey finds in the structure, as well as the specific provisions, of the Constitution a presumptive requirement that all statutes be "public-regarding." Combining that norm with the belief that most statutory enactments are not in fact designed to serve public-regarding purposes, Macey argues that courts are constitutionally obliged to enforce, not the legislative intent to provide private goods at public expense, but a hypothetical and constitutionally necessary intent to pursue the public interest. Macey's position involves, therefore, judicial activism of a quite swashbuckling variety.

Interestingly, Macey's and Easterbrook's approaches can lead to the same result. Both, for example, discuss the case of *Silkwood v. Kerr-McGee Corp.*,[8] and a look at their analysis of that case is revealing concerning the limitations of either interpretive approach. The underlying facts of the case — or a version of them — have become well known from the movie *Silkwood*. The narrow interpretive issue in *Silkwood*, as it reached the Supreme Court of the United States, was just this: Did the Atomic Energy Act of 1954, which established a comprehensive system of federal regulation of the production and use of radioactive materials, prohibit an award of punitive damages to Karen Silkwood's estate under state law? In a five-four decision, the Supreme Court held that the jury's ten-million-dollar award of punitive damages could stand.

Both Easterbrook and Macey agree with the majority opinion, but they reach that agreement by strikingly different paths. In Easterbrook's view, the Atomic Energy Act, because a licensing statute, is almost certainly private interest legislation. He looks, therefore, to see what sort of bargain the atomic energy industry was able to get on the question of the application of state tort law to nuclear accidents. He discovers that the Atomic Energy Act preserves state remedies, while the Price-Anderson Act limits the total exposure of a corporation for any particular incident to $250 million. Easterbrook gleans from these statutory provisions that the industry probably wanted complete protection from tort liability, but was unable to obtain it. The Court should, therefore, not give the atomic energy producers the benefit of a bargain they were unable to make.

While Macey agrees that the Atomic Energy Act and the Price-Anderson Act represent private interest legislation (masquerading under a thin veneer of public protection), he views the Supreme Court's majority opinion in *Silkwood* as having given the relevant statutes a public interest interpretation. On its face, the Atomic Energy Act is designed both to improve safety and to encourage "widespread participation in the development and utilization of atomic energy for peaceful purposes." But safety regulation has, in Macey's view, been inadequate — a result that he alleges was fully expected by the industry groups that he hypothesizes to have lobbied for the act. Hence, in order to further the public interest in safety, the Court should allow state trial juries to award punitive damages, even if those damages are a hundred times greater than the maximum fine available to the Nuclear Regulatory Commission under the statute. Although, according to Macey, the punitive damages award in *Silkwood* was "in direct conflict with the special interest goal [of the legislation]" — to limit the tort liability of those supplying nuclear power — the Court should ignore the underlying political reality and further the aspirational safety purposes of this statute as stated in its preamble.[9]

I hardly object to courts taking a sophisticated view of the public versus private interest aspects of legislation. But Easterbrook and Macey seem to be in the grip of a vision that makes them accept unsupported hypotheses much too readily. Both authors write, for example, as if there were some clear consensus in the public policy, legal, or political science literatures that licensing statutes are enacted primarily for the benefit of regulated parties. But this idea is, to say the least, deeply controversial. They cite no support for this general proposition, and I can find none. Moreover, both authors ignore the very substantial practical difficulty of determining how the legislation they analyzed serves private interest goals, even if one is committed to the general proposition that statutes usually are designed to do so.

Presumably, the engine driving Easterbrook's and Macey's conclusion that licensing is a proxy for private interest legislation is the view that licensing is sought to protect existing firms from competition. But, if so, consider the situation in *Silkwood*. The relevant "interests" here would be those of the electrical utility industry as it was constituted at the time of the passage of the Atomic Energy and the Price-Anderson Acts. There were no nuclear-fired generating plants at this stage. The significant underlying material interest in imposing a licensing requirement then might have been the interest of coal and petroleum producers (and transporters), who wanted to limit the substitution of nuclear energy for fossil fuel. On this view the licensing scheme, by restricting entry, would be peculiarly for the benefit of the fossil fuel industry. But that industry would presumably be delighted by the availability of punitive damages against nuclear-powered electrical plants. Given that reading of the private interest history of the statutes in question, Macey and Easterbrook have gotten the result backwards.

I cannot, of course, claim that I have the analysis of the "real" interest underlying the Atomic Energy Act right and that Macey and Easterbrook have it wrong. Indeed, I can conceive of a number of other plausible private interest stories. It may be, for example, that the real interests at work are the interests of the specialty construction industry, uranium producers, holders of long-term uranium contracts, or whoever. The point is only that "positive theory" at this level of generality is indistinguishable from ideology. Hypotheses rapidly become facts because the "facts" are difficult or impossible to find.

The Macey approach might seem defensible, nevertheless, because arguably public choice theory is doing no work in his interpretive regime. He could be viewed as telling the judiciary only that it has a constitutional duty to promote the public interest through interpretation, whatever the politics of legislative enactment. But notice the difficulties with this posture. First, it seems clear that Macey's idea of the public interest to be served is highly dependent on its opposition to the private interest he imagines to have had an overweening influence on the legislation to be interpreted. Otherwise it is hard to understand how Macey knows that safety has not been pursued at an appropriate level under the Atomic Energy Act. The notion that a regulatory regime that has resulted in the virtual abandonment of the nuclear power industry in the United States has nevertheless been too lax seems to need at least some explanation.

Second, while one might easily agree with some weak form of Macey's interpretive thesis — "When in doubt, nudge statutes in the direction of some public interest goal" — that is not the methodology suggested. The idea here is to treat statutes just like the common law. That a provision is a legislative creation is to have no particular weight.

This is an extremely strong form of judicial monitoring via interpretation. I can think of no justification for such a judicial posture that does not rely on the belief that legislatures generally are not attempting to implement some vision of the public interest when enacting a statute. For if one believed that legislatures were enacting such visions, and that there are multiple public values that inevitably lead to public-interested compromises, then interpreting all specific clauses as subordinate to any broadly stated purpose, as Macey proposes, looks like nothing more than judicial revision. Nor is this "Council of Revision" constrained by even that degree of "modesty" often thought to be induced by articulating revisionary questions as ones of judicial *review* rather than judicial *interpretation*.

In short, the Easterbrook and Macey attempts to use public choice to inform statutory interpretation seem remarkably unhelpful. Easterbrook's approach appears to be conceptually confused both about interest group bargaining models and about the nature of contract theory and practice. He apparently employs some public welfare notion as a normative underpinning for the judicial posture recommended, but these ideas are never brought to the surface or explored. Macey engages in heroic assumptions about historical facts and suggests that courts should revise statutes to promote the public welfare, notwithstanding the strong belief that the public interest is seldom if ever considered in the legislative process. The constitutional justification for this theory of "interpretation as revision" is similar to the one I endorse as a basis for reinvigorated judicial review. But Macey would apply it to all statutes all of the time. Not only is this approach indiscriminate, but, as I shall demonstrate later, interpretive revision of this sort invades legislative prerogatives in a more dramatic and nonreversible fashion than judicial invalidation of the same statute.

Not all the legal literature seeking to apply public choice theory to statutory interpretation has been so rambunctious. Moderating his views somewhat after taking on direct responsibility for legislative interpretation, Judge Richard Posner offers a more discriminating approach.[10] In his view, statutes may be of at least four types: statutes pursuing the public interest economically defined (correction of market failures); statutes pursuing the public interest defined in other ways (such as the just distribution of wealth); statutes expressing a public sentiment not easily explained in either efficiency or distributional terms (such as the regulation of pornography); and legislation furthering the interest of narrow interest groups.

Posner suggests that we first classify legislation and then pursue different interpretative strategies depending on the type of legislation presented for interpretation. Public interest legislation should receive a broad purposive construction, while narrow interest group legislation should get the treatment suggested by Easterbrook. Posner specifically objects to the use of presumptions one way or another concerning the nature of legislation. He criticized Guido Calabresi's book on statutory obsolescence,[11] for example, because Calabresi, without any explicit justification, uniformly assumes a public interest perspective on legislation. Presumably, he would feel the same way about Easterbrook's and Macey's standard presupposition that public law is usually a "private interest deal."

"Judicious" as it may appear, Judge Posner's approach is unworkable in most cases. Consider the legislative scheme at issue in *Silkwood*. Should we agree with Easterbrook and Macey that this is private interest legislation because it contains exclusive licensing provisions and limitations on liability? Or perhaps because private interests lobbied for its passage? I certainly would be hesitant to so conclude unless I were utilizing Easterbrook's and Macey's presumptions — a methodology that Posner enjoins us to avoid. Licensing of a technology that has the capacity to produce massive and irreversible catastrophe hardly seems conclusive evidence of a private interest viewpoint. Nor does a limitation of liability under circumstances of enormous uncertainty but potentially great public gain. Nor would I be convinced by the undoubted presence in the legislative process of those who perceived the incidence of public benefits under the legislation to be skewed in their direction. Some such presence can be identified in virtually all legislation.

The public or private character of the Atomic Energy and Price-Anderson Acts seems rather hopelessly indeterminate. Moreover, I suspect that the same situation would obtain with respect to most legislation. When asked to choose between a public interest and a private interest perspective, we will almost always have to vote our presuppositions, not our analysis of the evidence. And the public choice literature simply does not establish a basis for believing in one or another of those presuppositions. Nor does it in any way validate the utility of the interpretative approaches that the three preceding authors have suggested.

William Eskridge's attempt to provide a systematic classification of legislation along with attendant interpretive methodologies suffers from problems similar to Posner's efforts. Eskridge uses Michael Hayes's and James Q. Wilson's classifications of legislation according to the distribution of the legislation's benefits and costs.[12] This classification scheme, combined with some basic ideas from interest group theory, provokes Eskridge to provide both predictions about what sort of legislation will emerge from legislatures, and an analysis of the degree to which one should be concerned that a particular type of legislation is the result of competition between narrow self-interested groups or organizations. Each of the four types of legislation that is generated by Eskridge's two-by-two matrix then has an appropriate form of interpretation attached to it.

The Eskridge approach is an advance over its predecessor's application of public choice ideas to statutory construction. He uses public choice theory itself to develop his classification scheme. His approach, based on ideas about the supply and demand of legislation, thus has more analytic bite than Posner's intuitive categorization of the legislative territory. His conclusions are less grotesque parodies than Easterbrook's or Macey's of legislative life as revealed both within and outside of the public choice literature.

Even so, it would be extremely dangerous to adopt the Eskridge approach as a set of interpretive rules. We need not pursue the difficulty in great detail. Like Posner's classification system, Eskridge's is not self-defining or self-applying. More important, it is vague or ambiguous at its core. Legislation has multiple distributions of costs and benefits. Moreover, those distributions may change over the life of the legislation. I have grave difficulty assigning even superficially easy cases, like Social Security pensions or the National Labor Relations Act, much less our old friends the Atomic Energy and Price-Anderson Acts, to one box in Eskridge's matrix.

These classification difficulties relate to a more fundamental problem. Eskridge's assortment of interpretive approaches seems to flow in some mysterious way from the positive analysis of the underlying structure of the legislation. The only hint of why comes from Eskridge's suggestion that the courts, when interpreting, are about the business of remedying "dysfunctions" in the

Table 4.1. Eskridge's Typology of Legislation

Distributed benefit/distributed cost	Distributed benefit/concentrated cost
Danger: The legislature's failure to update the law as society and the underlying problem change. **Response:** Courts can help maintain a statute's usefulness by expanding it to new situations and by developing the statute in common-law fashion. **Caveat:** Courts should be reluctant to create special exceptions for organized groups.	**Danger:** Regulated groups' evasion of duties, as agencies are "captured" by groups. Regulation becomes a means to exclude competition. **Response:** Courts can monitor agency enforcement and private compliance, and can open up procedures to allow excluded groups to be heard. Courts should seek to make the original public goal work.
Concentrated benefit/distributed cost	Concentrated benefit/concentrated cost
Danger: Rent-seeking by special interest groups, at the expense of the general public. **Response:** Courts can narrowly construe the statute to minimize the benefits. Courts should err in favor of stinginess with public largesse. **Caveat:** Rule of stinginess not applicable if statute really serves a public purpose.	**Danger:** The statutory "deal" often grows unexpectedly lopsided over time. **Response:** Courts can fine-tune the statutory arrangement to reflect new circumstances. **Caveat:** Err against very much judicial updating unless affected groups are systematically unable to get legislative attention.

legislative process. But surely we need a better-articulated normative view of what courts should be doing, along with some positive explanation of what we should expect from courts before we can begin to assess the usefulness of Eskridge's rules of thumb.[13]

Eskridge, however, offers his model much more as a set of caveats, not as a set of interpretive rules. If we are unhappy with adopting a broad presumption about either private interests or public interests as the dominant explanations for legislation, Eskridge's typology begins to tell us something about where we might expect the process of legislative enactment to be characterized by one or another of these perspectives. It suggests where we might be more or less worried about misjudging legislative intent by using the wrong presuppositions. It provides opportunities for local insights into the dynamics of particular types of statutes; it helps to lead the mind toward appropriately complicated visions of what legislation is about without losing all pretense to be more than a "garbage can" theory. Understood in this way, the Eskridge typology has the advantage of beating the currently available alternatives. Although the contribution is modest, any "usable" idea probably will be.

Statutory Construction from a "Voting Theory" Perspective

Judge, now Justice, Antonin Scalia stimulated some considerable portion of the contemporary interest in interpretive methodology by his attacks on the use of legislative history as a guide to the interpretation of statutes.[14] Scalia's basic position is both clear and controversial. In his view the law is embodied in the text of the statute. Nothing else has been enacted by the Congress or signed by the president. Hence, a court that resorts to prestatutory materials that were not enacted usurps the legislative function — or perhaps, more accurately, threatens to turn it over to particular legislators who expressed their opinions, or to staff writers who compiled the legislative reports that accompany bills to the floor. On this view, using legislative history is (usually) unconstitutional.

Scalia's is a hard-edged, but hardly an unsophisticated, position. Although it has been caricatured as a variant of the long discredited "plain meaning" rule, it is in fact an argument that stresses the use of statutory language as the best evidence of the interpretation of the law. Scalia is perfectly prepared to read legislative texts within the context of the total statute of which they are a part, other statutes related to the same subject matter, and prior judicial opinions interpreting the same or related texts. Scalia believes that his approach reinforces the legislative process as it was envisioned by the Constitution and thus enhances the democratic process as a whole.[15]

Public choice scholars have noticed that his "textualist" approach to interpretation might be supported by certain implications drawn from the Arrovian impossibility theorem. Scalia's basic idea, after all, is that the judge's duty is to construe statutory language, not to divine legislative intent. Voting theorists might well argue that this is a wise approach given the impossibility of mapping collective choices onto individual preferences. Looking for legislative intent is a search for a mythical beast. The Congress as a body has no intent. And the relationship between the individual intentions or preferences of the legislators who voted for a bill and the outcome of the legislative process cannot be discovered. As Kenneth Shepsle, and others before him, have put it, "Congress is a 'they,' not an 'it.' "[16] Legislative intent, Shepsle goes on to argue, is an oxymoron.

If Shepsle is correct, then Scalia's approach receives substantial support. For if legislative intent means the aggregation of the intentions of the members of the legislature, and we have little or no reason to believe that any particular piece of legislation will accurately portray those intentions, then we have no reason to go rummaging about in legislative history for expressions of intent by members of the Congress. As historians, we may be interested in what they thought as individuals, but those thoughts have no particular bearing, nor could they, on the (fictitious) intent of the legislature. Scalia not only has a constitutional grounding for his argument, he is eminently sensible to eschew a search for the undiscoverable.

While there is force to Scalia's separated-powers argument, it is hardly airtight. Even if one concedes that the appropriate approach of a court when construing a statute is to search for "statutory meaning" rather than "legislative intent," it is far from clear that repairing to the legislative history in some way invades the appropriate powers of the legislature. To be sure, Scalia is correct to assert that a court will enforce only the statute, not some utterance by a single legislator or even a legislative committee. But that is not the point of looking at legislative history materials. The idea is not to give the them the "force of law," but to use them to try to understand the meaning of the legal text. There may be reasons for believing that giving appropriate weight to such evidence is extraordinarily difficult, but that prudential concern is a far cry from Scalia's constitutional slam dunk.

Similarly, not all public choice theorists would agree with Shepsle that a search for legislative intent is conceptually confused. McNollgast (a pseudonym for Matthew McCubbins, Roger Noll, and Barry Weingast) argue that there is nothing in Arrovian voting theory to undermine the meaningfulness of legislative intent.[17] They take an institutionalist view of the Congress in which it is important to notice that the Congress has delegated certain lawmaking activities to subgroups within the body — committees and the chambers' leaders — who have control over the agenda and the progress of particular bills. Legislative decisions do not cycle endlessly until cut off by some arbitrary feature of the legislative process, as in the standard Arrovian model of multiple voters voting over multiple issues. Instead, the Congress organizes itself to exclude certain preference orderings from the agenda and to give certain people vetoes or dictatorial powers with respect to the progress of a bill. This is purposive or intentional activity that may often lead to compromise, but not to indeterminate or random outputs. Legislative processes purposefully violate Arrow's criteria for a "fair" voting procedure in order to create one that can produce stable outcomes and meaningful products.

Indeed, McNollgast believe that by emphasizing what might be called the "agency" side of public choice analysis, they can inform the search for legislative intent and aid judges in appropriately interpreting statutory terms.

McNollgast encourage us to focus on what they call the "enacting coalition," that is, the legislators who in fact voted for a particular piece of legislation. (Opponents' intentions are irrelevant — they did not want the legislation. They may only give some indirect evidence of what the majority wanted by offering alternatives that are rejected.) Once we have narrowed the search for whose intentions matter, two questions remain: Which voices in the enacting coalition are most important, and how can we tell that legislative statements are sincere rather than strategic?

In answering these questions, McNollgast analyze the organization of the Congress and the relatively stable procedures and institutions through which the Congress orders its business. These processes clearly delegate authority to particular members concerning matters within their jurisdiction. Those members have proposal responsibilities and veto points which make their intentions particularly salient concerning the meaning of the compromise that is ultimately voted by the enacting coalition.

But, McNollgast warn us, we should not always listen even to legislators who have been granted special legislative authority. We should believe them only when misrepresenting their position could be costly to them, not when they are engaging in what McNollgast term "cheap talk." Thus, for example, the president has every reason to be candid about what he wants when proposing legislation. If what he says is unreliable at this point in the process, he will quickly lose influence with all other players. On the other hand, we should discount presidential signing statements that attempt to put a presidential spin on enacted legislation. At that point in the process the game is over, and it is then costless for the president to offer an opinion about the "true meaning" of the statue.

From a normative standpoint, McNollgast argue that courts and administrators have an obligation (and a reason) to be faithful agents of the legislature. Hence, these agents should pay attention to the statements of intention that are provided by those to whom the legislative process has given formal authority, at least where those intentions are expressed in a context assuring that the relevant actors have reason to be candid.

While McNollgast have done a serviceable job of rehabilitating the notion of legislative intent and reinforcing the conventional use of legislative history, they have not necessarily developed either a feasible or a desirable approach to statutory interpretation. As they recognize, the determination of who is important is contextual; it changes with each piece of legislation. Moreover, separating out "cheap talk" from sincere utterances is no easy matter. The processes of both the House and the Senate are extraordinarily complex. Virtually all routine processes admit of exceptions, and cagey parliamentarians can play remarkably subtle games. Knowing what a legislator stands to lose by a strategic utterance involves more than just knowing the standard rules of the House and the Senate. It involves knowing the dynamics of particular bills and the alternatives that were available when processing the legislation in question.

Indeed, I am quite uncertain about how to evaluate McNollgast's examples of presidential utterances early and late in the legislative process. Should we view presidents as never staking out strategic positions that over- or understate their true preferences when introducing bills? And why should it be costless to misrepresent the "deal" made between the administration and the Congress when signing a bill? Is the Congress likely to treat a "welcher" the same way the next time around? In short, this "imaginative reconstruction" of the legislative process, to use Judge Posner's phrase, is enormously information demanding. If McNollgast mean to suggest that legislative history is reliable only when it can be deployed in this sophisticated fashion (using Bayesian decision theory in the bargain), they may have offered judges and administrators a tool that they cannot use.

Perhaps more important, the McNollgast argument from delegation makes a logical leap similar to Scalia's separation-of-powers argument for textualism. That the members of the Congress delegate authority to committees, subcommittees, and the like in order to get legislative business done does not necessarily mean that they delegate authority to those parties to determine what statutes mean. Why, for example, should we not presume that the members who vote for a bill rely on the courts or administrative agencies to interpret and apply legislation in a fashion that reinforces the general sentiments of the enacting coalition? Indeed, why is not such a presupposition a necessary safeguard against the potential information monopoly of the strategically placed players whose opinions McNollgast urge interpreters to heed?

We could presume that this delegation of interpretive authority was intended, of course, if we knew that the interpretive methodology that would be used by courts and administrators would be the one that McNollgast urge upon us. But if that were true, then the argument is circular. The authoritativeness of these particular statements by particular legislators flows from the interpretive methodology, and the interpretive methodology is justified because certain legislators' views are legally authoritative.

To see why this is the case, imagine by contrast that we knew that the interpretive methodology adopted by all interpreters would be Scalia's textualism. Under this assumption, the members of the legislature would know that legislative intent would have to be embodied in the language of the legislation itself in order to have force. Either baseline permits purposive legislative action, but in the second scenario there is no reason to presume that delegations of power to facilitate legislative action carry with them delegations of authority to determine legislative intent. The McNollgast advice to "listen to the dealmakers" would be preferable to Scalia's textualism only if we could give some further reasons for it, of either a normative or a prudential sort. That may be possible, but as this issue is joined, public choice visions of legislative organization seem to lead in two quite different directions.

Assume for the moment that we all agree that the search for "legislative intent," at least the "true purpose" of legislation, is the normatively appropriate activity for statutory interpreters. What does public choice analysis of legislative organization tell us about how meaningful the utterances of those with special responsibilities for bills should be? I think it tells us two quite different stories. Both are plausible, and empirical "testing" has been unable to determine which is the better view.

The first story emphasizes the degree to which those sitting on or in charge of various congressional committees are likely to be *un*representative of the whole of either House or the Congress. This should be true because legislators will want to sit on committees that are of the most intense interest to their constituents. After all, if legislators are rewarded with reelection by "bringing home the bacon," then they must be in a position to do so. And because legislators can, within some constraints, choose their committee assignments, committees and subcommittees should be populated mostly by those with the most intense preferences on the issues within their jurisdiction.

On this view of the "industrial organization of the Congress,"[18] the opinions of those who have the most control over bill X are likely to be quite unrepresentative of the median legislative supporter of the bill. Knowing this, legislators would not want interpreters to use the statements of committees, committee chairs, or bill managers as representing the general will of the enacting coalition. As faithful agents of the legislature, interpreters should, therefore, be wary of the pronouncements of these "issue extremists."

The second story emphasizes the extent to which the Congress as a whole is likely to be held accountable by voters for what the Congress does.[19] On this view, the majority and minority leadership will permit members to exercise some choice about their committee assignments. But the leadership will be careful to balance committees such that they are quite representative of the legislative body as a whole. For if the whole will be held accountable for actions that must be delegated to a part, the whole needs assurance that what the part produces will both reflect the views of the whole body and be explained to it candidly. On this account of legislative organization, the views expressed by floor managers, committee chairs, and committee reports are highly probative of "what the legislature meant" when it enacted the bill. For the legislature organizes itself to ensure that its committees truthfully reveal the intent and likely effects of legislation. When a majority votes for a bill, it thus ratifies the information supplied by its agents, including what those agents said about how the bill should be understood.

This latter story provides substantial support for the McNollgast approach —at least if we can distinguish between candid expression and the "cheap talk" that legislators permit their colleagues, but know to discount themselves. If further empirical research supports this vision of legislative organization, it will also support American courts' conventional view that the legislative history supplied by critical actors has some claim to represent the will of the legislative body itself. The cynical view that legislative history is always just something concocted for the gallery, the press, or the "folks back home" will have been refuted.

The Influence of Game Theory

The McNollgast analysis is actually in a game-theoretic mode. They attempt to use the structure of a particular game—the legislative process— and the costs and benefits of particular actions to particular parties within that game, to provide insight into the appropriate use of legislative history. As we have seen, while they can hardly claim to have provided a convincing resolution of the debate between those who favor and those who reject the use of legislative history, their analysis helps to avoid the facile application of Arrovian conclusions to legislative processes that are structured by different rules. They remind us that if we would focus on the legislature as creating legal texts, we must be prepared to look at a complex institutional decision process in considerable empirical detail. And they and their colleagues have suggested testable hypotheses about whether and what kind of legislative history legislators would be likely to want interpreters to use.

Game-theoretic approaches have other uses as well. They may help us to understand some of the effects of interpretive actions and the strategic considerations that may be involved in them. In particular, a simple game-theoretic, spacial model may help to reinforce ideas that most lawyers probably already have at an intuitive level but are prone to forget, while also suggesting some nonintuitive notions that institutional designers would do well to remember.

The preexisting intuition is captured in an old lawyers' quip: "I don't care who writes the laws as long as I get to interpret them." Few who utter this amusing banality realize just how powerful interpretation can be in our particular institutional system. For it is not just that the writers of laws may not have sufficient time or interest to correct interpretive mistakes, the structure of

Table 4.2. The Article I, Section 7 Game

Left		Q		I_2	P	C_1		C		S	I_1	H		Right

the legislative process will, in many instances, make it *impossible* for them to do so. Moreover—and here the counterintuitive idea surfaces—even if the legislature acts to "correct" an interpretation with which it disagrees, *it will almost never end up with its original policy reinstated, even if not a single member of the legislature has altered his or her preferences.*

In order to elaborate these ideas, we will adopt a simple linear model that William Eskridge and John Ferejohn employed to illustrate what they call the "Article I, Section 7 Game."[20] The basic story goes like this: The House (H), the Senate (S), and the president (P) are each involved in approving new legislation. Each institution will have slightly different preferences, but they often can compromise and adopt a policy.

In the simple one-dimensional model depicted by table 4.2, the preferences of the House, the Senate, and the president are situated from left to right along an imaginary line that connects points on a continuum of possible policies. The placement of the actors represents their preferred policy choices. Q represents the preenactment status quo, and C the "compromise" policy that has been embodied in new legislation. The statute is then interpreted and applied by an administrative agency or by a court. While either implementing institution may be attempting to carry out the true legislative intent, it may fail. Assume that the interpretation is either at I_1, or I_2. Can the legislative process overturn either of these erroneous interpretations?

The answer depends entirely upon where the agency or court interpretation falls on the left-to-right political spectrum defined by the one-dimensional model. If the interpretation remains within the outer boundaries defined by the preferences of the legislative players, as at I_1, nothing can be done. At least one of the players, perhaps two, will have been made better off by the interpretation. That is, the interpretation will be closer to their true preferences than was the compromise policy adopted. (In table 4.2, both S and H gain by I_1.) Hence, they will exercise their power to block the legislation by refusing to pass it, or by vetoing it. (Technically, the president's veto can be overridden, but in practice it almost never is.) In short, this interpretation of the statute sticks until at least one of the players in the legislative process changes its mind. (Eskridge and Ferejohn also demonstrate that the game can be made dynamic over time. If the original preferences of the institutions shift, agencies or courts can shift with them without fear of being overruled by new legislation, as long as they stay within the outer boundaries of the players' preferences.)

The situation is different if the interpretation falls outside the boundaries defined by the institutional positions, as at I_2. If we assume that each player is indifferent between policies that lie to its left or right, so long as they are equidistant from its most preferred position, then an interpretation that goes too far to either the left or the right can be called back within the boundaries defined by institutional preferences. If the interpretation is to the right of the rightmost player, the moderate and leftist player can offer up a new statute which adopts a policy that is to the left of the rightmost player but equidistant from or closer to its preferred point than the interpretation that is being overturned. A similar dynamic works if the interpretation is too far to the left, as in table 4.2. A new policy can be adopted somewhere between P and C_1.

Note, however, an interesting aspect of this "correction" of the erroneous interpretation. It does not put the policy back where the legislature had placed it originally (C). The interpretation shifts the status quo point and hence the terms of the bargain among the House, the Senate, and the president. In our example, the president will veto any bill to the right of C_1. Hence, while the legislative process can overturn an erroneous interpretation some of the time, it is most unlikely that it will ever be able to reverse an interpretation such that it reinstates the precise policy that was adopted originally.

In some sense we have all always understood that the tripartite division of legislative power favors the status quo. This simple game-theoretic model, however, strongly reinforces that intuition and gives us some additional insights. The first is that interpretation of the law establishes a status quo point that will have the stability that our form of government gives to any existing state of affairs. Less obvious, but equally important in appreciating the power of interpretation, even when the legislative process can overturn an interpretation, it literally cannot escape the force of the interpreter. Interpretation has rearranged the status quo and thus reconfigured the structure of subsequent legislative bargaining.

The public choice perspective has failed to give us a decisive methodology for construing statutes. This is hardly an unexpected result. No theory can succeed in that task without providing both a complete vision of the background constitutional presuppositions that should guide interpretation and a workable means for applying these guiding assumptions to particular cases. Because the normative and positive dimensions of this task incorporate (1) the ongoing political struggle over the meaning of American constitutionalism and (2) the endless hermeneutic controversy concerning the possibility and the dynamics of meaningful communication, "interpretation" is unlikely to be rendered noncontroversial by any particular analytical school's theoretical approach.

Indeed, certain public choice ideas have proved to be seriously unhelpful. The notion that legislation is a "deal" among private interests manages to disparage public action while shedding virtually no light on the realities of lawgiving or the appropriate approach to interpretation. Voting theory's focus on the potential for chaos in collective decision processes generates the spectre of meaningless legislation without coming to grips with the realities of legislative organization, or the ways in which legislative action is purposeful and, hence, interpretable. Public choice scholarship that tempers and refines these ideas often reveals just how far we are from truly usable knowledge, if by that we mean reliable guidance on how to interpret and apply particular statutory terms.

Yet there are contributions here that should not be missed. The public choice orientation focuses attention on the speaker—the legislator—and seeks to unravel the mystery of who this might sensibly be said to be. That the effect may be to render the notion of legislative speech even more problematic is a gain, not a loss. Save from some nostalgic, anthropomorphic perspective that is ultimately unsustainable, we are better off being skeptical that we really know what we are talking about when we utter words like "legislative intent." Public choice theorists are hardly the first to point this out, but their relentless analysis of the speaker makes this particular form of interpretive naiveté less and less possible.

Even more promising, the idea of multiple speakers, bound together by particular institutional rules for authoritative speech, begins to open up the study of interpretation to notions of strategic action and dynamic evolution. It focuses our attention on what is legitimate and possible within the rules of our particular lawgiving game. It reframes the issue of interpretative truth as one of authority or appropriateness.

These again are hardly new ideas on law or legal interpretation. Indeed, they are the lawyer's traditional fallback position where meaning is irreducibly controversial. But public choice's attempt to model the lawgiving game in a more rigorous fashion helps give some structure to flabby legal conceptions of "institutional roles" that often are invoked to stop thought and justify interpretive *ipse dixit*s. A game-theoretic perspective reveals that it is here that analysis might fruitfully begin.

To make this point more concretely, let us return briefly to the subject of Chapter 3, rationality review, and compare the lawyer's conventional wisdom about institutional roles in the contexts of judicial review of and judicial interpretation of statutes. The usual view goes something like this: Rationality review is strongly antimajoritarian because it forecloses the implementation of the will of the majority. It is thus a danger to democracy and requires extremely strong justifications, none of which have ever been wholly successful.

Judicial interpretation of statutes by contrast is not only inevitable, it can be structured to be prodemocratic, that is, to enforce the true will of the majority. Moreover, should the judiciary err, the injury to majoritarian governance is remediable by the legislature itself.

These positions are, of course, caricatures. Legal theorists and ordinary lawyers understand that American constitutionalism institutes a limited form of majoritarianism and emphasizes liberty as well as democracy. Constitutional scholars have detailed the subtle interactions between the Supreme Court's vision of particular constitutional texts and the demands of majoritarian sentiment. And no lawyer truly believes that enforcing majoritarian judgments exhausts the functions of statutory interpretation or that overturning the judicial construction of a statute is an easy matter.

These caricatures nonetheless shape legal thought in powerful ways. The assertion, for example, that the legislature can more easily reverse a judicial judgment that a statute lacks a rational basis than correct a faulty construction of a statute strikes the legal mind as bizarre. Yet that is surely the import of the Article 1, Section 7 game depicted in table 4.2. Were C struck down as irrational, the legislature would be returned precisely to Q. And from there it might return to, or very close to, C, having now provided a more persuasive predicate for the reasonableness of its actions. Indeed, administrative agencies do this repeatedly when their policies are overturned as "arbitrary."

In short, a court overturning a statute on irrationality grounds may invade legislative prerogatives for public choice hardly at all. By contrast, a court misconstruing the legislature's statutes may often disempower it from implementing anything very close to the legislators' most preferred policy.

This line of thought has practical consequences. For example, courts often invoke the maxim that they should construe statutes to avoid serious questions of constitutionality. The rationale for this preference is that it keeps the judiciary within its appropriate constitutional role of enforcing the legislative will so far as it can. Yet our prior analysis suggests that this approach may be precisely backwards. If these "invalidation-avoiding" interpretations are also likely to be different from what the court thinks the legislature intended — as they often are, else why invoke the maxim — then the court is probably both misconstruing the statute and making its construction uncorrectable. A truly restrained court, that is, one intent on enhancing opportunities for implementing the legislative will, would do better to confront the constitutional question head on. Not only is the court likely to find some way to sustain the statute in any event; even if it invalidates the law, it at least returns the legislature to the status quo ante and gives the legislature a more realistic chance of concocting a constitutional policy that is close to its most-preferred position.

5

Explaining Administrative Process

Most public law is legislative in origin but administrative in content. Statutes empower and instruct administrators, but only at a relatively general level. This is obvious in many statutory regimes. When Congress tells the Interstate Commerce Commission to disapprove "unreasonable or discriminatory" railroad rates, the Federal Communications Commission to license broadcasters when in the "public interest," or the Food and Drug Administration to regulate foods and drugs for "safety," it has not said much. The operative law will emerge from the rules adopted and the decisions handed down by the administrators who implement these statutes.

Over the past several decades Congress has tended to be more specific, and, in the process, to enact much longer and more detailed statutes. Yet, these "mega-statutes" simply call forth increasingly detailed rules and decisions from the administrators who must implement them. Administrative regulations and administrative adjudications dwarf, both in number and in practical effect, the legislative output of the Congress and the decisions of the courts. Although hardly discernible from a reading of either our eighteenth-century Constitution or the contemporary popular press, we live in an administrative state. And although the examples I have given feature federal officials, the situation is little different at the state level.

Thus, while the press reports endlessly on the machinations of national and state politicians, citizens mostly encounter administrators. We vote for our congressperson, state legislator or mayor, but we deal primarily with the IRS, the Social Security Administration, the Department of Motor Vehicles, and the local building inspector or tax assessor's office. These are the "devoted public servants" who lead us through the labyrinthian requirements of modern law, or the "pointy-headed bureaucrats" who make our lives miserable.

The everyday, numerical, and experiential dominance of administrative over legislative or judicial lawmaking seems both unavoidable and troubling. Unavoidable because as we have demanded more from government we have necessarily demanded more administrators to carry out the programs and policies adopted. Troubling because administrative governance affronts our common understanding of how American democracy is supposed to operate. The Constitution says virtually nothing about administration beyond empowering the Congress to create "Departments" and providing for the appointment of "officers of the United States." And while the president is charged to "see that the laws are faithfully executed," the idea that administrators make law, decide legal claims, or operate outside of the executive branch has troubled legal theorists since the federal government's first forays into civilian regulatory activity. Citizens, meanwhile, wonder what it means to have a "democracy" run importantly by unknown, "faceless" bureaucrats, or to have "legal rights" that can be enforced only in administrative tribunals.

The historic role of administrative law has been to address these concerns for legal and political accountability in an increasingly administrative state. And because those concerns are both serious and persistent, this particular subpart of constitutional law has always been hotly contested ground. Respectable scholarly opinion still ranges from a belief that most of the apparatus of the administrative state is unconstitutional, to the belief that administrative law's continuous attempts to ensure legal and political accountability are both constitutionally unnecessary and governmentally dysfunctional.

In this and the following three chapters, I will address three issues: First, why does administrative law take the shape that it does? What is it really all about? Here we pit the standard stories of the legal culture against revisionist interpretations that have emerged from the public choice literature. The question is simple: Who has the most persuasive argument? The answer is complex. Resolution may in the end turn on who has the burden of proof.

Second, I will assess the claim of some public choice scholars that broad delegations of lawmaking power to administrators are undesirable and should be unconstitutional. I will argue by contrast that, properly understood, public choice ideas suggest the constitutional appropriateness and democratic desirability of conferring lawmaking powers on appointed officials. Chapters 7 and

8 use some game-theoretic strands of public choice theory to explore the reasons for contemporary regulatory gridlock and the likely influences of presidents, Congresses, and courts on administrative policymaking.

This chapter takes up a very general set of questions: What explains the shape of the administrative decision processes that we observe? Why are administrative functions structured in particular ways by special and general statutes, agency rules, and judicial decisions? What is the real role of "administrative law," by which is generally meant "administrative procedure," in the modern administrative state?

THE WORLD OF THE LEGAL IDEALIST

Answers to these questions abound in the legal literature. In an influential article Richard Stewart argues, for example, that much of modern American administrative law is constructed to facilitate pluralist participation in administrative decisionmaking. More recently, Cass Sunstein has argued that administrative law is designed to promote the republican value of deliberative rationality and to limit the influence of special interest pleading. Indeed, the legal literature bristles with claims concerning the normative purposes of administrative process and processes, ranging from "fairness" to "efficiency" and utilizing a host of other ideas as well—"openness," "accountability," "legitimacy," "rationality," to name but a few.[1]

Little attention has been paid to the structure of these claims. This inattention is perhaps explained by noting that, whatever their distinctive normative perspectives, lawyers' arguments about how administrative processes should be constructed or understood proceed from a basic methodological agreement. On this view, call it the "idealist's vision," administrative processes are part of the general fabric of American public and constitutional law. The law of administrative procedure contributes, as does all such law, to the construction of an operationally effective and symbolically appropriate normative regime. To put the matter slightly differently, administrative procedural requirements imbedded in law shape administrative decisionmaking in accordance with our fundamental (but perhaps malleable) images of the legitimacy of state action. That is administrative procedure's purpose and its explanation.

REALIST CRITIQUES

One need not be of a particularly skeptical turn of mind to find much of the conventional lawyerly discussion of administrative process less than revealing. For example, attention to the content of the norms summoned by ordinary legal discourse leads quite easily to the suspicion that something more is afoot here than the rhetoric reveals. How could terms as "open-textured" as *rationality* or *fairness* possibly structure or constrain administrative action? Given resourceful packaging, could not any process be said to further one, or all, of the ideas that populate administrative law's normative universe — particularly if these notions must be "balanced" against each other in application? Surely, this is merely law as comforting ideology, not law as a set of conceptual tools that can be used to generate determinate processes for the control of administrative action. One need not investigate institutional behavior in any detail to suspect that the normative discourse of administrative process is inadequate to the tasks of political or legal control that are its putative purposes.[2]

Whatever the complexity of its normative preoccupations, therefore, administrative law scholarship seems to exhibit a certain naiveté. In carrying forward its interpretive enterprise, it has tended to ignore behavioral questions about how its concepts are generated, structured, and maintained. It has failed to ask hard questions about whether its ideological pretensions are in any way connected to the realities of bureaucratic governance. That is, like most fields of law, administrative law remains ripe for a continuing "realist" revolution that focuses attention on administrative process as the product of political struggle, rather than as the product of normative, idealist elaboration. In the current intellectual climate, critical legal studies (CLS) and public choice theory are the principal contenders for the realist throne. And so it has come to pass that Gerald Frug, in an elegant CLS critique, has explained how the normative structure of administrative (and corporate) law serves to maintain an ideology of bureaucracy that both legitimates and masks coercion.[3] Administrative procedure assures us of the objectivity of administration even as it subjects us to the discretionary dominion of administrators. As such, the law's stories of bureaucratic legitimacy are preeminently "mechanism[s] of deception."[4]

Public choice theorists, in particular the McNollgast team, have weighed in with a similarly bleak view.[5] They argue that administrative processes can be understood as the means by which political victors maintain the gains from successful interest group struggle at the legislative level. Administrative decision structures are the devices through which legislative principals control the actions of potentially deviant administrative agents. Legislatures can thereby deliver on the electoral deals that maintain them in office. In both the CLS and public choice accounts, the normative rhetoric of the law, the crucial data analyzed in both the legal literature and judicial opinions, is largely epiphenomenal — a product or constituent of more fundamental underlying material processes that are obscured, if not misrepresented, by lawyers' talk.

TOWARD A COMPARATIVE TEST

To a degree, idealist and realist explanations of administrative procedure are noncomparable perspectives on the same phenomena. Lawyers and legal scholars provide an internal interpretation of process purposes and goals articulated in the normative vernacular of American political and constitutional ideology. Realists are "external" or "critical" observers looking past the law's internally prescribed rhetoric to explain process phenomena in terms of material interests and political power. Idealists, by ignoring issues of behavioral motivation, seem to view expressed intentions as relatively nonproblematic guides to what is being done and why. Realists tend to combine rhetoric, objective interests, and concrete behaviors to construct both their whats and their whys, either through the development and testing of behavioral hypotheses (public choice) or through the reflexive or dialectical examination of rhetoric and practice (CLS). These two perspectives not only look at different data — idealists at expressed purposes; realists at implicit (sometimes hidden) interests or ideology — they have dramatically different methodologies for the interpretation of behavior and conflicting ideas of what could count as a reason for action.

Given this radical disjunction between the two approaches (to say nothing of the intellectual gulf that divides CLS and public choice realists), mediation of their rival claims may be impossible. If methodology determines both evidence and its interpretation, then to ask who has the best explanation of American administrative processes may simply pose an issue of taste. Each explanation may be adequate within the terms of its own methodology, but hopelessly inadequate, or indeed obviously false, from the perspective of the alternative visions. The "best" explanation then becomes the one that best fits the analyst's own preferences concerning the style of explanatory stories.

But perhaps methodological bias might also provide a way past methodological relativism. If what we see depends upon what we look for and how we look for it, then the choice of evidentiary base and interpretive stance should privilege the theory whose methodology is chosen. Precisely because of this privileging, there emerges a possible test of the power of administrative process (and perhaps other sorts of legal) storytelling. For, if we privilege one style by adopting its methods, and it still fails to beat its competitors, then we should at least be very skeptical that it should be adopted as the primary account of the phenomena to be explained. Can such a comparative test be constructed?

Comparative testing across methodologies requires a somewhat heroic act of translation. Stories emerging out of different intellectual commitments must be given structures that are both coherent in their own terms and can be accommodated by the privileged methodology. Moreover, once that is accomplished, some divergent implications from each type of story must be specified. Otherwise we will have no test. The task of the second part of this chapter, therefore, is to attempt to provide the necessary translations and to describe the process implications of each theory as translated. The third section will attempt to marshal some evidence concerning which process implications are best confirmed.

As mention of "testing" and "confirmation" in the previous paragraphs perhaps already suggests, the methodology to be privileged here is that of public choice theory. The attempt is to specify coherent models of the purposes for procedural arrangements and then to describe the processes likely to implement those purposes. Each model will state a standard behavioral hypothesis of the form: "If the purposes to be served are these, then we should expect the procedures we observe to be like this."

Models of Administrative Procedure

IDEALIST VISIONS OF LEGISLATION, ADMINISTRATION, AND ADMINISTRATIVE LAW

Let us return to the changing visions of law and governance that I have employed before, but with a greater emphasis on the role of administrative institutions. During the crucial middle decades of this century, say, from the 1930s through the early 1970s, the vision of legislation and administration that seems to have dominated legal consciousness was a vision of government as a well-ordered input/output machine. Into the machine went social problems and political values; out of the machine came legislative programs that would make social reality conform to social ideals. The new activist state was purposive and pragmatic. Collective purposes — visions of the public interest — were shaped by the macropolitical processes of electoral and legislative debates. Concrete realizations of those purposes were achieved through the practical application of the expertise possessed by administrators to whom various policy domains were delegated.

Over this period dramatic changes took place in the social vision of just which public problems were most pressing and which institutional devices most efficacious in addressing them. New Deal problems of infrastructure disorganization, economic distortion, and worker insecurity gave way to the Great Society's focus on the negative externalities of superabundance and the incompleteness of the welfare state. The image of expert administration, meaning an independent commission operating as a specialized tribunal, was replaced by the image of a technocratically expert bureau, acting through techniques that were primarily quasilegislative. But throughout these four or five decades, skeptics to the contrary notwithstanding, the dominant images in both our political and our legal rhetoric celebrated the progressive translation of widely approved public ideas into concrete programmatic benefits. Failures to realize public purposes were viewed as failures of imagination — either poor conceptualization of problems or an improper fit between social issues and institutional techniques.[6]

This idealist vision also encompassed an idealist administrative law. From this perspective, legal control of administration effectuated basic liberal or pluralist democratic values. To be sure, administrative law was a flexible regime which accommodated great variety in institutional designs and in allocations of administrative power. This flexibility was crucial to the overall picture of political programs as exercises in pragmatic problem solving. Indeed, the shift toward "pragmatism" was the great triumph of the New Deal's administrative lawyers. Beset by vigorous, sometimes vicious, attacks from conservative lawyers, and even leading academic theorists, they responded by burying the critics in facts.[7] Rigid delimitation of legislative and executive functions, for example, was rejected. Virtually complete delegations of policy choice from the legislature to administrators were permitted in the interests of programmatic efficacy.[8] Nor did the separation of powers demand executive control over officers whose independence and expert judgment might be compromised by political interference.[9]

Yet, administrative law was not all flexible accommodation to the administrative enthusiasms of the moment. Judicial review was designed to keep administrators within their jurisdictions and harnessed to the values and purposes expressed in the macropolitical processes of legislation and electoral accountability. Moreover, procedural protections for both individuals and groups, backed again by judicial enforcement, reinforced the image of citizens as rights holders in the new administrative state and supported participation in the micropolitical processes of administration.

Mediation of the tension between the ideals of governmental efficacy and of self-, or participatory, governance defined the central issues for administrative law and administrative lawyers. Working out how democracy was to be structured and maintained in this new activist, administrative state was hardly easy. But there seemed little doubt that the construction of an effective public law for the pursuit of public purposes motivated and guided the enterprise. The activist administrative law that emerged over this period, and that still provides the dominant image of what administrative law is about, was something of a pastiche of liberal and pluralist political programs. A closer look at how these two normative visions differ, and yet can be combined, will provide a sharper picture of contemporary idealist legal consciousness and its implications for administrative process.

Liberal democratic ideals of limited government and citizen rights, ideas that had supported ideological opposition to the rise of the administrative state, were eroded but not wholly supplanted during the middle decades of this century. Indeed, this opposition had arisen during the Progressive era and had been expressed by the leaders of the bar.[10] Opposition was not based just on antipathy toward an activist social agenda. It included a liberal legal ideology that focused as much on procedure and remedies as on the substance of programs.[11] Liberal democratic legality in administrative decisionmaking can be envisioned as entailing a number of connected institutional arrangements aimed at preserving individual rights through the maintenance of the "rule of law." Fundamental to that essentially Madisonian program is policy choice firmly attached to a constrained legislative process — that is, one accountable to the electorate, one subject to the checks of bicameralism and the presidential veto, and one confined by the substantive limits prescribed in federal power-sharing arrangements.

Limited, accountable, and "checked" policymaking cannot, however, eliminate all conflict between state power and individual rights, nor are these structural, constitutional features self-implementing. Liberal democratic constitutionalism demanded further that decisions affecting individual rights be made in accordance with due process of law, and that there be an opportunity for judicial testing of the legality of any exercise of power altering those rights.[12] Implementing these notions of procedural regularity and substantive legality in the administrative sphere dictates many of the subsidiary features of administrative process, including at least (a) process transparency (published norms, open proceedings, and reason giving) and (b) decision rationality (adequate factfinding and objective rationalization of decisions in terms of the relevant statutory norms and the evidence of record). The lynchpin of the whole enterprise is judicial review to assure that substantive and procedural rights are protected.[13]

According to the now standard story, as New Deal state activism triumphed in the postwar years over laissez-faire constitutionalism, liberal legality in administrative law beat a hasty retreat. The demand for a tight connection between legislative choice and administrative action expressed in statutory standards or criteria collapsed. A similar fate befell the idea that "due process" entailed judicial, or at least formal adjudicatory, process. In the hands of progressive judges, the notion of individual rights became as much a shield for administrative discretion as a protection for private interests.[14] Judicial review for solid record evidence and cogent instrumental rationalization of decision-making gave way before deferential invocations of expertise and the translation of legal issues (for courts) into questions of fact (for administrators).[15]

Yet, this apparent relaxation of legal constraints on administrative decision procedures neither wholly jettisoned liberal democratic ideas nor abandoned the defense of dominant constitutional presuppositions against the corrosive proliferation of administrative discretion. That defense, however, was coming to be understood in terms of a new model of normative pluralism.[16] And within that model old ideas were given a new shape and new forms of implementation.

The demand for statutory standards via the "nondelegation" doctrine might be more formal than real, but administrative legality still entailed nonarbitrariness — the articulation of reasons connecting discrete decisions to general norms or policies. Where were those policies to be found, if not in statutes? The answer was in administrative rules and prior administrative adjudications.[17] Administrators could be expected, indeed required, to generate their own law, and they could then be held accountable to it. Moreover, this process of administrative lawmaking need not be wholly self-referential. Indeed, it could not be if "administrative accountability" was to be more than a fiction.

There thus emerged a complex idea of procedural legality or process rationality comprised of several elements. One strand of this notion focused again on substantive rights, not as impediments to the development of substantive policy, but as claims to procedural protection from error in the application of that policy. Moreover, these substantive rights, now backed by judicially constructed procedural defenses, were themselves the product of state action, the creations of particular regulatory and social welfare regimes. Administration thus came to entail the procedural inclusion of clients and claimants whose legal interests were an artifact of the administrative state.[18] Process claimants might only have the substantive "rights" that the state gave them, but courts policing administrative legality could ensure that the provision of legal rights carried with them access to the procedural levers necessary to make those rights meaningful.[19]

Significant as those protections might have been, formal process rights attached to individual adjudications could have left administrative policy development via general rulemaking adrift in a legal void of pure administrative discretion. The courts experimented with a host of techniques to fill that void. The Administrative Procedure Act (APA) was reinterpreted to create new "rights" to judicial review that evaded the old rights-based limitations on standing, ripeness, and reviewability.[20] Procedural innovation at the judicial level sought to align the fact gathering and reason giving of the administrative policy process more with the judicialized techniques of agency adjudication.[21] Judges defended universal access to rule-making policy processes by extraordinarily rigorous demands for notice of proposed administrative action and rational justification for policy choice in the face of vigorous protest by agency opponents.[22] Putative beneficiaries of agency protection or largesse were given increasing power to force policy development from lethargic or recalcitrant administrators.[23] While these developments can be described in a terminology reminiscent of liberal legality — as attempts to limit administrative discretion by rendering administrators accountable to the substantive demands of statutory regimes and to the procedural requirements of the constitution and the APA — the particular form of control employed, call it "proceduralism," had other normative bases.

The proceduralist project in administrative law is the micropolitical analogue of John Hart Ely's influential vision of the function of constitutional adjudication.[24] On this view, judicial review is justified by the necessity to maintain reasonable access for all groups to a political process whose democratic character consists precisely in its responsiveness or potential responsiveness to the wishes of those groups. Similarly, the normative, pluralist vision of administrative processes sees both process design and judicial policing of the implementation of those designs primarily as devices for providing policy access to relevant political forces or interests. Administrative legality entails policymaking that accommodates these interests procedurally by giving them serious consideration in the development of substantive norms.

Given the conventional "new wine in old bottles" techniques of legal development, it is perhaps not surprising that the pluralist and liberal projects can be carried on using essentially the same legal concepts. Demands for process transparency and decision rationality can be used both to protect rights and limit government (liberalism) and to assure access and an appropriate accommodation of interests (pluralism). This may be a happy feature of administrative law: new arrangements can be accommodated without the stress of developing a new politico-legal vocabulary. But from the vantage point of our current project — the description of the procedural implications of a normative account of administrative law — the capaciousness of the legal categories is something of a problem. It suggests that legal structures and processes may be given multiple normative interpretations. Their purposes, therefore, remain ambiguous.

Consider, for example, the administrative-process implications of the basic commitments of liberal legality and normative pluralism. Liberal legality, as I have said, features the protection of individual rights. Normative pluralism, on the other hand, is primarily concerned with the accommodation of competing interests. It might be imagined, therefore, that institutional designers seeking to implement these two different normative programs would produce quite different process or decisionmaking structures. A rights-protecting administrative process, for example, might demand formal procedures of a familiar sort: specific notice of claims contrary to existing private rights, allocation of the burden of proof to the state where it proposes to diminish or withdraw rights; full disclosure of all facts and arguments that support the state's claim; full opportunity for rightsholders (but not others) to contest claims and arguments by confrontation and cross-examination; decisionmaking by a neutral adjudicator; decisionmaking based wholly on the facts and arguments of record in the proceeding; and so on.

By contrast, interest accommodation would seem to imagine an informal process. Here, for example, there need be no clear specification or division between participants and "deciders." Sharply defined burdens of proof, rights of confrontation, or limitations to record evidence would get in the way of a negotiated resolution which takes account of the interests of all parties. Indeed, interest accommodation seems to require a highly flexible process of political bargaining in which facts and values are not kept critically distinct, and in which "parties" may be added or subtracted freely as subject matter shifts or is redefined. While the formal adjudicatory proceeding is restricted to those who, strictly speaking, have claims of right with respect to determinate remedies, the informal process is one in which "stakeholders" arrange and rearrange themselves with respect to a proposed outcome which is itself subject to debate, negotiation, and, perhaps, radical revision.

Looked at in this way, the administrative-process implications of liberal legalism and normative pluralism seem remarkably distinct. We should be able to scan American administrative procedures to see whether they seem constructed on one or the other model. But, alas, the facts are difficult to find.

On the one hand, we do find numerous instances of formal adjudication in American administrative law. It is often both a feature of statutory regimes and a requirement of the Constitution. The structure of American administrative law thus evidences a commitment to the rights-protection ideals of liberal legalism. On the other hand, most administrative policy processes are characterized by an extraordinary degree of flexibility. Informal rulemaking processes, for example, generally take place over extended periods with multiple parties, shifting agendas, and eventual compromise. No one has a right to any particular outcome, nor are "rights" at stake.

In addition, rights to formal process in American administrative law are seldom, if ever, nonproblematic. At the constitutional level, they entail a sort of cost-benefit analysis which weighs the general interests of groups who claim particular process rights against other social interests in the effectuation of administrative programs.[25] Moreover, administrative capacities to redefine issues in general rather than specific terms, and thereby to determine the substantive relevance of individual facts and circumstances to administrative decisionmaking, make formal hearing rights almost wholly dependent on the necessities of administration within particular programs.[26] Individual procedural rights in American administrative law thus have a social basis, which is inseparable from the overall accommodation of interests developed in the implementation of substantive public purposes.

These interpretive uncertainties suggest that there may be major difficulties in developing a set of determinate and specific process characteristics that would implement the major visions of constitutionalism and administrative legality to which legal idealists have traditionally subscribed. It may be possible to interpret every instance of administrative structure or process as furthering the goals of liberal legality or normative pluralism, or of both simultaneously. This is particularly true if we allow procedures also to be compromises between, or syntheses of, these often simultaneously held visions.

The interpretive capaciousness of legal idealist categories does not, of course, eliminate the possibility of distinguishing liberal or pluralist normative commitments, and their procedural analogues, from radically different ones. Secret and coercive state processes without minimal aspects of notice, opportunity to participate, reason giving, and the like could hardly be part of either a liberal or a pluralist normative administrative program. Thus, on some grosser dimensions of process explanation, such as who has control over the structure of decision processes, liberal legality and normative pluralism may have implications that differ sharply from their realist competitors.

Liberal legality, for example, should certainly be highly skeptical of administrative procedural discretion. The protection of rights, including procedural rights, requires that other institutions, in particular courts, have effective control over the way in which decisions can be made. As I noted in Chapter 3, it is this feature of liberal constitutionalism that has made judicial review, at least in the American context, virtually the exclusive topic of constitutional theory. Does the normative-pluralist strand of legal idealism give similar prominence to court control of administrative process?

Pluralist processes might be thought, on the contrary, to feature broad discretion on the part of administrative decisionmakers to modify and adapt processes to accommodate relevant interests. Yet, the pluralist vision of administrative law in post–New Deal America has hardly deemphasized courts as the source of process norms. The role of courts has not been so much reduced as shifted, from the control of administrators' *substantive* discretion to control of their *procedural* discretion. Thus, for example, the "due process revolution" in administrative adjudication and the construction of a new "rational process" paradigm for administrative rulemaking have been described in the legal literature largely as court-centered activities.[27] Moreover, "rights" to participation in both formal and informal processes of agency policymaking were broadened and enforced by permitting dramatically broadened access to courts, which could then both structure and police the process rationality of administration.[28]

Thus, although a normative pluralist vision may imagine administrators to be engaged in broad-based interest accommodation, that accommodation must be legitimized by a process of decisionmaking that confers judicially enforceable *participatory* rights on affected interests. And both structuring and protecting those rights is a preeminently judicial function, accomplished through the interpretation of legislation, the Constitution, and the "common law" of administrative procedure.

The liberal-pluralist compromise that has shaped the legal idealist vision of American administrative procedure thus seems to require courts capable of structuring and controlling a process of legislative and agency procedural innovation that is directed at interest accommodation, but subject to conditions of widespread procedural rightsholding. The idealist conception of administrative law presumes, indeed features, control of administrative procedure by courts, rather than by agencies or legislatures. And on this dimension, if no other, it differs from the public choice model to which we now turn.

THE PUBLIC CHOICE THEORY OF ADMINISTRATIVE PROCESS

As usual, public choice theorists insist that we jettison our vision of governance as a benign input/output machine for the definition and effectuation of the public interest. In its place, governmental action is explained in terms of self-interested political bargaining in the pursuit of individual or group material interests. The black box of macropolitics and bureaucratic decisionmaking has been pried open to reveal copious opportunities for "rent-seeking" behavior both by the people's representatives and by the "experts" in charge of public programs. Moreover, if ubiquitous free rider difficulties induce rational ignorance in voters and radically skew the structure of pluralist interest group activity, then the self-interested manipulation of both legislative and administrative processes can go on largely unchecked by electoral restraints.

This revised, principal-agent perspective has reenergized a focus on institutional design and has generated explanations of the activist, administrative state radically different from those embedded in legal idealism. Rather than effectuating the public good while maintaining liberty and democratic control, public institutional arrangements are virtually all explained as devices to facilitate private gain at public expense. On this view, broad delegations of power and limitations on executive control structure politics in the interest of "iron triangles" of self-aggrandizing representatives, bureaucrats, and interest groups. Judicial review cements the gains from private deals for the use of public power, and agency processes are designed primarily to permit "capture" by the already advantaged. Pursuit of the "public interest" as a guide to understanding the structure and behavior of public institutions is thus replaced root and branch by hypotheses featuring pursuit of private material gain.

To be sure, the empirical record of this strand of public choice theory is one that should induce the utmost caution in its practitioners.[29] But public choice practitioners are not all wedded to interest group explanations. As we have seen, they work with a host of models having quite different assumptions and emerging out of differing "public choice" traditions. Their familial relationship is difficult to capture save in a core general presumption that political behavior is to be explained as the outcome of rational (and often strategic) action by relevantly situated individuals within some set of defined institutional boundaries. This variety, however, hardly makes public choice a nonstarter as a basis for constructing a good explanation of administrative process. What is needed is a more detailed theory with determinate procedural implications for testing. In the field of administrative process, the most ambitious effort to date is what I will call the "McNollgast hypothesis."[30]

The McNollgast hypothesis is relatively straightforward and, in the abstract, quite plausible. Electorally accountable officials, the president and the Congress, have a difficulty: They must often put the implementation of public policies in the hands of administrators who may have their own designs on the programs. Monitoring is always costly, as is the application of sometimes cumbersome sanctions. Moreover, the deviation of bureaucrats from politicians' desires may be inherently uncorrectable so long as the bureaucrats' actions remain within the set of options that might have been approved ex ante by some winning coalition. How can politicians control bureaucrats? The McNollgast answer is, "Through administrative process."

McNollgast posit that the two major control issues facing the Congress are problems (1) of information asymmetry and (2) of the erosion of an original legislative coalition over time. We will take the latter problem first because it illustrates a serious issue of vagueness in the model that is provided. One problem with the McNollgast hypothesis is that it may require amendment to make it produce "testable predictions."

To solve the problem of eroding legislative coalitions, administrative procedures would need to provide an opportunity whereby the constituencies that motivated the original legislative coalition could themselves act on implementing agencies to preserve the bargain struck at the legislative level. McNollgast hypothesize, therefore, that legislators will "stack the [administrative] procedural deck" in favor of the winning coalition.

So far so good, but there are some troublesome loose ends in this scenario. For example, why would the political controllers want to preserve the original policy position in the face of the erosion of the original legislative coalition? If the legislative coalition is one that is derivative from the demands of constituencies, then a change in the preferences of the legislative coalition should signal a change in the preferences of the constituencies. And if the desire for political control in this model is (as it seems to be) to cater to relevant constituencies in the pursuit of reelection (rather than to preserve some policy preferred on other grounds), then it is difficult to understand why the political principals — the legislators — *want* to preserve the old coalition at the administrative level. A new winning coalition of voters or interest groups desires a different policy. Preserving the old bargain denies supporters what they want — a good way to lose the next election.

McNollgast's refinement of the idea of "erosion" in their later work does not solve this problem.[31] Even if the legislature's inability to rectify administrative deviations is entirely a function of a change in the status quo point at which legislative bargaining begins, the status quo point for constituent interests has also changed. Hence the politically effective winning coalition for constituents will also have changed. Why it is politically advantageous to thwart this coalition still must be explained. The answer that legislators would want to prevent deviation ex ante in order to increase the value of the original deal merely raises further questions. The most important is this: If so, why were the administrators given the discretion to deviate from an ex ante known preferred position?

At another point in their discussion, McNollgast seem to address the issue of why administrators are given sufficient discretion to deviate from what appear to be the legislators' original objectives by suggesting that political controllers want to use administrative procedure as an "autopilot." By this they mean that administrative processes should allow dominant coalitions of constituents to work their will at the administrative level as their preferences change, without further activity on the part of legislative or presidential politicians. One can certainly imagine this being a desire of political principals. But it would presumably be accomplished by quite different processes than those that "stack the deck." Hence, no matter what procedures we find, either procedures that enfranchise original coalitions to resist alteration of legislative policy or procedures that permit flexible adaptation of policy pursuant to the coalition's new demands, we should presumably find the theory "proved." On this reading, as the social scientists say, there is no null hypothesis.

It might be, of course, that McNollgast are claiming that the same processes can be used both to stack the deck in favor of policies adopted at the behest of particular constituencies and simultaneously to provide those same constituents with the opportunity to force policy shifts as their preferences change. If so, then the theory suggests that we should be looking for processes that somehow enfranchise particular constituencies or interests independently of the relationship of procedural requirements to possible substantive outcomes. This might be evidenced, for example, by statutory provisions creating special personal access or decisional control for identifiable constituencies. But these sorts of statutes are quite rare at the federal level. Certain regulated agricultural marketing arrangements might qualify.[32] But we should not forget that it was the spectre of balkanized constituent-producer control of economic policy that energized the nondelegation doctrine in the 1930s. Since that time statutes have been much more universalistic in providing access to administrative processes and to judicial review of agency action.

If statutes fail to identify specially enfranchised constituents explicitly, then the determination of whether procedures satisfy the McNollgast hypothesis becomes difficult indeed. That some interests turn out to have an advantage in employing particular procedures is not very good evidence that they were the constituencies meant to be served by the legislation. Over time one would expect some such groups to emerge with respect to *any* statutory scheme. And historical inquiry into whether those benefitted were *really* members of the dominant coalition for passage of a particular statute is almost certain to founder on the inadequacy of the written record, if not on prior issues of how to operationalize the idea of "coalition" or what should count as evidence of "membership." Much modern legislation passes by lopsided majorities after extensive compromise that includes widely divergent viewpoints within the "winning coalition."

For present purposes, however, it is not necessary to solve these problems. If the McNollgast hypothesis is decoupled from the notion that legislator preferences are a function of constituent or interest group preferences, we can start simply by assuming that legislators do have preferences. And although this assumption does some violence to public choice theory as a whole — the theory of legislation has been divorced from a theory of elections — agency theory can be salvaged. The legislators (principals) who vote for programs can still be hypothesized to prefer that administrators (agents) carry out their instructions as specified in the statute. Moreover, because monitoring and control are costly, legislators should wish to reduce their own monitoring costs by empowering others to monitor administrators for them, whether or not those "others" were a part of the political coalition that motivated the legislation. This might be accomplished through standard forms of administrative procedure: the provision of specific beneficiary rights or statutory interests; defined processes through which these rights may be defended, if the agency attempts to deviate from them; and judicial review for their protection where procedures are inadequate at the administrative level.

For our "comparative testing" purposes, we need then only specify some implication of the public choice perspective that points toward different procedural implications than does an idealist vision. Here again, the obvious suggestion is the location of procedural control. While idealist legality seems to presume judicial control over process, the McNollgast hypothesis, both originally and as modified here, posits legislative control. After all, it is the need for low-cost legislative monitoring through control over procedural or structural design that motivates the behavioral hypothesis.

The requirement of retained or operative *legislative* control over process is particularly pointed with respect to the second (and as yet undiscussed) monitoring difficulty that McNollgast posit as ubiquitous in the congressional-bureaucratic principal-agent game: The bureaucracy's control over information. Thus, for example, if we find Congress structuring administrative processes in ways that require agencies to divulge politically relevant information to congressional monitors or their surrogates, then we may have some confirmation for the McNollgast hypothesis. To be sure, there is some overlap between this information-divulging idea and the openness and transparency demands of idealists' views of administrative law. But from the principal-agent perspective, the important element ought to be not just that information is made available, but what kind of information, to whom it is made available, and at whose request. If administrative law makes most information available to others, for example, in forms not particularly useful for congressional or legislative monitoring and through processes outside legislative control, then the McNollgast information hypothesis would not be confirmed.

It may be objected that this description oversimplifies the public choice vision. Legislators might employ courts and constituents as continuous monitors. Hence, provisions for judicial review or revelation of information to citizens through Freedom of Information Act requests could satisfy legislative monitoring requirements without any active oversight by the legislature itself. This is indeed possible. But if monitoring or access by anyone is to count as legislative control, so long as it is in any way facilitated by legislation, then we are back to the problem of nonfalsifiability. Everything will count as legislative control. It remains to be seen, therefore, if some more discriminating criteria can be developed to discern whether processes evidence legislative control or control primarily by others.

We thus have emerged from our excursion through legal idealist and public choice theories with divergent implications about the structure of administrative decisionmaking. Legal idealist theory describes control over administrative process as if it were preeminently a judicial task. Positive political theory posits an administrative process constructed by the legislature as a solution to its principal-agent problems concerning bureaucrats. If most administrative law is decided by courts, or perhaps by administrators themselves (as CLS theorists might well suggest), then the public choice hypothesis has at best modest explanatory power. It may explain why some procedures emerge, or why, everything else being held constant, legislators would seek to use statutorily specified processes as a control device, but it will fail to give us a unified vision or explanation of the complex and multifarious administrative processes that we now observe.

Assessing the Evidence

As the last paragraph suggests, at the level of "testing" the power of competing hypotheses, some further methodological problems become acute. For it is not entirely clear that even in their translated, "as if" form, idealist and public choice theories attempt to explain the same things. The normative idealist story may be a story that presumes only "ultimate control by the courts," not day-to-day judicial shaping of administrative procedure. The positive political theory approach, by contrast, may claim only that ceteris paribus, and at the margin, the Congress will attempt to control agency action through procedural design.

Because I do not believe that either normative idealist explanations or public choice analyses mean to deny their own importance by claiming that they only occasionally have bite, I will interpret them as contesting the same terrain, that is, as competitors for providing the dominant heuristic through which we are to understand the structure of American administrative law.

What then is to count as evidence of the plausibility or persuasiveness of one or another view? At one level the answer to that question is obvious. We are looking here for evidence of who has control over administrative procedures. We need then a definition of procedure and a definition of control. By "procedure" I will mean any structural or process characteristic which may affect administrative decisionmaking. This includes a huge number of potentially important structural or procedural issues: such things as an agency's organization, its location departmentally, the types of legal powers that it is provided, the internal procedures whereby those powers are exercised, the relationship between the agency decision process and the actions of other institutions (Congress, president, and judiciary), the conditions and forms of access to the agency by outside persons, the evidentiary and decision-process rules applicable to particular types of decisions, the forms of decisions, the structure of internal agency review and monitoring mechanisms, and so on. We are here using administrative process both in the broad sense that administrative lawyers would understand, and as synonymous with "the structure of decision-making."

By "control" is meant both the formal power to shape agency decision process and the use of that power to exclude procedural control by others. Moreover, we should be looking for exercises of formal authority over process which seem to have some significance in terms of the decision processes actually used. The search is for controls or powers that shape behavior.

Assessing the descriptive or predictive power of our competitive approaches over the vast array of procedural issues that populate the administrative process landscape, and in relation to the myriad agencies that occupy that same space, is the work of a lifetime, not a chapter. I can here give only an impressionistic analysis of the strengths and weaknesses of the legal idealists' and public choice theorists' hypotheses. To simplify matters further, we will consider only our privileged competitor, public choice, and focus primarily on the sorts of evidence that has been marshalled in support of the McNollgast hypothesis.

THE WORLD ACCORDING TO PUBLIC CHOICE

In this world one would expect to find a Congress intent upon using administrative process to insure agencies' fidelity to the congressional will. It should be continuously involved at all of the levels of procedural design that I have mentioned. In addition, we would expect the legislature to draft the procedural elements of statutes in great detail in order to control procedural meddling by the president (or the executive office of the president), the courts, and agencies themselves. Procedures should be specific and hand-tailored, not general and off-the-rack.

There is, indeed, some evidence for this view of legislative procedural design. The establishment of federal agencies' basic purposes, their structure within the executive branch or as independent agencies, and the articulation of their legal powers are always a matter of statutory specification. These fundamental aspects of the articulation of agency process are never within the control of the agency itself. And, while subject both to judicial review and judicial revision via construction, the statutory provision of administrative purposes, structures, and powers is a staple of congressional debate at the formation of new administrative agencies. These topics are often also revisited and subjected to legislative modification as experience accumulates over time. It is difficult to find any agency that has not had its charter legislatively modified in these respects, sometimes frequently. Moreover, save in extreme cases, the courts permit the Congress to make these arrangements free from external judicial control.[33]

Similarly, it is not uncommon to find congressional legislation saying something about agency internal structure, the participation of affected outside interests, required evidence for decisionmaking, decision-analytic techniques, and procedures for external review. However, as we move into these more particularistic aspects of agency process, hand-tailored legislative control seems to recede by comparison with generic provisions which leave huge areas for agency discretion, or for judicial or presidential specification.

I do not mean to suggest that one cannot find congressional attempts to control almost any aspect of process in some agencies at some times. The Congress's restructuring of the National Labor Relations Board in the Taft-Hartly Act is a notorious example.[34] Moreover, this particular restructuring reached fairly minute levels of procedural detail, such as who would write draft opinions for administrative law judges or the Labor Board. Indeed, any agency's processes may, because of political saliency, bring forth specific congressional action. Thus, for example, the Congress has statutorily specified such minutiae as the frequency of disability reexaminations by the Social Security Administration. And having tasted the bitter political fruits of its handiwork, Congress quickly returned to the Social Security Act to provide yet a further set of decision-process details to rescue the disability decisional structure from virtual collapse.[35] One suspects that a close look at the history of any agency will reveal some such episodes. If not, the agency has been leading an unusually quiet political life.

Yet these detailed and process-specific incursions into administrative process seem dwarfed by the degree to which the Congress acts generically and leaves the crucial details of procedural implementation to agencies, courts, and perhaps the president. Indeed, from the viewpoint of administrative lawyers who work with and observe the changes in agency processes, *agency* strategic control of process would seem to be the rule. All agencies have the (usually explicit and always inherent) power to adopt procedural and evidentiary rules. Quite often these rules radically alter the apparent procedural and evidentiary situation that one would have imagined from examining the legislative provisions. For example, under the 1962 New Drug Amendments, the Food and Drug Administration seems to be burdened with an impossible hearing procedure for removing ineffective drugs from the market. Yet, by deft articulation of evidentiary requirements, the agency has managed to banish thousands of drugs under the 1962 amendments while, in over thirty years of operation, providing the statutorily "required" hearings to only a handful of manufacturers.[36]

An agency's substantive policymaking also may render irrelevant precisely those factual issues about which constituency interests most wanted an opportunity for elaborate procedural protection. The examples of these devices are legion. The FCC has done it to broadcasters; the FPC has done it to gas producers; the Social Security Administration even does it to the disabled.[37] Procedural control from the legislative level is an extremely uncertain enterprise.

This is doubly or triply true when one recognizes that judicial review and central executive branch controls often proceduralize in ways that both are unanticipated by legislators at the time of enactment and have general effects across a huge number of policy domains. It seems virtually undeniable that the major procedural developments in American administrative law from the Administrative Procedure Act to the present have been the work largely of the courts or of the chief executive. The extension of hearing rights to new interests, the proceduralization of rulemaking, the liberalization of standing rights, the subjection of administrative inaction to judicial review that approximates review of administrative action, the routinization of cost-benefit analysis and the centralized coordination of agenda setting[38] — all have had profound effects on the strategic leverage of various groups who participate in the administrative process. But none of these developments contained an important legislative element. Nor is there much evidence of effective congressional action to limit agency, executive, or judicial procedural creativity.

Indeed, one of the striking things about American administrative process is the degree to which the Congress has proceduralized by generic rather than by particularistic or even agency-specific provisions. In addition to the Federal Administrative Procedure Act and the Freedom of Information Act, the Congress has within the last couple of decades made process demands on agencies through the Privacy Act, the Government in the Sunshine Act, the Federal Advisory Committee Act, the Regulatory Flexibility Act, the Intergovernmental Cooperation Act, and the National Environmental Policy Act, to name but a few "framework statutes." But, again, the crucial implementing details of these general statutes have been left almost exclusively to courts, to agencies themselves, or to centralized executive actors like the Office of Management and Budget. Thus, for example, the occasions for and content of environmental impact statements have been shaped largely by judicial construction.[39] And the salience of the environmental impact statement within particular agency processes is largely a function of the agency's own structural and procedural choices. Similarly, the demands of the Freedom of Information Act seem to be a joint product of judicial construction, the litigating guidelines established within the Justice Department concerning the defense of FOIA claims, and agency internal processes for information disclosure.[40]

These latter points are particularly important to the argument that McNollgast make concerning the use of administrative process to solve information asymmetries between agencies and the legislature. In the public choice view, the procedures for rulemaking in the Federal Administrative Procedure Act and the demands for administrative openness in the Freedom of Information Act and Government in the Sunshine Act are designed to protect political overseers from information asymmetries that arise because of bureaucrats' potential monopoly on information. But it is very hard to make a plausible case for this story.

First, the APA requirements on rulemaking are extraordinarily modest. They require only that the agency put a notice of a proposal in the Federal Register and allow thirty days for comments prior to its adoption. Since there is no requirement that the agency notice any rulemaking proceeding early in its deliberations, the APA itself would permit agencies to evade congressional control simply by waiting until they were well prepared to act and then moving, thirty days after the original notice, to adopt their final regulations. Thirty days is a nanosecond on the "geologic" congressional calendar. (Congress can, of course, act later by statutory amendment or otherwise, but in doing so it will have received no benefit from the rulemaking provisions of the APA.)

Moreover, to the extent that the comment period is supposed to provide a way of knowing something about the political saliency of particular proposals, the APA is very badly designed to inform the Congress. The comments all go to the agency, and may be docketed in ways that are inaccessible without substantial effort. There is no requirement that these comments be simultaneously forwarded to the Congress or that they be indexed, summarized, or otherwise made transparent to outsiders before the agency acts. To the extent that these simple APA requirements have been made more onerous since 1946, they have been made more onerous largely by judicial interpretation, not by anything the Congress has done.[41]

But there is a more fundamental difficulty with viewing the Administrative Procedure Act, even as interpreted by the courts, as providing an opportunity for the Congress to surmount information asymmetries that inhibit political control. The same procedures that to some degree promote information revelation simultaneously disable political intervention. Congressional intervention, other than through additional amendatory legislation, must take place on the administrative record.[42] Moreover, the requirements of rationalization of decisions in terms of that administrative record mean that "political" concerns cannot be given weight unless the factual record and statutory purposes justify it.[43]

Similar points can be made about the Freedom of Information Act. There is nothing in the FOIA that gives the Congress preferential access to agency information. Nor does the statute require that the agency disclose anything that would not in any event have been required to be disclosed to the Congress as a practical political matter on the request of a relevant committee or subcommittee. The channels for information from bureaus to the Congress do not need lubrication by the Freedom of Information Act. If any "grease" is required, it is provided instead by factional disagreements within most agencies themselves. As the general counsel of the Food and Drug Administration once said to me before a legislative hearing, "I hope I've been allowed to see all the FDA internal memoranda that Senator Kennedy has."

To be sure judicial policing of political pressure through procedural or substantive invalidation is not perfect. Diligent private interests, informed via FOIA requests, might apprise the Congress of information about which it would not have known to ask. My point is rather that if these general administrative procedures are designed to deal with information asymmetries between the Congress and bureaus, they are very badly designed. How much better for the Congress to have required that all regulations be laid on the table for ninety days, or six months, or some longer period, prior to being adopted. How much better for the Congress to have demanded, as the president has demanded for the Executive Branch, that agency agendas and large amounts of information and analysis be submitted directly to the Congress both before and during the course of rulemaking.

On this account, the principal-agent, legislative-control model seems, at best, radically incomplete. Moreover, the fact that the bureaucracy must take account of at least two political principals is glossed over as if it were of little importance. Yet, in the life of agencies and in the design of administrative structures, the Congress and the president seem to view this issue as of fundamental importance. The president is not just a participant in a legislative coalition. Or, if so, s/he is a participant who notoriously defects from the legislative understanding of the agreement, often as early as at the time that s/he signs the bill. Moreover, s/he is a defector who has independent power to shape agency process and structure. And where multiple principals are involved in the development of processes and structures, the directions of political controllers might easily be self-canceling. Competition between or among principals may eliminate, at least reduce, the power of all political principals.[44] A model that takes the principal-agent paradigm seriously must confront this issue.

Finally not only do the courts, the president, and federal agencies themselves act as independent developers of agency procedure — developers whom many observers are likely to view as more important to most agencies, at least on procedural issues, than is the Congress — the Congress also has the peculiar habit of delegating huge amounts of responsibility for the development of administrative processes to states and localities. Although federal spending as a proportion of gross national product has nearly tripled since the Eisenhower administration, the number of federal civilian employees as a percentage of the overall population has actually shrunk. This is true in part because the federal government during those years has constructed hundreds of programs which are administered by states and localities under state qualifying statutes and subject to the variety of state administrative requirements that inhabit both state administrative procedure acts and state common law. Why would a Congress desiring to control the implementation of federal programs (or federal spending) through administrative process make these vast delegations to agencies whose structure within state government and procedural requirements within state administrative law are almost completely outside its control?

If monitoring adherence to the specific preferences of a dominant legislative coalition were the principal, even a very important, explanation for the specification of administrative structures and processes, this would indeed be a monumental puzzle. One might, of course, posit that the dominant coalition in all these programs was composed of the implementing states and localities — or of others who preferred to wage administrative warfare at the state or local level. These hypotheses might even (sometimes) be true. But the story would have to be investigated in great detail in every case to rebut the plausible presumption that a Congress intent on the use of procedure as a monitoring device would not delegate huge chunks of procedural discretions to fifty separate legal and political systems.

I can only conclude that major insights into the structure and processes of federal administrative agencies as they actually operate are unlikely to flow from viewing agency structure and process primarily in terms of the monitoring and sanctioning problems that legislative controllers have with federal bureaucracies. That the public choice story has something to tell us I have little doubt. But the convincing parts of that story will not persuade aficionados of idealist explanation that their modes of analysis should be abandoned.

Multiple counterexamples do not demonstrate that a rational actor, principal-agent model has nothing to teach us about the development and design of administrative process. Indeed, a Congress that did not try to control for predictable bureaucratic failures would be irresponsible, as well as foolish. But this is to say only that public choice ideas reinforce a sense that statutory drafters are likely to have anyway. Agency processes and structures matter to "implementation," and implementation may determine legislative success or failure. Q.E.D.

So where does that leave us?

When I am in a cheerful mood, the inadequacy of all simple stories concerning the origins and evolution of administrative processes suggests to me that the modern administrative state is a construct of which Madison, Hamilton, and Jefferson might justly be proud. It is checked and balanced, motivated and constrained in ways so complex and continuous that there are no final victories in the political competition to control the exercise of administrative power. On more somber days, however, I am troubled by the possibility that the inadequacy of our theoretical perspectives may simply mean that we cannot recognize the degree to which the founders' hopes for combining individual liberty with effective governance have been disappointed by the growth of modern bureaucratic administration. The public choice fraternity seems to have mostly somber days. So long as we remain skeptical of the generalizability of their views, they can help us to employ appropriate discount factors when legal idealists begin to extol the virtues of due process and the rule of law.

6

Should Administrators Make Political Decisions?

Virtually all agency action begins with a statute. More important for purposes of administrative law, statutes provide the legitimating standard for much of agency decisionmaking. Save for a few executive functions specified in the Constitution, such as the powers to grant pardons and negotiate treaties, the agent — an executive officer or the administrative agency — has only those powers provided by its principal — the legislature. Legislative specification of agency jurisdiction, purposes, and powers thus provides the normative justification for administrative authority and implies an instrumental conception of administration — agencies are created and empowered in order to implement policy choices made in the legislative process.

It is hardly surprising, therefore, that one of the concerns of U.S. administrative law should be to regulate the linkage between legislative and administrative action. But legal doctrine confronts a world wonderfully more complex than the one a simplistic principal-agent analogy suggests. Statutes empower, direct, and constrain; but they often fail to decide critical issues of public policy. Indeed, in the real world of political action, where administrators often request and help to draft new statutes' authority for themselves, agencies may appear to behave more like independent entrepreneurs seeking funding from the Congress for projects of their own than like well-instructed agents implementing their principal's orders.

The descriptive inadequacy of the principal-agent paradigm thus seems to create a normative crisis of legitimacy in administration. For if agencies are prominent, perhaps primary policymakers pursuant to vague statutory authorizations, how can either political or legal control of agencies possibly work? Some lawyers and some members of the public choice fraternity believe this crisis is acute. I believe, in part on legal and in part on public choice grounds, that both are wrong.

Delegations and Constitutional Doctrine

Article I, section 1 of the United States Constitution provides: "All legislative Powers herein granted shall be vested in a Congress of the United States, which shall consist of a Senate and House of Representatives." Similar provisions appear in virtually every state constitution. For at least 150 years the Supreme Court's decisions were replete with categorical statements suggesting that Congress could not relinquish any of its power to enact legislation through grants of policymaking power to administrators. The following statement by the first Justice Harlan in *Field v. Clark* is typical: "That Congress cannot delegate legislative power to the President is a principle universally recognized as vital to the integrity and maintenance of the system of government ordained by the constitution."[1]

Yet in that case the Court upheld a provision of the Tariff Act of 1890 which authorized the president to suspend favorable tariff treatment for nations that imposed on American products any "exactions and duties . . . which . . . [he] deemed, that is, which he found to be, unequal and unreasonable." The Court theorized that the act simply accorded the president the authority to make the factual determination requisite for implementation of the policy prescribed by Congress. "He was the mere agent of the law-making department to ascertain and declare the event upon which . . . [the legislature's] expressed will was to take effect."[2] This argument is, of course, logically unassailable. All you need do is believe — counterfactually — that whether a tariff is "unreasonable" is a question of fact rather than a political judgment.

In decisions both before and after *Field v. Clark,* the Supreme Court upheld statutes that accorded the president, or occasionally other executive officers, a large role in formulating as well as implementing national policy. Many of these laws dealt with foreign affairs, a field in which Congress might have believed that the Constitution accorded the president an especially wide discretion in effectuating legislative judgment. The Court offered a variety of rationales for upholding such loose delegations of authority. Some laws were said merely to give the president authority to determine the "contingency" — a violation of the nation's neutrality rights by a foreign power — that brought congressional policy into force.[3] In other statutes, the Court suggested Congress had firmly established the general contours of public policy and simply left the president to "fill up the details" of regulation, even though such "filling up" might involve the power to declare conduct criminal.[4]

Perhaps the most widely quoted formulation of the "old" nondelegation doctrine appears in *J. W. Hampton, Jr. & Co. v. United States.*[5] The Court acknowledged that Congress could not feasibly prescribe in detail the rules governing every facet of federally regulated activity. Chief Justice Taft concluded from his reading of *Field v. Clark* and *United States v. Grimaud*: "If Congress shall lay down by legislative act an *intelligible principle* to which the person or body authorized to fix . . . rates is directed to conform, such legislative action is not a forbidden delegation of legislative power."[6]

In all these early decisions, the Court kept insisting that the Constitution forbade abdication of Congress's monopoly of legislative power. But not once did it invalidate any delegation Congress saw fit to make, and it upheld phrases such as "just and reasonable rates" for railroad regulation and "public interest, convenience, or necessity" for the issuance of broadcast licenses as establishing "meaningful standards" for agencies to apply. It therefore is not surprising that by the early 1930s, the "nondelegation doctrine" was thought to have become an empty formalism.[7]

However, in 1935, the Court for the first — and last — time struck down congressional enactments as unlawful delegations of legislative power. The Court did so in two cases dealing with separate sections of the National Industrial Recovery Act, an early piece of New Deal legislation that soon fell into disfavor with most elements of the Roosevelt constituency.

In *Panama Refining Co. v. Ryan,*[8] the provision at issue was section 9(c) of the National Industrial Recovery Act (NIRA). That section authorized, but did not require, the President to exclude from interstate commerce oil products "produced or withdrawn from storage in excess of the amount permitted to be produced or withdrawn from storage by any state law or valid regulation. . . ." Disobedience to an exclusion order was made a crime punishable by fine and imprisonment. Section 9(c) provided no criteria on which the president was to base his action, and the Court refused to find the requisite guiding principles in the act's declaration of policy, which listed many competing objectives apparently without preference. Nor did the act require the president "to ascertain and proclaim the conditions prevailing in the industry which made the prohibition necessary." Canvasing its previous precedents, the Court declared: "Thus, in every case in which the question has been raised, the Court has recognized that there are limits of delegation which there is no constitutional authority to transcend. We think that section 9(c) goes beyond those limits. As to the transportation of oil production in excess of state permission, the Congress has declared no policy, has established no standard, has laid down no rule. There is no requirement, no definition of circumstances and conditions in which the transportation is to be allowed or prohibited."[9] With but a single dissent, the Court thus struck down the "hot oil" provisions of the NIRA.

Four months after the *Panama Refining* decision, in *A. L. A. Schechter Poultry Corp. v. United States*,[10] the Court invalidated section 3 of the same Act, which empowered the President to approve industry codes of "fair competition" upon submission by trade associations or business groups. The only conditions limiting the president's power were that the groups submitting codes for approval had to be "truly representative" of the industry, could impose no "inequitable restrictions on admission to membership," and could not "be designed to promote monopolies or to eliminate or oppress small enterprises . . . [or] operate to discriminate against them." Upon adoption, a code became the standard of fair competition for an industry, and its violation became a criminal misdemeanor, carrying a fine of up to five hundred dollars. Justice Cardozo, who had been the lone dissenter in *Panama Refining,* agreed with the majority in *Schechter*. "The delegated power of legislation which has found expression in this Code," he declared, "is not canalized within banks that keep it from overflowing. It is unconfined and vagrant."[11]

Since the *Schechter* case, the Supreme Court has not invalidated a single statute on the basis of excessive delegation. This result—not surprising, of course, given the history of the doctrine—cannot be explained by improvements since 1935 in the drafting of statutes.

The first post–New Deal nondelegation challenge to reach the Supreme Court signaled the Court's reversion to form. In *Yakus v. United States,* it upheld Congress's World War II delegation of authority to control prices, which was implemented by the Office of Price Administration (OPA). The Court said:

> Congress enacted the Emergency Price Control Act in pursuance of a defined policy and required that the prices fixed by the Administrator should further that policy and conform to standards prescribed by the Act. The boundaries of the field of the Administrator's permissible action are marked by the statute. It directs that the prices fixed shall effectuate the declared policy of the Act to stabilize commodity prices so as to prevent war-time inflation and its enumerated disruptive causes and effects. In addition the prices established must be fair and equitable, and in fixing them the Administrator is directed to give due consideration, so far as practicable, to prevailing prices during the

designated base period, with prescribed administrative adjustments to compensate for enumerated disturbing factors affecting prices. In short, the purposes of the Act specified in §1 denote the objective to be sought by the Administrator in fixing prices—the prevention of inflation and its enumerated consequences. The standards set out in §2 define the boundaries within which prices having that purpose must be fixed. It is enough to satisfy the statutory requirements that the Administrator finds that the prices fixed will tend to achieve that objective and will conform to those standards, and that the courts in an appropriate proceeding can see that substantial basis for those findings is not wanting.[12]

Although the Court struggled to distinguish *Panama Refining* and *Schechter*, the attempt was barely persuasive. *Yakus* treated as acceptable precisely the same grab bag of potentially inconsistent statutory directions for the exercise of executive authority that the prior cases had found empty. The Supreme Court has subsequently upheld many other grants of administrative authority in the face of plausible charges that they were no more specific than those found wanting in 1935.[13] Although most contemporary statutes of major political and economic significance contain provisions of great detail and complexity, they nevertheless often exhibit surprising vagueness precisely at the point of critical policy choice. Requirements for action that might otherwise provide clear guidance are continuously rendered discretionary by adverbial equivocation. "Feasible," "practicable," and "reasonable" are congressional favorites. The National Highway Traffic Safety Administration (NHTSA), for example, is exhorted to adopt regulations that "meet the need" for vehicle safety as long as those regulations are "practicable," "reasonable," and "appropriate."

The leniency of the Supreme Court in permitting delegations of authority to administrators has not gone unchallenged by commentators. These critiques of the toothless nondelegation doctrine come both from within and from outside the public choice fraternity. Critics of the more conventional type tend to emphasize the impact of broad delegations of authority to administrators on democratic accountability and the rule of law. Public choice commentators have similarly emphasized the political accountability difficulties that are generated by the broad policy choices given to administrators, but they have been even more adamant in challenging the broad delegations of authority to agencies on the ground that they decrease public welfare.

We will look at these diverse criticisms of current constitutional doctrine both separately and in combined forms. In so doing, we will see public choice analysis playing a number of different roles. On the one hand, the public choice approach can answer questions—or at least claims that it can—that are an embarrassment to other forms of critique. On the other hand, the translation of public choice analysis into claims about public welfare turns out to be an embarrassment to the public choice fraternity itself. Indeed, I will argue that by thinking through the ways in which interest group pluralism may structure different forms of political contests, elections, and accountability systems, one can construct a public choice argument *for* broad delegations of authority to administrators that looks at least as good on both welfare and accountability grounds as do the critics' calls for specificity in statutory drafting.

Delegation, Accountability, and the Rule of Law

In *The End of Liberalism: Ideology, Policy, and the Crisis of Public Authority,* Theodore Lowi argues that modern toleration of broad delegations of policy making authority to administrators is part of a political tradition that is antithetical to law (that is, to rules or standards as distinguished from procedures).[14] In Lowi's view, the legislature's failure to prescribe policy inevitably results in a failure of government to develop coherent policy and ultimately in the replacement of law by ad hoc bargaining. In particular, Lowi contends that broad delegations will generally result, not in administrative rulemaking to determine policy, but in policy remaining permanently indeterminate. This is true, he argues, because in individual cases it will be too costly for affected parties to insist upon a clear statement of policy:

> Interest-group liberalism has little place for law because laws interfere with the political process.
> . . . In brief, law, in the liberal view, is too authoritative a use of authority. Authority has to be tentative and accessible to be acceptable. If authority is to be accommodated to the liberal myth that it is 'not power at all,' it must emerge out of individual bargains.
> . . . Delegation of power provides the legal basis for rendering a statute tentative enough to keep the political process in good working order all the way down from Congress to the hearing examiner, the meat inspector, the community action supervisor, and the individual clients with which they deal. Everyone can feel that he is part of one big policy-making family.[15]

Lowi provides the following imagined dialogue to illustrate his point:

> *Wages and Hours Regional*: Mr. Employer, we find that you owe your ten employees a total of $10,000 in back wages, plus fines, for having them take telephone messages while having lunch on the premises.
> *Employer*: I object. You interrogated my employees without my knowledge, and did not interrogate me at all. And, besides, where do you get off saying my boys were 'on call' because they heard the phone ring? Talk to my lawyer.

Regional: How about $5,000 in back pay and no fines?

Employer: Good God, now I'm really disgusted. I want in writing your official interpretation governing such a case: And aren't there rules about notice and hearings?

Regional: How about $2,500 in back pay?

Employer: Well, hell, I . . .

Regional: How about an exchange of memoranda indicating future compliance?

Employer: Mmm . . . [aside: Lawyers' fees . . . trips to testify . . . obligations to that damned congressman of ours . . . .]

Official memo from Regional, weeks later: You are hereby directed to cease.

Posted in employees' toilet: You are hereby directed to eat lunch off the premises.

This drama could have taken place in one long-distance call or in half a dozen letters strung out over many weeks. However, the demoralizing part is not what one might expect. It isn't 'bureaucracy.' . . . Disgust, disappointment, and distrust would arise in such a case because the agency appears 'gutless.' Its effort to avoid enunciating a rule may be rationalized as flexibility, but to most intelligent people directly involved in such a problem it can end in reduced respect — for the agency and for government. And meanwhile, no rule.

. . . Admittedly the complexity of modern life forces Congress into vagueness and generality in drafting its statutes. Admittedly the political pressure of social unrest forces Congress and the President into premature formulations that make delegation of power inevitable. But to take these causes and effects as natural and good, and then to build the system around them, is to doom the system to remaining always locked into the original causes and effects.[16]

Lowi is by no means alone in believing that the practice of broad delegation is a formula for bad government. In *Democracy and Distrust: A Theory of Judicial Review,* John Hart Ely views the failure of the "legislature" (Congress) to "legislate" (decide policy questions) as one of the major obstacles to a truly representative democracy.[17] "There can be little point in worrying about the distribution of the franchise and other personal political rights unless the important policy choices are being made by elected officials." In Ely's view, restricting legislative delegations will not produce perfect, only democratic, governance. "I'm not saying we may not still end up with a fair number of clowns as representatives, but at least then it will be because clowns are what we deserve."[18]

Similar sentiments seem to underlie the opinions by Justices Rehnquist and Burger in *Industrial Union Department, AFL-CIO v. American Petroleum Institute* and *American Textile Manufacturers Institute, Inc. v. Donovan.*[19]

Both would have sent section 6(b)(5) of the Occupational Safety and Health Act back to Congress for further specification of the criteria by which the Occupational Safety and Health Administration should balance the objectives of protecting worker health and maintaining a healthy economy. The pertinent language of section 6(b)(5) directs OSHA, in regulating worker exposure to toxic chemicals, to prescribe the standard that "most adequately assures, to the extent feasible . . . that no employee will suffer material impairment of health or functional capacity even if such employee has regular exposure to the hazard . . . for the period of his working life." Union representatives claimed that the instruction obliged OSHA to mandate the use of whatever available technology an industry could afford to install without bankrupting itself, while employer groups insisted that the agency was required to weigh the costs of controls against health benefits in deciding what standard is "feasible." Adoption of the first interpretation could in some instances force employers to spend hundreds of millions of dollars, while acceptance of the latter version would substantially reduce protection for workers in industries where control technology was expensive.

According to Justice Rehnquist concurring in the judgment of the majority in *Industrial Union Department*: "In drafting § 6(b)(5), Congress was faced with a clear, if difficult, choice between balancing statistical lives and industrial resources or authorizing the Secretary to elevate human life above all concerns save massive dislocation . . . . That Congress chose . . . to pass this difficult choice on to the Secretary is evident from the spectral quality of the standard it selected."[20] In *Donovan*, Rehnquist dissented and, joined by Chief Justice Burger, suggested that the "spectral" language of section 6(b)(5) masked a policy disagreement so profound that had Congress been required to resolve it, "there would have been no bill for the President to sign."[21]

The Lowi-Ely-Rehnquist critique dramatizes an apparently serious flaw in American government — a legislature fleeing from choice on critical issues, not by postponing action, but by adopting vague statutes conferring policymaking power on administrators who will themselves be deeply compromised by their lack of clear statutory authority. Thus, it is suggested, we blunder our way into an administrative state that has traded its democratic values for little or no increase in effective governance.

The delegitimation critics might be divided further into two camps. Lowi seems to make an argument from authoritativeness; Ely and Justice Rehnquist seem to be making arguments about the need for accountability. Let us examine these arguments in turn.

Lowi's position is certainly familiar. A consistent strain of our constitutional politics asserts that legitimacy flows from "the rule of law." By that is meant a system of objective and accessible commands, law which can be seen to flow from collective agreement rather than from the exercise of discretion or preference by those persons who happen to be in positions of authority. By reducing discretion, and thereby the possibility for the exercise of the individual preferences of officials, specific rules reinforce the rule of law.

Yet, while focusing on the rule of law and its undeniable importance in maintaining liberty, we should not forget the apparently equal importance of a contradictory demand: the demand for justice in individual cases. Moreover, the demand for justice seems inextricably linked to the flexibility and generality of legal norms, that is, to the use of vague principles (reasonableness, fairness, fault, and the like) rather than precise rules. Were one to doubt either the ubiquitous human desire for justice or its connection to general norms, Thibout and Walker have demonstrated, in an impressive series of cross-national clinical trials, a demand for the absence of law in the sense (legal rules) that Lowi uses that term. Indeed, these findings lead Thibout and Walker to argue that law must consist exclusively of these broad general principles in order for any adjudicatory system to appear just. And, of course, any set of general principles that would allow elaborate contextualization of circumstances before authoritative judgment would, of necessity, also allow the exercise of broad discretion by those charged with developing middle-level policies and deciding concrete cases.

This is not to say that Lowi is wrong to remind us about the demand for authoritativeness. But it is surely not the case that legitimacy is subsumed in authority, even were we to agree that the latter is nonproblematically implemented by statutory precision.

The Ely-Rehnquist demand for legislative decisionmaking as a prerequisite to accountability is similarly incomplete, and even more perplexing. In Ely's vernacular, I find it difficult to understand why we do not presently have exactly the "clowns . . . we deserve." The dynamics of accountability apparently involve voters willing to vote upon the basis of their representative's record in the legislature. Assuming that our current representatives in the legislature vote for laws that contain vague delegations of authority, we are presumably holding them accountable for that at the polls. How is it that we are not being represented?

Moreover, the sort of specific issue accountability that Ely seems to applaud, indeed to advocate, is hardly transparently desirable. Do we really want to choose our representatives (or hold them accountable) on the basis of specific votes concerning specific legislation which, but for constitutional necessity (a nondelegation doctrine with bite), they would have cast in more general terms? How exactly does it help us in choosing legislators to judge them on the basis of preference expressions that are not the expressions they would give, but for the constitutional necessity of being specific?

Even if we were to imagine that statutory precision would be informative, it is hard to envisage how rational voter calculation is appreciably improved. When one votes for Congressperson X, presumably one votes on the basis of a prediction about what X will do in the next time period in the legislature. How much better off are voters likely to be in making that prediction — that is, in determining how well Congressperson X is likely to represent them over a range of presently unspecified issues — by knowing that he or she voted yes or no on the specific language in certain specific bills in some preceding legislature?

After all, the voter will also know that X could not have controlled all or even a substantial portion of the language of those bills. Votes must have been cast "all things considered." Therefore, when making a general appraisal of X's likely behavior in the future, it is surely much more important that voters know the general ideological tendencies that inform those votes (prolabor, probusiness, prodisarmament, prodefense) than that X votes for or against the particular language of particular bill. I know of no one who argues that statutory vagueness prevents the electorate from becoming informed on the general proclivities of their representatives. Without more elaboration, Ely's notion that vague statutory language somehow severs the electoral connection can be viewed only as deeply puzzling. Indeed, I will later argue that he may have the true situation exactly backwards.

The Contributions of Public Choice to the Nondelegation Debate

If we were to subscribe to the McNollgast vision of administrative procedure discussed in the preceding chapter, it might provide Lowi with a counterattack on the argument from regulatory reasonableness. For one might hear Lowi replying, "But, don't you see, it is not the opportunity for reasonableness that is being provided. Rather, administrative procedure provides a means for the continuous policing of administrators by interest groups that have been empowered both by the legislature's broad delegation of authority and by the procedural constraints that they are permitted to impose on the agency." And, were we to assume that there is surely something to the McNollgast story about administrative procedure, Lowi has a point. The vision he offers of individual capacity to hold administrators to the demands of the rule of law, is intuitively more appealing than administration as the free play of interest group politics.

But the public choice vision will not really save the Lowi critique. For, in fact, Lowi seems to be caught in something of a conceptual muddle. He has implicitly equated law with statute. But he has given no reason for concluding that law as made by administrators, including administrative practice that includes settlement, is less authoritative law than law as enacted by the legislature. We often complain about "bureaucracy" precisely because it is "rulish" and it is clear that courts are prepared to hold agencies both to their rules and to their customary norms. Viewed in this way, it is not clear that Lowi's complaint really is about the absence of rules. Instead, Lowi seems to have smuggled in an undeveloped premise about the superior *democratic* authority of statutes as compared with administrative policy. But if that is his argument about political *authority*, it collapses into the sort of *accountability* complaints that are echoed by John Hart Ely and Chief Justice Rehnquist.

Here again public choice theorists have come partially to the rescue. For some scholars have claimed that vague delegations are precisely a device for avoiding responsibility in the face of difficult political decisions and perhaps intractable interest group conflict. In short, the public choice literature suggests that Ely is right. Vague delegations are a means to reduce accountability. But they also go further. From a public choice perspective, not only are vague delegations reducing accountability in American governance, they are systematically reducing public welfare in the bargain.

The most elaborate exposition of this view, building on the work of Morris Fiorina and others, is by Peter Aranson, Ernest Gellhorn, and Glen Robinson, *A Theory of Legislative Delegation*.[22] The Aranson, Gellhorn, and Robinson (AGR) thesis is fairly straightforward. The authors first ask when one should expect that legislators would be willing to confer broad authority on administrators to determine policy. They discern two such situations. In the first, legislators recognize that legislation is likely to benefit one group of constituents while imposing substantial costs on another group. In order to claim credit with the former constituency, while avoiding potentially energetic opposition from the second group in the next election, legislators pass a vague statute. They can then claim credit for the general action benefiting the first constituency, while shifting the responsibility for focused harms to the implementing decisions of administrators.

The second set of circumstances yielding vague statutes is one in which legislators again confront opposing groups in their constituencies. But all groups favor some action to the status quo. They merely are unable to agree on any single course of action. Passing a vague statute in effect creates a public policy lottery—an action preferred by all the opposing groups to no action at all. Who gains and who loses among these contending interests will then be determined by administrative action.

Having identified circumstances under which they would predict vague statutes — that is, statutes conferring broad discretionary authority on administrators — Aranson, Gellhorn, and Robinson then ask whether these are circumstances that are likely to produce welfare-enhancing legislation. Their answer is a resounding no. In their view, virtually all legislation is designed to produce "private goods at public expense." Moreover, they consistently imply that the net benefits of these "private goods" are negative, that is, the public costs of producing the private goods are greater than the benefits received by the private interest groups who receive them. Because vague delegations reduce the cost to legislatures of legislating, we get more of this "private goods" legislation than we otherwise would. A reinvigorated nondelegation doctrine would increase the costs of legislating, reduce the number of (private goods) bills that were enacted, and thereby enhance general welfare. Aranson, Gellhorn, and Robinson recognize that prohibiting vague delegations would also inhibit some "public interest" legislation. But given their belief about the relative incidence of private interest versus public interest legislation, these losses would be more than offset by the gains from reduced legislative output.

We will first consider the claim that vague delegations of authority to administrators are systematically driving down public welfare. As we shall see, this attempt to translate public choice theory into a brand of welfare economics cannot succeed. And as I noted in Chapter 2, no one has been able to devise empirical tests that would convince those not already persuaded that most legislation merely generates private benefits at public expense.

Statutory Vagueness and the General Welfare

Assume first the hypothetical scenario in which the legislature creates a public policy lottery by charging an agency to do something about some issue, but without charging it specifically with what to do. In the AGR account, the legislature does this in order to satisfy diverse demands for action when there is no consensus on what the action should be. By hypothesis, all the actors demanding that the legislature do something are risk-acceptant, that is, they prefer the lottery to the status quo. Assuming rational expectations (as AGR seem to do), this implies that every actor will favor giving implementing decisions to administrators within the bounds of the legislatively established lottery.

Aranson and his colleagues present this situation as one of pernicious legislative action. Yet it is extremely difficult to discern why. The legislature has been perfectly responsive (representative) and has by definition enhanced general welfare (everyone preferred the lottery to the status quo). To be sure, the administrative agency's implementing action may not be to choose the best possible policy. And perhaps AGR believe that if forced to act specifically the legislature would have chosen such a policy, thus eliminating the possibility of administrative error. But given these authors' general views of legislative behavior, one is hard pressed to imagine how their argument would proceed.

The welfare argument flowing from the alternative AGR scenario is less puzzling. Here, remember, the reelection-oriented legislator attempts to take credit for the beneficial outcomes of legislation while avoiding responsibility for the legislation's costs — what numerous authors refer to as the creation of a "fiscal illusion."

What then are the welfare consequences of this credit-claiming, blame-avoiding behavior on the part of legislators? AGR argue that it is negative. That claim rests on a much more general proposition — that the free play of political life, assuming self-interested constituents and self-interested legislators, makes all legislation disbeneficial (or most of it, anyway). But this is an argument that proves too much. At the very least, given the generality of these premises, AGR should advocate a constitutional rule which somehow requires that the legislature be limited to specific legislation whenever it wants to be vague, and to vague legislation whenever it finds it easier to be specific. Although presented as an argument against vague delegations, the argument is really an argument against all legislation.

What are the bases for this pessimistic view? Precisely the views we reviewed in Chapter 2. The first proposition is that legislators are oriented primarily to their own reelection. Thus they will consider legislative actions from the perspective of their ability to claim credit with relevant constituencies. Second, because legislators represent different constituencies with different interests, all of them will find it useful to make trades with each other (logrolling) so that the demands of a wide variety of constituencies can be satisfied. Finally, even where the costs of legislation affect all constituencies equally, bare-majority coalitions of the beneficiaries of legislation remain possible, provided that the benefits of legislation exceed one-half its costs. Given this possibility, the goal of all legislation (or, sometimes, most legislation) can be presumed to be the satisfaction of some coalition of private groups at a public cost that exceeds the legislation's benefits to the coalition. And notwithstanding these routinely negative results, voters will not chuck the legislators out because of something called "high voter perceptual thresholds." Voters can see the direct benefits to them but are relatively impervious to the high indirect costs of benefits to others.

The empirical gaps and logical leaps in this argument are quite wonderful. First, all politics is interest group politics. All legislation and all legislator-constituency relationships are "pure pork barrel." Legislation with respect to abortion, prayer in the public schools, environmental protection, and river and harbor improvements can all be modeled in precisely the same way. More critical, a possibility theorem (it can happen) is transformed into a behavioral prediction (it will happen). Because bare-majority coalitions could pass disbeneficial legislation, they do. The system is maintained by a combination of logrolling (allowing all legislators to play the same game) and electoral ignorance (fiscal illusion). In this worst-case scenario, neither the balkanization of power in subcommittees nor the decline of party discipline seems to inhibit logrolling. Ideology (a belief in civil rights or environmental protection) neither broadens the benefits of legislation beyond bare-majority coalitions nor limits (for example, a general belief in individual autonomy or small government) the legislators' ability to pass (remember the presidential veto?) welfare-reducing statutes.

Quite apart from the doubts engendered by modest reflection on the empirical bases of this attempt to extract welfare consequences from (sometimes axiomatically diverse) public choice theorems, the analysis presented appears quite incoherent when placed in the context of a choice between vague or specific legislation. Presumably, vague delegations foster the march toward welfare-reducing results by reducing legislative decision costs.[23] But there is a problem with using logrolling as one of the major driving forces behind the proposed worst-case scenario and attributing welfare losses to delegation of authority to administrators. The problem is simple: Vague delegations seem to inhibit logrolling. Delegations of power transfer policy decisions to the jurisdiction of administrative agencies which have grave legal difficulties, and little apparent incentive, to trade values across programs. Any delegation thus restricts the policy space across which logrolling can be orchestrated and thereby limits the number of deals available to legislators in the next time period. The only way to cure this defect — to keep policy within the legislative space where logrolling can continue — would be to maintain all apparently delegated policy questions continuously on the legislative agenda. But if that were true, there would in fact be no delegation and no savings in legislative decision costs. Delegation would be irrelevant because nonexistent.

This difficulty might be solved if all possible legislative deals could be constructed within a particular piece of legislation. If there is indeed wide diversity of interests, there seem to be two techniques available for accomplishing all logrolling within a single bill. The first is a breathtakingly broad delegation: a pure policy lottery — completely standardless legislation that restricts neither policy choice nor jurisdiction. For even a determinate subject matter would restrict some trades, thus excluding some legislators and their constituents from logrolling. This would in turn produce incentives to blow the whistle on the fiscal illusion, and then the whole story begins to unravel. Ignoring for present purpose the obvious nonexistence of such delegations, there is, as I have noted, no a priori basis for presuming that the welfare consequences of pure policy lotteries are negative. Indeed, if demanded by voters with rational expectations, continuous play in such lotteries should produce general welfare gains.

A moment's reflection, however, reveals why the pure policy lottery is likely to remain a mere conceptual category. It seems extremely unlikely that all groups will prefer any *conceivable* change with respect to every *possible* issue to the status quo. These are the preferences of revolutionaries, not of American interest groups. Logrolling by special interests in the presence of fiscal illusions seems much more likely to produce a disparate set of specific statutory provisions. Such statutes can give everyone something, while confining the bargain to a particular time period, thus leaving open fulsome opportunities for multilateral trades in the future.

In short, while AGR's general theory of legislation may capture the dynamics and welfare consequences of certain classes of legislation — appropriations bills for defense installations or for river and harbor improvements — it is a theory which seems to explain specific, not vague, legislation. And to the extent that we believe that such "Christmas tree bills" are indeed instances of private interest legislation that reduce general welfare, we should *favor* statutory vagueness as a potential correction. Perhaps the Defense Department or the Army Corps of Engineers could avoid at least some of the worthless projects that pure pork-barrel politics produce. Indeed, the recent use of a "base-closing commission" to remove that issue partially from political bargaining is an example of just such a move.

Thus, without exploring further the empirical naivete of this apparently hard-headed approach (bare-majority legislation, for example, is virtually nonexistent), it appears that the theory has nothing to offer that would support a limitation on the legislature's capacity to delegate discretion to administrators. For the analysis offered cannot even make out a plausible theoretical case for the systematically negative welfare effects of vague delegations.

Statutory Vagueness and Electoral Accountability

Public choice objections to vague delegations on welfare economics grounds may be unpersuasive. Nevertheless, if the public choice approach reinforces Ely's complaint about the destruction of electoral accountability, vague delegations may yet prove to have sufficiently unhappy consequences for democratic governance that we should like to constrain them more than does current Supreme Court doctrine. Yet these stories about legislators systematically tricking their constituents through the simple device of a vague statute seem highly problematic. Remember my earlier critique of the Ely position. Do we really want to choose representatives or hold them accountable on the basis of *specific* votes concerning *specific* legislation which, but for constitutional necessity (a nondelegation doctrine with bite), they would have cast in more general terms? And do we really believe that voters get better information from specific votes on specific legislation than from knowing the general ideological proclivities of their legislators or candidates?

David Schoenbrod clearly seems to believe that more specific information is always better information for purposes of democratic accountability. In his view, "delegation allows legislators to convey information selectively, withholding opinions about the hard choices while providing opinions that embrace popular aspirations. The Clean Air Act and many other regulatory statutes have passed by wide margins for this reason, not because Congress reached a consensus on difficult subjects." Schoenbrod continues: "The ideological poses that legislators strike and the laws that emerge from agencies often bear little resemblance to each other. . . . Indeed delegation makes it possible for legislators to espouse internally inconsistent ideologies (for example, avoiding economic dislocation and protecting health). They need not join issue over inconsistencies because they are talking at the symbolic level of goals rather than at the concrete level of laws."[24]

To summarize, Schoenbrod's argument is that broad delegations provide legislators with the opportunity to provide information selectively, to legislate without reaching consensus, and to disguise inconsistent positions. I have no quarrel with Schoenbrod that legislators do all of these things in the context of broad delegations of authority to administrators. My argument is that not all of these things are unqualifiedly bad, and that those things that do reduce accountability are equally available to legislators in the context of enacting highly specific legislation.

As previously suggested, I do not believe that failure to reach consensus on detail should disable legislators from legislating because I see no reason to believe that it has negative consequences either for public welfare or for political accountability. A decision to go forward notwithstanding continuing ambiguity or disagreement about the details of implementation is a decision that the polity is better off legislating generally than maintaining the status quo. Citizens may disagree, but they can also hold legislators accountable for their choice. If citizens want more specific statutes, or fear that legislating without serious agreement on implementing details is dangerous, they can, after all, throw the bums out.

To be sure, it may be argued that this requires a significant level of sophistication on the part of voters. But that is precisely the problem with the suggestion that broad delegations of authority in legislation enhance the ability of representatives either to dissemble or to be inconsistent, by comparison with more specific legislative action. The sad truth is that legislators can as easily convey information selectively or take up inconsistent positions in specific statutes as in more general ones.

The Clean Air Act that Schoenbrod uses as an example for his view as easily supports mine. There are indeed some critical gaps in this statute and its many amendments that leave substantial policy discretion to administrators. On the other hand, the statute goes on for hundreds of pages, many of them containing hypertechnical provisions that few citizens could possibly understand. Moreover, to the extent that the Clean Air Act and its amendments do things that dramatically depart from citizens' expectation, I would suggest that they are largely in the detailed provisions, not in the broad aspirational sections. Voters do not read bills and would have little chance of understanding most of them if they did. Hence, legislators can selectively convey information about legislation whether they legislate specifically or generally.

Nor does specificity help voters police for inconsistency in legislators' ideological positions. Indeed, it would seem to me much easier for a voter to detect the inconsistency in a legislator's statement that he or she intended "to protect the public health through strict air quality regulation while avoiding any serious economic dislocation" than by attempting to figure out that the specific provisions of a bill were indeed trading off these values and in precisely what ways.

Consider a different, but now well-known, example: The most specific legislation that comes out of the Congress these days is perhaps the gargantuan and mind-numbingly detailed legislation drafted by the Budget, Appropriations, and Finance Committees. But an Omnibus Budget Reconciliation Act can hardly be carried, much less read. And perhaps nowhere in American politics do legislators make better use of selective information and creative incoherence than in explaining to the American people what has been done in constructing the federal budget.

The long and short of the matter seems to be this: No one has been able to demonstrate any systematic relationship between improving accountability, or enhancing the public welfare, or respecting the rule of law, and the specificity of legislation. Plausible abstract hypotheses can be connected with selective examples to demonstrate that both generality and specificity can impair one or all of the public values I have been discussing. If that is the case, then surely the Supreme Court has been wise to leave the choice of statutory generality to the legislature itself.

The Affirmative Case for Broad Delegations

Let's review the bidding. We seem to have no strong reason to believe that broad delegations of authority either delegitimize governance or produce systematically negative welfare effects. In theory, at least, legitimacy may flow from general statutory principles, implemented by administrative rules and decisions, as well as from precise statutory rules. Nor is there a cogent a priori argument that broad delegations of authority sever the electoral connection. Moreover, to the extent that disbeneficial legislation results from unrestrained vote trading across issues, broad delegations have no determinate welfare effects. Viewing broad delegations as acts of self-paternalism by legislators, constraining further disbeneficial deals, seems as plausible as the notion that vague delegations somehow facilitate logrolling. The most critical thing that might be said about vague delegations producing policy lotteries is that the outcome may satisfy the "winning coalition," to use McNollgast's terminology only ex ante, that is, until the administrative delegate "spins the wheel" and chooses a determinate policy. The case against broad delegations thus seems quite weak. But is there anything that can be said that would tend to favor broad delegations of authority to administrators? Or is this perhaps a debate in which whoever has the burden of persuasion loses?

WELFARE EFFECTS

Were we to assume that the welfare effects of legislation, both specific and vague, were random in specific instances and neutral overall, we should at least be interested in reducing the administrative costs of legislating and of implementing what was legislated.[25] These administrative costs seem to be of two kinds: the direct costs of making and carrying out decisions and the error costs of faulty policymaking and implementation. At the implementation stage, these error costs may, of course, result from what have come to be known as "agency costs" (the divergence of the agent's purposes from those of the principal),[26] as well as from simple mistakes. Hence, while division of functions may have certain efficiency properties (specialization and the like), it also entails monitoring to detect breaches of duty as well as simple errors on the part of the agent. And statutory specificity has obvious advantages from the standpoint of monitoring compliance.

Is there any reason to believe, nevertheless, that broad delegations of authority will often reduce the sum of decision, agency, and error costs? A wide range of commentators have certainly believed so. Indeed, as AGR point out, the possibility of such cost reductions is the commonest form of argument in support of broad delegations of authority. Yet, those same authors seem quite right when they emphasize that the possibility of cost savings is not a conclusive argument for this form of governmental division of authority. There must also be some reason to believe that the legislature will not only be able to discern when vague delegations entail cost reductions, but will also be motivated to realize those gains when they are available.

A weaker prodelegation case can nevertheless be supported. If we are unconvinced by the AGR thesis that broad delegations are on balance welfare-reducing, then it makes sense to have the delegation device available for use when and if it would reduce the sum of decision, error, and agency costs. The challenge then is to design other constitutional constraints that will prod the legislature in the direction of welfare-enhancing legislation. Indeed, it seems quite odd to constrain the legislature by denying it an efficient decision process in order to reduce welfare losses. Substantive prohibitions are much more to the point.

The policy lottery scenario reinforces this form of argument. If delegations are responsive to demands for a policy lottery, then there is reason to believe that the legislation itself has at least mildly positive, rather than merely neutral, effects. Hence, providing an efficient decision technique encourages the passage of welfare-enhancing legislation in addition to preventing waste. However, because such delegations entail choosing a "winning" policy in a constrained lottery, we must confront the problem of predicting whether agency action will in fact enhance welfare when taken. One way that the agency would fail to make a welfare-enhancing move would be to act outside its jurisdiction. But that sort of administrative error or usurpation is the easiest sort to constrain through legal controls, such as judicial review.

Agency actions within its jurisdiction (the lottery space defined by the statute) may nevertheless fail to capture all the welfare gains potentially available and may even have negative net welfare effects. Does judicial review or Office of Management and Budget oversight ensure that agency choices will always have positive welfare effects? Hardly. Yet it is also clear that executive branch requirements that cost-benefit analyses of agency regulations be prepared, and court demands that agency explanations for rules demonstrate a reasoned assessment of competing values, surely press agencies in the direction of cost-minimizing or welfare-enhancing action. No such constraints would operate on specific legislative choices.

The much-discussed case of *Chevron, U.S.A., Inc. v. Natural Resources*

Defense Council Inc.,[27] provides an illustration of both the strengths and the weaknesses of administrative law as a means for ensuring that broad delegations of power to administrators yield welfare-enhancing outcomes. The case provides, as well, some interesting judicial discussion of the legislature's reasons for making such delegations.

Chevron involved review of the Environmental Protection Agency's so-called bubble policy. Pursuant to a regulation adopted in 1981, facilities emitting substances into the ambient air were allowed to install new equipment not meeting all the conditions in their air quality permits, provided that they made offsetting changes that prevented those alterations from adversely affecting the quality of the emissions emanating from whole plants. Respondent NRDC claimed that each source of pollution in an existing plant was a "stationary source" within the meaning of the Clean Air Act. Because that act prohibits any increase in emissions from any "stationary source" in "non-attainment" areas, the NRDC argued that the flexibility sought to be introduced by the bubble regulations was not permissible in those areas of the country (nonattainment areas) that were required to improve, not merely maintain, their air quality.

The Supreme Court held that the EPA could treat a whole plant as one "stationary source" (the bubble policy), even though for other purposes the EPA treated each emitting location as a stationary source. After parsing the statute and the legislative history, the Court concluded that Congress had no discernible specific intent either to encourage or to inhibit the use of the bubble technique. Rather, the Court viewed the statute as establishing only a general framework for administrative action. Congress sought to accommodate in some fashion demands for both environmental quality and economic growth. Because here the EPA seemed to have made a "reasoned" trade-off between those interests, the Court concluded that its judicial, reviewing function was at an end.

In short, the EPA had been given jurisdiction to balance environmental and economic values in arriving at a specific policy choice, and it had done so in an apparently reasonable fashion. Without directly addressing the potential non-delegation issue raised by a statute that, as interpreted, clearly conferred administrative power to make critical value choices, the Court said, "Congress intended to accommodate both [economic and environmental] interests but did not do so itself on the level of specificity presented by these cases. Perhaps that body consciously desired the administrator to strike the balance at this level, thinking that those with great expertise and charged with the responsibility for administering the provision would be in a better position to do so; perhaps it simply did not consider the question at this level; and perhaps

Congress was unable to forge a coalition on either side of the question, and those on each side decided to take their chances with the scheme devised by the agency. For judicial purposes it matters not which of these things occurred."[28]

In short, the Court seems to be telling us that whether the Congress was explicitly attempting to enhance welfare by taking into account the gains from specialization, or the uncertainties inherent in dealing with specific contingencies at the legislative level, or alternatively was constructing a policy lottery to reduce decision costs at the legislative level, the constitutional situation was the same. In either case the legislation was valid and the judicial role was to assist the legislature in realizing these potential gains by ensuring that agency action was within its jurisdiction (that is, the choice was from the set of alternatives established by the particular lottery) and "reasoned" (connected to the principal's purposes and free from excessive error).

We cannot, of course, conclude from the *Chevron* decision, and the EPA's handling of the Clean Air Act's broad delegation of authority at issue in that case, that broad delegations subject to judicial review are likely to be welfare-enhancing. Few agency choices seem as clearly cost-effective as the bubble policy. Nor is it certain that the Court would interpret the Clean Air Act as conferring authority to "accommodate" environmental and economic values only by making choices that yielded a net gain in social welfare. Indeed, in the very next paragraph the Court suggested that it may not have been thinking in welfare terms at all. The opinion continued:

> Judges are not experts in the field and are not part of either political branch of the Government. Courts must, in some cases, reconcile competing political interests, but not on the basis of the judges' personal policy preferences. In contrast, an agency to which Congress has delegated policy-making responsibilities may, within the limits of that delegation, properly rely upon the incumbent administration's views of wise policy to inform its judgment. While agencies are not directly accountable to the people, the Chief Executive is, and it is clearly appropriate for the political branch of the Government to make such policy choices — resolving the competing interests which Congress itself either inadvertently did not resolve, or intentionally left to be resolved by the agency charged with the administration of the statute in light of everyday realities.[29]

This latter argument seems to premise the acceptability of EPA's policy choice on a quite different ground — the greater accountability of administrators to the electorate, through their connection with the chief executive, than that of courts, which are much further removed from electoral politics. Following the Court's lead, it seems time for us to return to themes of accountability, responsiveness, and legitimation. The welfare arguments for permitting delegation of policy choice to administrators are hardly overwhelming. And there is in the second quotation from the *Chevron* opinion the germ of an idea that could establish the superiority of vague delegations to specific statutory enactment as a technique of accountability, and thus of legitimation.

Accountability in a Presidential System

Strangely enough, it may make sense to imagine the delegation of political authority to administrators as a device for improving the responsiveness of government to the desires of the general electorate. This argument can be made even if we accept many of the insights of the political and economic literature that premises its predictions of congressional and voter behavior on a direct linkage between benefits transferred to constituents and the election or reelection of representatives. All we need do is not forget there are also presidential elections and that, as the Supreme Court reminds us in *Chevron*, presidents are heads of administrations.

Assume then that voters view the election of representatives to Congress through the lens of the most cynical interpretation of the modern public choice literature on congressional behavior. In short, the voter chooses a representative for that representative's effectiveness in supplying governmental goods and services to the local district, including the voter. The representative is a good representative or a bad representative depending upon his or her ability to provide the district with at least its fair share of governmental largesse. In this view, the congressperson's position on various issues of national interest is of modest, if any, importance. The only question is, Does he or she "bring home the bacon."

The voter's vision of presidential electoral politics is arguably quite different. The president has no particular constituency to which he or she has special responsibility to deliver benefits. Presidents are hardly cut off from pork-barrel politics. Yet issues of national scope and the candidates' positions on those issues are the essence of presidential politics. Citizens vote for a president based almost wholly on a perception of the difference that one or another candidate might make to general governmental policies.

If this description of voting in national elections is reasonably plausible, then the utilization of vague delegations to administrative agencies takes on significance as a device for facilitating responsiveness to voter preferences expressed in presidential elections. The high transactions costs of legislating specifically suggests that legislative activity directed to the modification of administration mandates will be infrequent. Agencies will thus persist with their statutory empowering provisions relatively intact over substantial periods of time.

Voter preferences on the direction and intensity of governmental activities, however, are not likely to be so stable. Indeed, one can reasonably expect that a president will be able to affect policy in a four-year term only because being elected president entails acquiring the power to exercise, direct, or influence policy discretion. The group of executive officers we commonly call "the administration" matters only because of the relative malleability of the directives that administrators have in their charge. If congressional statutes were truly specific with respect to the actions that administrators were to take, presidential politics would be a mere beauty contest. For, in the absence of a parliamentary system, or a system of strict party loyalty, specific statutes would mean that presidents and administrations could respond to voter preferences only if they were able to convince the legislature to make specific changes in the existing set of specific statutes. Arguments for specific statutory provisions constraining administrative discretion may therefore reflect a desire merely for conservative, not responsive, governance.

Of course, the vision of a president or an administration having to negotiate with the Congress for changes in policy is not one that is without its own attractiveness. Surely, we desire some limits on the degree to which a president can view a national election as a referendum approving all the president's (or the president's colleagues') pet projects, whether disclosed or undisclosed during the campaign. Those who abhor the policies of any administration, for example, might surely be attracted to a system that would have required that particular president to act almost exclusively through proposals for legislative change. Yet it seems likely that the flexibility that is currently built into the processes of administrative governance by relatively broad delegations of statutory authority permits a more appropriate degree of administrative, or administration, responsiveness to the voter's will than would a strict nondelegation doctrine. For if we were to be serious about restricting the discretion of administrators, we would have to go much beyond what most nondelegation theorists seem to presume would represent clear congressional choices.

This last point is so neglected in the nondelegation literature that it is worth elaborating. While most discussions of the nondelegation doctrine focus on the question of substantive criteria for decision, establishing criteria is but one aspect of the exercise of policy discretion. In the formation of regulatory policy, for example, at least the following general types of questions have to he answered: What subjects are to be on the regulatory agenda? What are their priorities? By what criteria are regulations to be formulated? Within what period of time are they to be adopted? What are the priorities for the utilization of enforcement machinery with respect to adopted policies? What are the rules and procedures by which the relevant facts about the application of legal rules will be found? What are the rules by which facts and law will be combined to yield legal conclusions, that is, "findings," that there have or have not been violations of the regulations? What exceptions or justifications are relevant with respect to noncompliance? If violations are found, what corrective action or remedies will be prescribed?

Each of these questions can, of course, be broken down into a multitude of others, and the answer to each question is a policy choice. Virtually any issue that can be specifically controlled by legislative answers to one of these questions can be reopened and redetermined when considering another. Thus, for example, even if Congress had adopted as legislation every specific and detailed rule that subsequently has been adopted by the Occupational Safety and Health Administration, the influence of the OSHA statute might have been vastly different—indeed, was vastly different—in the Carter and Reagan administrations. In the broadest term, the statute had a different meaning in the years 1976 to 1980 than in the years 1980 to 1988.

Were the Congress to attempt to make statutory meaning uniform over time, it would have to specify the most extraordinarily elaborate criteria for exercising enforcement initiative, for finding facts, for engaging in contextual interpretation, and for determining remedial action. Indeed, to insure uniformity it would have to specify some objective criteria for all these judgments and some algorithm by which they were unified into decisions. Squeezing discretion out of a statutory-administrative system is indeed so difficult that one is tempted to posit a "Law of Conservation of Administrative Discretion." According to that law, the amount of discretion in an administrative system is always constant. Elimination of discretion at one choice point merely causes the discretion that had been exercised there to migrate elsewhere in the system.

If Congress were able to adopt specific regulatory criteria in some particular instance, say, the OSHA statute, it would only have begun the process of making the real regulatory choices itself. Nor will it do to suggest that activities beyond the setting of substantive criteria fail to raise the broad policy issues that concern nondelegation theorists. How the facts will be found often determines who wins and who loses. What cases are important enough to pursue entails policy discretion of the broadest sort. When to withhold remedial sanctions or alternatively to make an example of some offender raises issues of basic moral and political values. In short, as Aranson, Gellhorn, and Robinson recognize, making legislation specific and congressional choice determinative means addressing all these issues in great detail.

Such a strategy would, of course, result in wonderfully wooden administrative behavior and on that ground alone be highly objectionable.[30] More important for present purposes, were Congress forced to try to repeal the Law of Conservation of Administrative Discretion in order to comply with a reinvigorated nondelegation doctrine, it would eliminate executive responsiveness to shifts in voter preferences. For in this scenario, the high transaction costs of specific legislation will give an enormous advantage to the status quo, and the status quo will be susceptible to change only by a statute of the same kind.

Responsiveness to diversity in voter preferences is not limited to changes through time. It is surely plausible to imagine that, given a large land area and a heterogeneous citizenry, governmental responsiveness also entails situational variance at any one time. If our laws were truly specific, this would also be impossible. We could not, for example, have a Social Security Disability program which harnesses the national government's advantage in the collection of taxes for redistributional purposes and employs a national general criterion of disability, while permitting flexible application that takes account of local attachment to the work ethic, local employment opportunities, and other variations that are likely to be peculiar to particular regions of the country. In short, we could not have laws that say, "Do something, but be reasonable and take account of local differences." Or at least we could not have them if our idea of democratic responsiveness is that the Congress as a body should make all the decisions necessary to give determinant meaning to the statutes that it passes.

In fact, as the fraternity of antidelegation theorists often laments, Congress seldom enacts such statutes. The extraordinary delegitimizing effect of rules that are so specific that they cannot he made responsive across either space or time suggests to me that this "failure" is a major benefit. Responsiveness to the will of the people is not a unitary phenomenon that can be embodied in a single institution. Broad delegations recognize that tight accountability linkages at one point in the governmental system may reduce the responsiveness of the system as a whole.

There is one additional reason to believe that broad delegations to administrators might improve responsiveness. As voting theorists seldom tire of telling us, when three or more alternative policies exist, there is the everpresent possibility of a voting cycle which can be broken only by resort to some form of dictatorship result. Legislators must, therefore, often delegate decisive authority somewhere in order to decide. There are any number of ways to deal with this problem — rules committees, forced deadlines, random selection, allocations of vetoes, and the like.[31] Lumping alternatives together in a broad or vague statutory pronouncement and delegating choice to administrators is but another way of avoiding voting cycles through the establishment of dictators.

But dictators may also be responsive. (One should remember that both Hobbes and Machiavelli gave elaborate counsels of prudence to him who would be king.) And if the choice is among rules committees, random selection, and providing vetoes to particular parties or delegations to administrators, the legislature may sensibly conclude that the last is likely to be the more responsive mechanism.[32] Administrators at least operate within a set of legal rules (administrative law) that keep them within their jurisdiction, require them to operate with a modicum of explanation and participation of the affected interests, police them for consistency, and protect them from the importuning of congressmen and others who would like to carry logrolling into the administrative process. In short, if Arrow's theorem makes us uncertain about the responsiveness of majority-rule voting procedures to citizens' or even legislators' desires, perhaps vague delegations to administrators can be a technique for avoiding the more disheartening aspects of breaking out of voting cycles.[33]

Moreover, delegations to administrators may become particularly attractive where the alternative preference orderings that would produce collective intransitivities are interpreted as conditional on alternative perceptions of states of the world. For in this situation it is possible that administrative research, fact finding, or "natural" experimentation with alternative policies will produce a unified view or construction of reality that ultimately yields a rational or transitive collective ordering of preferences. Interpreted in this way, delegation to experts becomes a form of consensus building that, far from taking decisions out of politics, seeks to give political choice a form in which potential collective agreement can be discovered and its benefits realized.

THE RULE OF LAW

Note, moreover, that this final example suggests that delegations to administrators may indeed promote the rule of law, and thus at least partially answer the Lowi critique. Even in the accounts of public choice theorists like McNollgast, administrative procedures are wonderfully complex and are meant to be constraining. They can be enforced in courts of law to ensure that those who are empowered by the procedures in fact have that political power available to them. Moreover, as case after case in the law reports illustrates, the rationality test with respect to administrative policymaking has remarkable power by comparison with its analogue as applied to statutes. While I have argued that it is not necessarily desirable to have the form of lax rationality review now applied to legislatures, it is clearly the case that while such review is lax where statutes are concerned, quite the contrary is true concerning administrative regulations. Indeed, the courts have made this point explicitly by striking down administrative requirements for lack of a good rationale while *in the same case* upholding legislative requirements that were similarly lacking in empirical justification. The reason for the distinction was put laconically by the court in just these terms: "no administrative law test applies to acts of the legislature." In short, to the extent that by the "rule of law" or by "authoritativeness" one means the capacity to ensure legality through judicial review, administrative processes score much higher on this criterion than do legislative processes. Delegating authority to administrators thus reinforces checks for both procedural and substantive legality that might otherwise be missing.

Having critiqued the case against delegations of policy choice to administrators and argued for my own form of "prodelegation" doctrine, I do not want to try to take that argument any further. The point has been not to decide the nondelegation doctrine issue conclusively one way or the other, but rather to illustrate concretely both dangers and advantages from using public choice analysis to illuminate public law issues. From that perspective some basic lessons seem pretty clear.

First, public welfare rabbits cannot be made to jump out of public choice hats. Public choice can help us to better understand how certain choice procedures structure or allocate decisional powers. It can help us to see possibilities for strategic behavior and strategic equilibria that yield likely outcomes in particular decision processes having particular structures and stakes. But it cannot itself tell us anything about whether those outcomes will be welfare enhancing or welfare reducing.

Second, we must be vigilant to guard against the seductive powers of partial analyses. The nondelegation case was littered with fragmented theoretical constructs. To give but three examples, democracy was equated with legislative majoritarianism, while ignoring the role of the presidency and how interest group action might differentially affect national and local electoral processes. The "agency costs" of delegations were treated without consideration of the information and decision costs that they also make relevant. "Logrolling" was analyzed without any consideration of how agency delegators changed the structure of the "logrolling game."

Finally, we should take from this discussion a heightened awareness of the way applied public choice may forget some of the theory's own basic presuppositions. Public choice is premised on rational actor models. When concepts like "fiscal illusion" start being imported into the analysis, it is always a danger signal. Like the Marxists' old standby, "false consciousness," by explaining everything, it risks explaining nothing.

7

Legal Control of Administrative Policymaking
The "Judicial Review Game"

As late as the presidency of John F. Kennedy, the principal image of federal administrative action was the adjudication of a case — a prosecution by the Federal Trade Commission, an enforcement action by the National Labor Relations Board, a licensing proceeding before the Federal Communications or Federal Power Commissions, or a rate proceeding at the Interstate Commerce Commission.[1] More than thirty years later, when Americans think of "regulation" they tend to think of the adoption of general rules concerning workplace safety by the Occupational and Safety Health Administration, or of rules governing air or water quality by the Environmental Protection Agency.[2] Nor is rulemaking the exclusive province of post–New Frontier agencies designed with that regulatory technique prominently in mind. The politically salient activities of old-line agencies — Federal Trade Commission regulation of charm school and funeral home practices, or Federal Power Commission deregulation of natural gas pipeline prices — often feature rulemaking rather than adjudication.

This "paradigm shift" was in part evolutionary, but it also contained critical elements of conscious redesign of the administrative process. Regulatory reform movements in the 1960s emphasized rulemaking and extolled its virtues of efficiency, fairness, and political accountability. While Kenneth Culp Davis may have been more hyperbolic than most in characterizing rulemaking as "one of the greatest inventions of modern government,"[3] he was hardly alone in the belief that a shift from adjudication to rulemaking would reenergize federal policymaking, while simultaneously making it more rational and more democratic.

Today's reformers tend to view rulemaking by federal administrative agencies more as a problem than as a solution. From one perspective, rulemaking is a problem precisely because it has been the instrument by which large, previously unregulated sectors of the economy have been subjected to costly federal edict.[4] Regulatory reform, in this view, lies precisely in reducing the reach of rulemaking authority and in making it subject to a realistic appraisal of the costs and benefits of governmental intervention.

From a different substantive or political perspective, rulemaking is equally strenuously criticized as having failed to live up to its promise. The brave new agencies of the 1960s and 1970s may have imposed many costs on society, but they have made only halting progress toward the safer and healthier world that was then envisioned. Regulatory program after regulatory program is years, if not decades, behind in completing (sometimes in addressing) its announced or statutorily mandated agenda. The older commissions that experimented with rulemaking in the 1960s and 1970s as a response to charges of inefficiency, unfairness, and lack of accountability have largely returned to their more familiar adjudicatory processes. The machinery of federal rulemaking is widely viewed as so creaky and accident-prone that administrators will resort to almost any other technique to attempt to get their jobs done.[5]

Although to some (perhaps a large) degree, these competing visions describe a dispute about policy or politics, a dispute in which the troubles with "rulemaking" or "the regulatory process" are really procedural placeholders for some substantive disagreement, there is also a sense in which the two sets of critics might perceive a common problem. While proregulation forces are constant in their calls for a more effective and timely rulemaking process, deregulators often have a similar interest.[6] The rulemaking processes of regulation are also the policy processes by which deregulation might be, sometimes must be, pursued. Thus proregulatory laments concerning the inability of the Occupational Safety and Health Administration to generate rules regulating the large number of toxic substances found in American workplaces might find a mirror image in deregulatory frustrations concerning OSHA's torpidity in revising archaic, but statutorily mandated, rules adopted twenty years ago. The EPA may have missed hundreds of deadlines in issuing rules to protect the environment, but a regulatory process that drives the Federal Energy Regulatory Commission to virtually abandon its initiatives to reintroduce market discipline in energy pricing is no friend of "deregulation" either. If policymaking by rule has become moribund or "ossified," as some have argued,[7] there is a need to reconsider the structure of agency rulemaking as a mechanism of governance, quite apart from that mechanism's substantive effects in particular instances. This chapter seeks to address that general institutional question.

We will first review some of the standard legal, political science, and management literature that has addressed the problem of agency rulemaking. As this review will demonstrate, commentators have developed both "external" (constraints by external forces) and "internal" ("bad management") accounts of why administrative rulemaking processes fail to fulfill the aspirations that the political process seems to have held for them. Deploying some standard "game-theoretic" techniques familiar in the public choice literature, this chapter and the next will analyze two external hypotheses: (1) that rulemaking is curtailed by legal controls via judicial review and (2) that rulemaking suffers from a stultifying set of political checks and balances representing congressional-presidential battles for policy authority. Game theory dramatizes the power of external legal and political controls on the administrative process. More important, the standard understandings of "the problem" besetting agency rulemaking and its solutions look very different when approached from the strategic perspective that game theory provides.

To summarize the argument of these two chapters, most fights about judicial review of agency action have revolved around *who* could seek review, *what* could be reviewed, or *how* review should be focused or substantively constrained. A game-theoretic analysis, combined with the consideration of the likely efficacy of other reform approaches, suggests, by contrast, that *when* review can be sought may be the most important question to consider.

Similarly, political control of administrative action is generally seen either as a question of how or how much the Congress can or should control the actions of administrators (topics we have pursued in prior chapters) or as a contest between the president and the Congress for political control of administration. A game-theoretic approach reveals the incompleteness of these analyses. Whether and how political influence over agency policymaking should be reformed depends critically on how one specifies the real interests that are at work in congressional control and presidential oversight. More interestingly, the players in the separation of powers game turn out not to be just the president and the Congress, but the president, the House, the Senate, and the judiciary. Explicit recognition of the greater complexity of the "separation of powers game" may critically affect the attractiveness of alternative institutional designs for creating an effective and accountable policymaking bureaucracy.

The Retreat from Rulemaking and Its Causes

The past decade's case study literature on the performance of America's administrative agencies details an agency-by-agency retreat from rulemaking. In *The Struggle for Auto Safety,* David Harfst and I concluded:

> NHTSA's regulatory behavior can be described concisely. [Although it was] established as a rulemaking agency to force the technology of automobile safety design, NHTSA's promulgated rules have had extremely modest effects in forcing the development of innovative safety technology. The rules that have become operational have required already-developed technologies, many of which were in wide-spread, if not universal, use in the automobile industry at the time of the standards' promulgation. Since the mid-1970s, NHTSA has instead concentrated on its statutory power to force the recall of motor vehicles that contain defects related to safety performance. It has re-treated to the old, and from the reformist perspective, despised form of legal regulation — case-by-case adjudication — which requires little, if any, techno-logical sophistication and which has no known effects on vehicle safety.[8]

Similar stories are told across the spectrum of consumer health and safety agencies. Terrence Scanlon described the CPSC as "easing itself out of rule-making, [and] learning to use its adjudicatory powers to achieve the same results."[9] Sidney Shapiro and Thomas McGarity note that the Occupational Safety and Health Administration in its seventeen-year history has completed only twenty-four substance-specific health regulations and has no worker-protection standards, or inadequate ones, for more than half of the 110 chemi-cals that the National Cancer Institute regards as confirmed or suspected carcinogens in workplaces.[10] The litany continues at other types of agencies, ranging from the Federal Energy Regulatory Commission[11] to the Federal Trade Commission[12] to the EPA.[13]

It is, of course, possible that the case study literature misdescribes contem-porary rulemaking in general, or that the abandonment of rulemaking is a matter of modest concern given the alternative techniques that agencies may use to enunciate policies and implement programs. Neither of these happy conclusions, however, seems able to withstand serious analysis.

A look at federal statutory requirements and the staffing of federal ad-ministrative agencies would suggest that rulemaking is now a more impor-tant technique than ever before in the effectuation of legislation programs — whether those programs be programs of regulation or of deregulation. The statutory demand for regulatory action is continuously increasing, while the personnel and resources available to regulatory agencies are in decline. Because it is well known that adjudication is a much more labor-intensive technique for policy formulation and implementation than is rulemaking, it hardly seems likely that agencies can be taking up the slack by moving from rulemaking to adjudication. In many cases, agencies cannot legally accomplish the same things by adjudication that they can by rulemaking. While the FTC might well be able (resource constraints aside) to do most things that it could do by rulemaking through a formal adjudicatory process, the same is not true for the EPA or for the National Highway Traffic Administration.

Moreover, the other techniques for making and implementing agency policy without rules or formal adjudications have unhappy consequences from the standpoint of both political oversight and the rule of law. They involve what is known colloquially as the "informal" regulatory process. Here agencies attempt to work their will through raised eyebrows, negotiations, after-dinner speeches, and, importantly, concessions to those who have the power to force them into more formal modes of action. In short, the loss of rulemaking efficacy is potentially a real loss, not just in policymaking capacities, but also in the transparency and accountability of regulatory agencies for the policies that they adopt and implement.

These observations lead to an obvious question: If the retreat from rulemaking has dire consequences, why are agencies engaging in a process of reinventing themselves that reduces their efficacy? And why are political and legal controllers permitting this process to continue given its unhappy consequences for regulatory efficacy, political accountability, and the rule of law?

Generally speaking, there are two classes of answer to this question. One focuses on the internal agency process and its managerial competence. In short form, the answer is that the rulemaking process is imploding because agencies are badly managed.

This explanation cannot be ignored totally. Good management beats bad management, and virtually no one believes all agencies, or private firms for that matter, are well managed. For several reasons, however, I will not pursue this "internal hypothesis." First, the current state of knowledge concerning the efficacy of particular managerial techniques is quite limited. In a recent unpublished survey of the literature on the management of rulemaking, Cornelius Kerwin, dean of the School of Public Affairs at American University, concludes that "existing case studies are better at identifying what their authors consider shortcomings in the management of rules than at establishing which structures and techniques materially improve rulemaking."

Second, few scholars in the field of organizational theory believe that there is a single best way to organize and manage bureaucratic undertakings. General recommendations or conclusions tend to be poorly supported, subject to so many exceptions that they provide little guidance, or bromides that do little more than repeat the conventional wisdom. The first three conclusions in a "managerialist" study of agency rulemaking done for the Administrative Conference of the United States[14] are illustrative:

The first conclusion, for example, states: "Structural reorganizations frequently do not result in any fundamental improvement to internal systems." This statement is poorly supported by the study. It is based on one episode. Moreover, it seems to contradict the only strong recommendation the study makes, that the "team" structure is the only effective one for the rulemaking process. Both statements cannot be correct — at least at the same place and time.

The second conclusion is that "an adversarial atmosphere often develops among technical experts, legal counsel and other staff offices working together on a regulatory project." In one sense this is a bromide — it is well understood that professional roles and institutional roles create conflicting perspectives. The implicit suggestion, however, is that "adversariness" is an ill to be avoided. Which, of course, is true — except to the extent that adversariness is needed in order to plumb the depths of particular policy issues and ensure that agency processes do not become exercises in "group think." In short, organizations should have enough adversariness, but not too much.

The third conclusion states: "To ensure accountability, federal agencies frequently retain signature authority at the higher levels. This results in inefficiency and staff/line coordination problems." Perhaps. But, as the first phrase of the conclusion states, retaining high-level authority ensures accountability. There is a trade-off here, and the conclusion tells us little about how to deal with it.

Indeed, one might imagine these three conclusions as giving an agency rulemaking manager the following advice: "Don't bother with structural reorganizations; avoid adversariness and decentralize decisionmaking" — is this not structural? — "in order to increase efficiency." A particular manager might sensibly respond, "I intend to reorganize my agency to preserve my authority and to ensure adversarial presentation of differing opinions. Why? Because, given my agency's external environment, ensuring accountability is the most critical managerial issue that I face and, believe me, I am going to be held personally responsible for whatever policy emerges."

In short, as my hypothetical agency manager's response suggested, internal structure may well be a function of the external environment. When one looks inside an agency and finds certain internal conditions that seem dysfunctional in pursuing the agency's rulemaking task, one may be looking at simple bad management. Or one may be looking at a response to some external stimulus or requirement. Because agencies must structure themselves and operate internally in order to succeed or survive in the external environment, this latter explanation will often be promising. Indeed, the ACUS study's third conclusion, by referring to accountability, recognizes the influence of external factors on internal arrangements.

I am perhaps predisposed to view internal structure and operation as responsive to external constraints. Harfst and I describe in great detail the ways in which the power structure and rulemaking processes within the National Highway Traffic Safety Administration were reshaped over the course of two decades to protect the agency against external threats. In the process, lawyers and economists achieved at least parity with, and perhaps dominance over, safety engineers. That these changes thwarted the rulemaking process and shifted the agency's enforcement strategies toward a recall regime having little safety payoff was not the result of "bad management." These internal changes were necessary in order that the agency could survive in its political and legal environment. And the threatening nature of that environment for other agencies seems to be well documented by other case studies. If one wants to improve rulemaking performance, one would do well to attend first to external environmental factors.

JUDICIAL REVIEW

For a number of commentators, judicial review is a prime suspect in the investigation of the abandonment of rulemaking by federal regulatory and other agencies. Losses in court because of uncertainties concerning the "practicability" of its rules have made the NHTSA cautious about using any safety technologies that are not already "road-tested." This has been particularly debilitating for an agency whose statutory mission is to "force the technology" of automobile safety.

In addition, the courts' insistence on responsiveness to outside commentators has caused the NHTSA to structure a highly iterative, and therefore time-consuming, rulemaking process. Delay in turn affects outcomes. Remands of certain crucial rules have altered the political timing of the agency's policy development. Rules that might have been successful at one period have become impossible to promulgate and implement as administrations and congressional personnel change. The willingness of the courts to second-guess the agency has also reinforced the adversarial posture of parties who would be adversely affected either by the agency's rules or by its inaction or vacillation. This view is supported in part by other NHTSA observers,[15] and similar complaints about judicial review are echoed by other commentators with reference to the FTC, FERC, and EPA.

While some commentators argue that some courts are simply too strict with respect to some agencies in reviewing their rules, most seem to argue that the real impediment created by judicial review is uncertainty. Because the courts are relatively uninformed about what is important among the many issues thrown up by parties seeking review of a rule, and because they are technically and scientifically unsophisticated in analyzing the issues that they perceive to be critical to a rule's "reasonableness," the perception in the agencies is that anything can happen. This produces defensive rulemaking, if not abandonment of the rulemaking process.

THINKING ABOUT REFORM

Judicial review is clearly not the sole external contributor to the "ossification" of rulemaking, as the next chapter will detail. Moreover, the American legal system is deeply attached to judicial review of administrative action as a means of attempting to ensure both legality and political accountability. We want the judiciary to rein in arbitrary or unauthorized administrative action, and we view the opportunity for judicial review as a major guarantee of the openness, and hence the political accountability, of the administrative process. Stamping out judicial review is not a sensible or politically viable idea. Reform instead requires a normative vision of how agency rulemaking should function and a strategic vision of how judicial review can be made to support, rather than retard, pursuit of that vision.

A normative vision that fits the practices of American administrative law is not very difficult to articulate. The development of agency rulemaking processes over the past twenty-five years highlights two major concerns: (1) that rulemaking be structured to provide fair opportunities for participation by affected interests, and (2) that it produce reasonable policy choices given the goals of the program and the relevant facts (however complex and uncertain these may be). Built into these notions of fairness and reasonableness are subsidiary norms of timeliness and resource conservation. A process too long-delayed or too expensive may become both unfair and unreasonable.

How should the external environment be structured to promote a fair and reasonable rulemaking process? Once again, abstract description is easy. Private participants should have equal access to decisionmakers and use that access to inform the agency concerning both "the facts" and the proper contextual understanding of the goals that the particular program should promote. External political institutions (Congress and the executive) should seek to assure both that programs are diligently implemented and that particular programmatic missions do not become ends in themselves — so disconnected from broader understandings of the place of the program in overall societal values that they produce unreasonable results. Legal review by the courts should assure that the authority exercised is authority legitimately conferred, that it is neither misused nor neglected, and that the basic norms of participatory fairness and substantive nonarbitrariness are respected.

The challenge, of course, is to design the procedural and institutional mechanisms that will facilitate this ideal external environment without simultaneously encouraging the abusive use of multiple mechanisms for external influence or control. How can checks and balances be established without creating "obstacles" instead? How can we deal with the all too obvious tendency of seriously affected parties to manipulate these needed external constraints for personal or partisan advantage? Or, to put the matter more cheerfully, how can private interest be harnessed to the public purpose of a fair and reasonable rulemaking process?

This last, more positive, formulation of the institutional design issue may also give us some analytic purchase on the problem. In short, if we think like public choice analysts, who would view "abuse" of the rulemaking process as a natural outgrowth of private interests, we have redefined our problem as a problem in the management of incentives. What we want to do, somehow, is to structure procedures and institutional relationships such that the incentives to exert influence by information and persuasion are maintained, as are checks on legality and political "tunnel vision," while opportunities for strategic obstructionism are eliminated. Not so easy, as any institutional architect knows; but there may be some insights to be garnered here, nonetheless. While incentives hardly translate directly into behaviors, careful attention to the incentives built into current arrangements might convince us that improvements are possible, that is, that we can eliminate some opportunities for abuse without simultaneously losing the valuable checks and balances that the external environment of rulemaking provides.

To get a grip on this analytic handle on rulemaking reform,,I have borrowed from public choice to develop something called the "rulemaking review game." The basic idea of the game is quite simple. It assumes that to the extent that an opponent of rulemaking (regulatory or deregulatory) perceives the use of an external obstacle to rulemaking to have a higher expected value than failing to use it, that external constraint will be activated. The question then will be whether we can discover, in current rulemaking processes, situations in which we would like to change the incentives of actors and thus change their calculations about whether to actuate some external constraint. If so, we have found a place where we would like to reshape the rules of the game in the interests of a better rulemaking process.

A Game-Theoretic Analysis of Judicial Review

Game theory is a subdiscipline in mathematics and economics which seeks to model the way in which choices should be made by rational actors, that is, actors who are seeking to maximize their own returns given certain available alternatives.[16] There is no claim by game theorists that actors will *necessarily* behave rationally. The game-theoretic structure merely makes clear what an actor's incentives are and how that actor might maximize its expected returns.

Obviously, when deciding whether to bring a legal action or whether to comply with an agency regulation, a regulated party may not behave in accordance with a simple game-theoretic structure. Hence, for example, a party who objects ideologically to any and all regulation might have very high negative payoffs to compliance, whereas a party that prides itself on being a "good citizen" might have high negative returns from resistance to regulatory requirements, even when it believes these requirements are illegal. In the illustrations that follow, I will not attempt to capture these sorts of preferences, although in most cases the game structure could be modified to take account of them. Instead, I will speak in terms of straightforward economic costs and benefits assumed to influence the modal person or firm.

TO COMPLY OR NOT TO COMPLY

Imagine for illustrative purposes that we are considering a regulation by the National Highway Traffic Safety Administration which requires that certain equipment be included in new passenger cars. Under current law, such a regulation is immediately appealable to a court of appeals. Because NHTSA regulations almost always allow significant lead times for compliance, failure to comply pending an immediate appeal will usually impose no costs on the manufacturers. The question for the manufacturers then is whether to begin immediately to work toward compliance or to challenge the rule in court.

To simplify matters further, we will ask first only whether a manufacturer will comply or not. We will then consider whether the manufacturer will bring an action to seek to invalidate the rule. The two questions are obviously connected, because if the rule remains in effect, a noncomplying manufacturer will at some point begin to incur penalties. For present purposes, however, we will assume that some firm will attack the rule and that during the pendency of that action there will be no penalties for noncompliance. Because there are no penalties for noncompliance, the strategic situation is not one in which the manufacturers view themselves as in a "game" with the federal agency. The important question for them, instead, is what their competitive position will

Table 7.1. Preenforcement Review Game 1

Assumptions: Appeal stays enforcement
           Compliance costs = 5 for each time period
           Sole complier loses additional 2 in market share

		Chrysler (others)	
		Comply	Not Comply
	Comply	-5, -5	-7, 0
G.M.			
	Not Comply	0, -7	0, 0

Payoff (G.M., Chrysler, or others)

be vis-à-vis other manufacturers should they comply or not comply with the rule.

Preenforcement Review Game 1 (table 7.1) illustrates this competitive situation. It makes the following assumptions: Compliance is costly and costs are relatively uniform. Here we assume that there is a compliance cost of 5 for each model year. There is a further cost of 2 if the manufacturer is the only one to comply, because that manufacturer's costs and prices will go up relative to its competitors and it will lose some market share. These numbers are arbitrary, but the structure of the current game does not make that important so long as no manufacturer receives benefits from compliance. The direct costs of compliance have been made greater than the market share losses from sole compliance because that represents the usual structure of demand elasticity in the automobile market — manufacturers do not lose a dollar in revenues for every dollar in increased price of their automobiles.

Looking at the two-by-two game set out in the table, it is not hard to see where G.M. and Chrysler (which is a placeholder for the other members of the industry) will end up. No one will comply. The lower right-hand quadrant is what is called a "dominant strategy" for each player. This is the action that each player will take no matter what the other player in the game does. To be sure, G.M. would prefer to be in the lower left-hand quadrant and Chrysler in the upper right-hand, but competitors have no reason to give each other the satisfaction of complying and losing market share when noncompliance is costless. It would appear that with preenforcement review no manufacturer would ever comply prior to the deadline. Presumably they would always seek judicial review because suit at least delays, and may eliminate, the need to comply.

BUT WILL THEY SUE?

The assumption that manufacturers will always sue, however, is unrealistic. To be sure, it is always in a manufacturer's interest for *someone* to sue,

Table 7.2. The Who Will Sue Game

Assumptions: Preenforcement review with stay of enforcement

                Compliance costs = 5

                Litigation costs = 1

                Probability rule invalid on preenforcement review = .5

                Probability agency will enforce if no one sues or complies = 1.0

		Chrysler (others)	
		Sue	Not Sue
	Sue	2.0, 2.0	1.5, 3.0
G.M.			
	Not Sue	3.0, 1.5	0, 0

Payoff (G.M., Chrysler, or others)

but it is in the interest of each manufacturer not to be the manufacturer who does sue. If someone else sues, all manufacturers get the benefit of the litigation (assuming it is carried out competently), and only those who join the litigation as parties will have to pay for it. This is a classic "free-rider" problem in which everyone wants to free-ride on somebody else's effort. This is the same idea that motivates much of interest group theory's predictions concerning the differential success of groups in political markets.[17] In some circumstances the free-rider aspect of the situation will mean that no one will sue. How likely are we to see that result?

The answer is, not very likely, and for a number of reasons. First, this free-rider problem can be solved by creating an industry association that will bring suit on behalf of everyone. If there is a precommitment to the association sufficient to give it litigating funds, the free-rider issue is solved. Also, in industries like the automobile industry where there are few manufacturers and top executives are well known to each other, there are significant social (and perhaps ultimately economic) costs to welching on one's fair share of expenses necessary to promote the "common good" of the industry. Finally, even in the absence of an effective association or social pressure, the likelihood of suit is quite high. We can see this by looking at the Who Will Sue Game (table 7.2). Here we have kept the compliance cost equal to 5 and added an assumption concerning litigation costs, that is, that they would be at most 20 percent of compliance costs. In addition, we have assumed that the probability is .5 that the rule will be held invalid. Recent experience suggests that this is not an unrealistic probability.

The logic of the payoffs in table 7.2 is just this: If a manufacturer sues it will pay litigation costs of 1 but will avoid compliance costs of 2.5, that is, compliance costs of 5 multiplied by the probability that the rule will be held invalid. Hence, the total payoff from immediate suit is 1.5, if the manufacturer sues alone, or 2.0, if both sue and divide the costs of litigation. Obviously, the manufacturer is better off if someone else sues, but it does not. In that scenario, it gets the 2.5 avoidance of compliance costs and also avoids paying its share of the litigation costs (in a two-manufacturer world: $1 \div 2 = .5$). If nobody sues, the payoff for everybody is 0. There are no gains from suit if no one sues.

Given this set of payoffs, the outcome of the game is indeterminate but the probability of suit is quite high. No player has a dominant strategy. G.M. would like not to sue if Chrysler is going to sue, but G.M. does not know whether Chrysler will; and vice versa for Chrysler. The situation is rather like the infamous teenage game of "chicken." G.M. and Chrysler would like to bluff each other into suing while not themselves suing. However, given that each is better off if it sues than it would be if no one sues, it is rational to chicken out and bring suit yourself. But in order to maintain credibility or "face" for future bluffs, there is also some possibility that neither will sue, even though it would be individually rational for them to do so.

There is, however, a mathematical equilibrium to the game. Indeed, there are three. If one or the other sues, then its competitor need not. We end up in either the lower left-hand or the upper right-hand box. These are stable positions once reached; neither player could individually change its mind and make itself better off. Of course, both could sue out of solidarity, precommitment, or stupidity, but this is not a stable equilibrium because either could withdraw and make itself better off. Because both parties know all this ex ante, the best strategy for each player — that is, the strategy that has the highest expected value — is a randomized approach that has each manufacturer sometimes sue and sometimes not. Whether a party sues or not does not have to be "random" in the statistical sense so long as it is not predictable by the other party. It is also possible to calculate the probability that someone will bring suit. The probability is quite high — 91 percent.[18]

The incentives created by immediate preenforcement review of rules are fairly straightforward. If there are no penalties for noncompliance, it is in no one's interest to comply. And, even with a free-rider problem, the chances are extremely high that litigation will ensue.

Thus far, of course, we have only been talking about suit by regulated parties. But beneficiaries may sue as well if they think that the rule is too weak. How should we model their possible payoffs in the Preenforcement Review Game combined with the Who Will Sue Game? It would seem that the structure of the games beneficiaries play should be similar to that modeled for regulated parties. Beneficiaries have immediate losses from their failure to achieve greater protection by a stronger rule that gives them incentives to sue.

These incentives are symmetrical to the incentives given regulated parties to avoid compliance costs. If we assume that on average benefits equal costs and that litigation is equally costly for each side, then the games are identical and we should expect a similar 91 percent probability that some beneficiary will sue if the rule is recognized as weak. And, of course, the rule could easily look both too weak to beneficiaries and too strong to regulated parties.

We know, of course, that the chances of suit cannot be over 100 percent. The chances that a beneficiary group or regulated party will sue must, however, approach that probability because the "review or not game" between beneficiaries and regulatees should look very much like the basic Preenforcement Review Game 1. Not challenging a "compromise" rule may be the best cooperative result, but it is not a dominant strategy if the "payoffs" to regulated and benefited parties of overturning the rule are equivalent.

THE POWER OF PENALTIES

The game-theoretic situation changes drastically if there is a penalty for noncompliance pending the determination of the validity of a rule. Preenforcement Review Game 2 (table 7.3) alters the situation of Game 1 simply by adding a penalty that is sufficient to deter, that is, that exceeds the gains from noncompliance. Because compliance costs are 5 and market share losses from sole compliance are 2, the penalty would have to be more than 7 to provide a deterrent. With this structure of payoffs, the dominant strategy in the game shifts from the lower right-hand to the upper left-hand corner — everyone complies.

But once again, this game is too simple. First, it is not certain that the penalty will be incurred. After all, the rule might be declared invalid and no penalty would be due. At the very least we need to modify the game to reflect the probabilities of success on appeal. Moreover, success on appeal in this game may be more complicated than the situation described in the Who Will Sue Game. It seems likely, given the payoffs in Preenforcement Review Game 2, that some member of the industry will comply rather than sue. And in the face of compliance, a substantial number of legal arguments concerning the validity of the rule will lose credibility. Many attacks on agency regulations are based on their "unreasonableness," and by "unreasonable" or "arbitrary" the affected parties often mean that the rule requires conduct that is technically infeasible or unreasonably costly. Neither of those grounds will be very plausible to a reviewing court in the face of compliance by one of the regulated parties. Hence, the probability of success changes if someone complies. The question of whether to comply or sue becomes a more complex, probabilistic issue.

Table 7.3. Preenforcement Review Game 2

Assumptions: Appeal does not stay enforcement
         Compliance = 5
         Market share loss from sole compliance = 2
         Penalty = 8

		Chrysler (others)	
		Comply	Not Comply
	Comply	-5, -5	-7, -8
G.M.			
	Not Comply	-8, -7	-8, -8

Payoff (G.M., Chrysler, or others)

THE COMPLY-OR-SUE CALCULATION

The simplest way to illustrate the situation facing a member of the regulated industry where there is no preenforcement review, or where such review does not toll the accrual of penalties, is by a "decision tree." The assumptions underlying this decision tree build on our prior ones. Once again the assumptions are arbitrary, but perhaps not unreasonable.

The idea of the decision tree is simply to trace out all the possible alternative actions available to a player, calculate the expected value of each alternative action, and then see what the total expected value is of a decision to act in a particular way — here either to sue or to comply. We assume in this decision tree that the actor, "G.M.," cannot at the time it makes a decision to comply or to sue know whether it will be successful in its suit or whether some other party may comply in the meantime. Because the actor has no information about the other party's decisions, it simply views the probability that someone else will comply as a chance probability, or .5. Hence, Chrysler, which is the first mover in this game, may comply or not comply, with a probability of .5 for each action. If Chrysler complies, then the probabilities are .9 that the rule will be held valid and .1 that it will be held invalid. But on the branch of the tree where Chrysler does not comply, the probability of either validity or invalidity are .5. The task then is simply to trace out the values for each branch of G.M.'s possible actions. G.M. can decide only to comply or to sue, but it will be doing so in one of four different worlds.

To see how the computation has been done, consider the top branch. There G.M. decides to comply and the expected value of this decision is its actual cost or benefit (here − 5 in compliance costs) times the probability that that state of the world is in fact the one in which Chrysler is complying. To get the

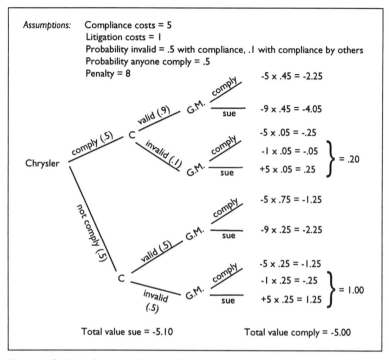

Fig. 7.1. The Comply-or-Sue Decision Tree

probability for that state of the world, one takes the probability that Chrysler has complied (.5) times the probability that the rule will be valid given that Chrysler has complied (.9) and multiples that fraction by the compliance costs. In the branch second from the top, the probabilities remain the same because it is sill the comply/valid world, but the payoffs are modified to reflect the fact that in this state of the world G.M. would lose the lawsuit, incurring penalty costs of 8 and litigation costs of 1. The only situation in which there are positive returns from any action is when G.M. sues and the rule is held invalid. In those circumstances it pays the cost of litigation (-1) but it gains by forgoing the costs of compliance ($+5$).

When all the values are multiplied by the probability that that action is taken in a particular state of the world, one can then total up the expected value of suing and the expected value of complying. Given the total values that emerge from this particular decision tree, G.M. would be almost indifferent as between suing or complying. A slight change in the values that are plugged into the decision tree would shift the balance in one direction or another.

The decision tree thus teaches several important lessons. First, once again, it illustrates that without a penalty for noncompliance the balance of the benefits or costs from litigating or complying will strongly favor litigation. For here the question is close even with penalties. But second, it does not follow that putting a penalty into the system ensures that no one will ever challenge agency action. Indeed, even with a penalty that is greater than the sum of compliance costs and market share losses, an actor whose disbenefits from compliance were only slightly greater than those we have assigned G.M. in this example would still find it rational to bring suit or, what is the same thing, to fail to comply and resist enforcement by raising the potential invalidity of the rule as a defense.

But there is a third lesson here that has been implicit in the whole analysis and that should now be brought front and center: To the extent that judicial review is a contributing factor in "ossifying" the rulemaking process, that problem may not lie in the conventional direction most often debated, that is, the relative stringency of the standard or scope of review. Judicial stringency is but one factor bearing on the likelihood of success in appealing a rule and on the payoffs to appeal versus compliance. The timing of review and the conditions on its availability also shape that calculation, as does the level of compliance costs. There are potentially a large number of policy options here for recalibrating the game so that it has an "appropriate" or "balanced" set of incentives.

Evaluating Policies

Assume for the moment that we believe the charge that judicial review debilitates rulemaking in roughly the ways that prior researchers have described. What policy levers would we like to pull to rectify the situation — remembering all the while that judicial review is a good as well as a bad; that in addition to inducing error, aggravating obstructionism, and demoralizing policymakers, judicial review may also protect against unfairness, irrationality, and nonaccountability?

ATTACKING "SCOPE" OR "STRINGENCY" PROBLEMS

Lawyers argue interminably over the appropriate scope of judicial review.[19] Congress has many times attempted to modulate the stringency of judicial review by changing the verbal formulae on scope of review. Contrary to the Administrative Procedure Act (APA) formulation, "substantial evidence" review was made part of the review provisions for informal rulemaking in a number of the newer regulatory agencies.[20] And a completely different formulation from those found in the act was utilized when judicial review was made available for veterans' claims.[21] In at least some cases — the famous *Universal Camera*[22] case is perhaps the premier example — the courts have believed that legislative reformulation of the review standard was telling them something important about the political branches' expectations concerning the scope of judicial surveillance of agency decision-making.

Yet, some commentators would argue that it is unclear whether "arbitrary and capricious" actually means anything different than "substantial evidence."[23] And where some find the general tenor of judicial review reveals continuing, if episodic, "hard looks," others see "soft glances" or some other metaphoric judicial posture as the new trend. Meanwhile, some of our most experienced judges have told us that how hard they look at any particular agency's determinations depends on a whole host of historical and contextual factors that outrun legislative formulation.[24] There thus seems much wisdom in John Mendeloff's suggestion that the real question in any review proceeding is reasonableness, and that "reasonableness is largely in the eye of the beholder."[25]

Do not overread the argument here. It would certainly make a difference in the judicial review game to change the probabilities of success in one way or another. The payoffs in the game are highly contingent upon those probabilities. Yet it seems a virtually forlorn hope that we might reduce the uncertainties that drive the adversary litigation process by working hard on the question of the scope or stringency of judicial review. New legislative language might put a spin on the process. But, given the other contextual factors that influence the scope of judicial review, even that spin might not be very long-lasting.

Moreover, we know from the literature on civil litigation[26] that the number of suits brought to trial is a function not of the standard for judgment, but of the degree to which plaintiffs and defendants similarly assess the "stakes" in the lawsuit and plaintiff's likelihood of success, that is, the expected value of going to trial. Given the multitude of issues available to be litigated in almost any preenforcement review proceeding and the vagueness of any applicable review standard, the chances that regulated parties, beneficiaries, and the government will assess the likelihood of a successful review differently seems high. In addition, all of these "players" are "repeat players," so that the "stakes" may be different for each, leading to different expected values of litigation even when probability estimates concerning a plaintiff's success in a particular suit are identical. In short, "settlement" of preenforcement review proceedings seems deeply problematic.

There is the additional concern that attempts to reduce the intrusiveness of judicial surveillance, by telling judges to be more respectful of administrative discretion, is neither politically popular nor constitutionally appropriate. To the extent that the Congress has seriously debated any general change in the scope of judicial review of rulemaking, it has largely sought to make review more penetrating, not more deferential. Telling the courts to lay off may be a political nonstarter, even if we believed that altered verbal formulae were efficacious or appropriate.

CHANGING THE STAKES

The preceding game-theoretic models, however arbitrary their quantitative assumptions, also demonstrate quite graphically how changing the stakes in the game matters. Almost no better engine for promoting litigation rather than compliance can be imagined than a scheme that permits immediate review while avoiding all compliance and penalty costs. For while lawyers and litigation are expensive, most major rulemaking proceedings involve issues of such importance to at least *some* firms or individuals that the compliance burden imposed or potential benefits forgone will dwarf the expected costs of litigation.

There might, therefore, be much wisdom in John Mendeloff's further suggestion that trench warfare in the rulemaking process might be avoided by systematic attempts to ease compliance burdens. (He is particularly critical of the OSHA statute which seems to leave the administrator no choice but to impose extremely costly regulatory requirements.) There are indeed many ways to reduce compliance burdens. Lengthening time periods for compliance tends to reduce costs, as do less stringent or less broadly applicable standards. Market-like devices for trading among regulated parties to minimize overall compliance costs also have much to recommend them. Yet, this "reduce the stakes" strategy has some severe problems. One is that it seems to argue that the solution to the problem of too little rulemaking is to do less, or less of significance. In many cases, reducing the stakes is a strategy for solving a problem by surrendering to it.[27]

There is, however, a deeper difficulty. Mendeloff's argument and the stylized game structures that have been portrayed here both tend to assume homogenous compliance costs. The clear fact of the matter, however, is that regulation disfavors (or benefits) some parties more than others.[28] Indeed, for some parties compliance costs may not be "costs," if by that we mean deadweight losses. Sometimes they are investments in future profitability. General Motors did not join with its American automotive competitor/colleagues in attacking the original passive restraints rule, for example, because it held the patents on the airbag technology and expected to reap significant competitive advantage from the regulation. It later waged religious warfare against the National Highway Traffic Safety Administration over that same rule in part because the agency's vacillating prescriptions (through no particular fault of its own) denied G.M. some very handsome profits.

The differential costs of compliance have particular relevance to deregulatory rulemaking. Existing regulations may have radically different effects within industries and their removal will benefit some parts of an industry more than others. Hence, reducing the stakes would have to mean something more than simply reducing regulatory burdens in order to have a significant impact on the use of legal process to wage regulatory warfare. The Investment Company Institute, for example, is surely one of the most litigious trade associations ever formed. Yet its efforts in the judicial arena are more often directed at maintaining regulatory burdens on financial intermediaries outside the scope of its membership list than at fighting battles for a freer market.[29]

Thus, policies that attempt to reduce adversarial obstructionism by reducing the stakes in regulation might virtually have to mimic legislative logrolling. In order to assure nonadversariness, agencies would really be looking for rules or rule relaxations that "fairly" distributed the benefits and costs over all the affected interests, including various classes of regulatory beneficiaries. In this guise, the proposal begins to look either like agency surrender (or "capture") or, more optimistically, a proposal for regulatory negotiation. And while "reg neg" clearly has its place, no one believes that most of the far-flung rulemaking activities of the federal bureaucracy can be reshaped into a negotiating format.[30]

We surely should be concerned about the imbalance in the stakes that results from significant discontinuities in the burdens of complying and litigating. But given the differential benefits and burdens borne by regulated parties, or by the potential beneficiaries of regulations that have been delayed or repealed, it will not be easy to design systems that place the right amount of weight on one or another end of the scales. Incentives for legal combat seem ubiquitous whether rulemakers are regulating, deregulating, or not regulating.

TIMING

Looking at the timing of judicial review is in some sense just another way of stating the stakes problem. The modern penchant for immediate preenforcement review often means that regulated or deregulated parties can choose between litigation and compliance at a time when the litigation alternative is relatively costless. Regulations often have lead times that extend well beyond the point at which an appeal would predictably be concluded, and stays of the effective date of a rulemaking action may be available to protect parties against potentially wasteful compliance efforts in the interim. Yet a concentration on timing as a discrete issue may suggest problems and reform opportunities that would otherwise be missed.

In certain circumstances, for example, the timing of review has complex interactions with the probabilities for a successful appeal. If the availability of immediate review eliminates the incentives of all parties to begin compliance efforts, then it also eliminates the incentives that might otherwise exist to solve some of the feasibility and practicability issues that may loom large in the litigation. Time and again, National Highway Traffic Safety Administration regulations foundered on the shoals of practicability or reasonableness. Yet over time it became clear that many of the technological problems that convinced courts to remand rules to the agency could be solved. Moreover, they might have been solved much earlier had attempts at compliance preceded resort to the judiciary.

The timing of review also radically reshapes the focus of litigation. Review in an enforcement context often concentrates on one or a few issues of particular moment to a particular firm. Preenforcement review invites, and usually produces, the invocation of a laundry list of potential frailties in a rule's substantive content or procedural regularity. The multiplicity of issues available, combined with the unavailability of evidence concerning genuine attempts to comply with the rule, dramatically increase the uncertainties of judicial review.

More than twenty years ago, Paul Verkuil warned us about the shift in the quality of review that would likely result from shifts in timing. In Verkuil's words

> One consequence of the early preenforcement review of rules in the Courts of Appeal is a new focus on rulemaking that, it is believed, will contribute to the creation of a new rulemaking model. In the past, when a rule was reviewable only after enforcement, considerable time could elapse before the rulemaking procedures and the factual basis for the rule were tested. As a result, review of the circumstances surrounding the rule's enactment was secondary and somewhat obscured by time; the main issue was the rule's application to the particular respondent before the court. But with a final order requirement tied more closely to notions of finality and ripeness, rulemaking review can take place almost instantly and the focus on rulemaking process may be much sharper. In this sense earlier review means closer review, which itself leads to a vigorous judicial scrutiny of the rulemaking model.[31]

The critical insight in Verkuil's analysis is his location of the focal point of judicial interest as the "model" of agency rulemaking. Much later Harfst and I dubbed this approach "proceduralized rationality review." Rather than take on the *Lochner*-ian task of substantive rationality review, the courts have "proceduralized" the issues as questions of the adequacy of the agency's explanation; or its responsiveness to objections raised by the rule's opponents; or the adequacy of the "notice" afforded parties, who claim that they would have responded differently had they but known the agency's true plans, or the facts or "methodologies" that it intended to rely upon.[32] The irony, of course, is that these attempts at *avoiding* judicial intrusion on administrative agencies' substantive judgments may have produced uncertainties and "defensive" rulemaking that have contributed much to its "ossification."

All of this suggests that there may be something more to the notion of changing the timing of review than merely its potential strategic significance in shifting incentives toward compliance rather than litigation. It has some "appropriateness" advantages over attempts to alter the scope of review toward soft glances or, even more ambitiously, to reintroduce "nonreviewability" of policy choices as a serious option.[33] To deny immediate review is not to deny review totally. The traditional individual "right" to independent judicial judgment is preserved. Timing also seems more amenable to legislative control than does an attempt to alter scope by revised verbal formulae. In addition, review at the application stage tends to ameliorate the "political" aspects of review (the sense that it is little more than a policy dispute fueled by competitive rent seeking), while simultaneously focusing issues and providing a better information base. "Enforcement" or "implementation" review thus puts the judiciary in a better position to defend its judgments against claims of either incompetence or "political" interference.

There are surely problems with this approach to reform. First, recent developments in congressional legislation and judicial lawmaking have tended almost uniformly in the opposite direction.[34] Preenforcement review has become the norm, and with increasing frequency later review in enforcement proceedings has been barred.[35] The congressional impulse has been to provide an opportunity for quick resolution of claims of invalidity on the theory that legal certainty would benefit both the agency and affected interests.

But inattention to the way in which this resolution of the timing issue shapes the incentives for litigation may have produced perverse results. Not only has the resolution of controversy not been particularly swift, many resolutions may have been unnecessary. And the usual disposition, remand, produces uncertainty plus delay. A period of attempted compliance, experimentation, and negotiation between the agency and affected parties, induced by the unavailability of immediate review, might well produce better rules, swifter compliance, and less litigation. Moving back toward the older regime of rulemaking review primarily at the time of enforcement thus has much to recommend it. For unnecessary judicial review simultaneously stultifies the policy process while imperiling judicial *and* administrative legitimacy.

We must, of course, be careful about the generality of such conclusions. While preenforcement review may have been particularly dysfunctional in the context of standard setting at the National Highway Traffic Safety Administration, it may be extremely important to permit preenforcement review elsewhere, for example, of EPA air quality standards. Those regulations set goals that are implemented through a complex state-federal process which may demand legal certainty in order to mobilize political resources, whatever the costs in legal adversariness. Nor does preenforcement review structure compliance/litigation incentives in the same fashion in other programs. Changes in Federal Energy Regulatory Commission or Securities and Exchange Commission accounting rules can be implemented with very short lead times. Here the option to litigate rather than to comply is sharply constrained, absent a stay of the rule pending the judicial outcome. In other programs, affected parties may find almost any rule providing legal certainty preferable to an unstructured licensing or prosecutorial system. Hence, the prospect of unbalanced incentives to litigate rather than to comply is much less prominent. Moreover, as respects deregulatory rulemaking, there may be little choice but to view the rule as either ripe for review when issued or effectively nonreviewable.

An additional difficulty with attempts to modulate the timing of judicial review is that timing is not just a function of congressional policy. A long line of Supreme Court jurisprudence has reinterpreted the provisions of both the Administrative Procedure Act and other generic legislation to permit preenforcement review. Later congressional statutes that provide for preenforcement review of the rulemaking efforts of specific agencies might be viewed as an effort by Congress to regulate the availability of preenforcement review rather than a legislative attempt to broaden and deepen the Supreme Court's initiative. At the very least, preenforcement review of rules should not be seen as a legislative demand forced upon an unwilling judiciary. Significant congressional action will be required to shift the current conventional view that preenforcement review is presumptively available.

A public choice or game-theoretic approach to the question of judicial review of administrative rulemaking hardly leads in a single or a conclusive direction. Note, however, that here strategic rational actor models do seem to provide some purchase on pressing policy problems and to lead in directions that have tended to be ignored by legal reformers. Whereas I earlier juxtaposed legal idealism and public choice approaches as competitive explanations for the shape of the administrative process we observe, this chapter suggests a potential for cross-disciplinary synergy. Public choice can assist in the achievement of our ideals, not just reshape or mock them.

8

Separated Powers and Regulatory Policymaking

As portrayed in Chapter 7, preenforcement review combined with highly uncertain outcomes and interest group competition produced a legal stranglehold on the regulatory process. The courts functioned as robed roulette wheels churning out results — either "case dismissed" or "remanded to the agency for further development" — in a fashion that approximated chance. Delaying review where possible was suggested as a device for dampening the enthusiasm of the players in this apparently dysfunctional regulatory roulette.

To some degree, the standard complaints about political control of agency rulemaking by the president or the Congress replicate the judicial review scenario. But there are crucial differences. While the outcome of attempts at political control may be equally uncertain, the direction of the pressures on agencies from Congress and the Executive Office of the president have tended to be countervailing. Uncertainty results not from vague legal standards applied by relatively uninformed generalist judges, but from the risks inherent in interbranch competition for control over policy. This gives the "political oversight game" a somewhat different structure than the judicial review game and leads to different conclusions about appropriate reform strategies.

We will begin again by looking at contemporary complaints about political oversight of agency rulemaking. We will then analyze these complaints and reform proposals in very much the same interest group competition spirit that animated the judicial review analysis. Finally, we take up a revised perspective that features institutional competition among the president, the House, and the Senate. From this vantage point, both the stakes and the control techniques embedded in the political oversight game stand out in sharp relief. More important, analysis of this interinstitutional competition helps explain why the political institutions have failed to resist the establishment of the debilitating forms of adversarial legalism that the judicial review game emphasizes.

Politics and Rulemaking

EXECUTIVE OVERSIGHT

While judicial review arguably has been evenhandedly intrusive or constraining with respect to agency regulation and deregulation, executive oversight in the Regan-Bush years generally pressed agencies only in the direction of deregulation or nonregulation. Not surprisingly, these executive branch "reforms" were a lightening rod for proregulatory partisans, while garnering widespread support from antigovernmental and promarket forces. The academic and popular literature on the subject is, to put it gently, extensive. The debate is waged at all levels, from the technical soundness of cost-benefit analyses to the constitutionality of both executive oversight and congressional interference with it. This war is not only a war of words. Heavy political armament is also brought to bear. Presidents have given Office of Management and Budget directors and vice presidents considerable power to delay or quash agency initiatives. Congress meanwhile fights back with confirmation delays, funding quarantines, failures to reauthorize legislation facilitating executive review, and statutory provisions purporting to exempt agencies from all executive consultations.[1]

Whether these delays and displacements are good things or bad things depends importantly on one's perspective on the overall executive regulatory review process. If one's view is that the process produces better coordination of federal policy, more thoughtful regulation, and less costly intrusions into private activity, then delay and displacement are worth their costs. On the other hand, if one believes that executive oversight replaces expert regulation with political expediency, provides preferential access to the regulatory process by regulated interests, and subverts the congressional (and presumably the general political) will, the consequences of executive oversight appear negative.

Outside environmental regulation, which has been the OMB's major target, it is unclear whether regularized executive review through the OMB has had a dramatic impact on agency rulemaking. Because the Office of Information and Regulatory Analysis (OIRA) in the OMB has limited capacity to review agency rules, most rules, even those that satisfy the criteria for "major federal actions," pass through with little OIRA input.[2] Yet it is hard to judge just what impact OMB oversight has by looking at OIRA review patterns. As in the case of judicial review, agencies may organize themselves internally to avoid surprises at the OMB. If so, they will engage in a form of "self-censorship" that gives OMB review an enhanced impact.[3]

Moreover, executive review has often been more overtly political than the relatively technocratic process at the OIRA. Vice President George Bush was an active promoter of "regulatory relief" in the early Reagan years, and later, as president, he gave Dan Quayle a similar mandate through his Council on Competitiveness. While the OIRA might argue with more credibility that it was merely ensuring that regulatory priorities and regulations themselves were based on sound "regulatory analyses," vice presidential interventions have been rightly perceived as "political" rather than technocratic and are responding importantly to the complaints of a Republican president's major political constituency — the business community.

CONGRESSIONAL ACTION

While the actions of the federal judiciary and of the federal executive establishment are often viewed as delaying or derailing agency rulemaking efforts, much congressional activity is ostensibly directed toward forcing its pace. Over the past two decades, the Congress has included hundreds of action-forcing mandates, principally rulemaking deadlines, in federal agency legislation. The congressional tendency to demand action is in part a response to 1960s perceptions of a moribund and often "captured" agency regulatory process. That tendency has been sustained and consistently reenergized by the Congress's institutional competition with the Executive Office of the president as that office, mostly through the OMB, has increased its oversight and review of the agency regulatory process. A substantial period of Republican presidents and Democratic Congresses has given partisan political impetus to this constitutionally sanctioned institutional competition. If ever there were an instance of the fulfillment of Madison's expectation that "ambition [would check] ambition," the last two decades of regulatory politics have provided that example. In the Clinton administration, particularly after the 1994 elections, presidential-congressional roles may have been reversed. But, as we shall see, that does not alter the basic structure of the political competition.

Moreover, proregulatory Congresses versus deregulatory presidents is too simple a story for even the Reagan-Bush years. Congressional action has also been responsible for agency underperformance. For one thing, many observers agree that the Congress has routinely overpromised in its modern regulatory legislation.[4] Statute after statute has declared that problem after problem would be solved through agency regulatory action, with scant appreciation of the scientific or political complexity of the task that was being set. Moreover, as it became clear that many of the objectives sought in this legislation would require massive research and development efforts, Congress has not responded with funding levels that would make accomplishment of its objectives feasible. But neither has it relaxed the statutory timetables or reduced the agenda previously set for agency attention. To some extent, therefore, the sense that agency rulemaking is faltering is the result of ambitions that cannot possibly be met with the resources provided.

Congress also has acted directly to constrain the pace and direction of agency rulemaking. Before it was ruled unconstitutional — indeed afterward as well — Congress appended legislative veto provisions to hundreds of agency statutes. Many of these were attached to rulemaking provisions, thus suggesting serious congressional concern with the good sense of agency proposals or likely proposals.[5] Congress has also used highly specific "appropriations riders" to partially repeal or to delay agency rulemaking activities. And it has matched the executive branch in its willingness to impose analytic review requirements on agency regulatory activity.[6]

While overpromising, underfunding, and contributing to analytic overkill in its legislation, the Congress has seemed to direct its oversight activities primarily at chastising agencies for the slow pace of their regulatory efforts. The specter of administrative agencies failing to protect the public health and safety, as they have been ordered to do by congressional legislation, can often capture media attention and promote particular legislators' personal goals. If some suggestion of bad faith or scandal can be added to agency laxity in the face of an environmental or health crisis, so much the better. As a consequence, the oversight exposé is a popular form of Capital Hill recreation. And while obviously necessary and useful to some degree, congressional bureaucrat baiting has tended to delegitimate the administrative process politically and to further hamper the agency rulemaking process.[7]

The Congress also has a tendency to combine statutory analytic demands with procedural complexity. Not only must an agency analyze a problem itself, it must provide opportunities for outsiders to challenge its analyses and provide analyses of their own. The comments of outsiders, or their testimony and cross-examination, must then be taken into account by the agency in justifying the rationality or reasonableness of its rules. As we have seen, some commentators argue that procedural complexity in administrative rulemaking is the result of a congressional desire to maintain control over the bureaucracy in the interests of the coalition that passed the agency's statute.[8] Others suggest that procedural complexity is a legislative bone thrown to the unsuccessful opponents of regulatory legislation. Whatever the motivation, procedural complexity may render the regulatory program "cumbersome and unworkable."[9]

The plausibility of these lamentations concerning political oversight of agency regulatory efforts gives the vulgar public choice perspective on governmental activity much of its allure. Political life resembles a theater of the absurd where general public demand is satisfied by programs designed to fail and thus to protect the "special interests" who trade politicians money for votes. Access, participation, fair procedures, and rational analytic routines are all smoke and mirrors disguising the sordid business of politics as usual. What's more, the public often seems to believe the "blame the bureaucrats, not us" version of legislative responsibility that sound-bite journalism promotes. Nimbleness at credit claiming and blame avoidance, not the construction of sound policy processes, becomes the skill that ensures incumbency.

Of course, as I argued earlier, this bleak story cannot withstand rigorous analysis. Programs desired by the general public that impose *any* costs on focused interests should not pass. And the public choice version of the origins and functions of administrative procedure does no better than the stories of legal idealists. Yet there is surely enough here to be concerned about, whether it is interinstitutional competition or interest group capture. Let us return to a game-theoretic approach, first to examine the problem of interest group competition and political control, and then to look more broadly at how the competition among governmental institutions steers regulatory policy.

Games, Presidents, and Congresses

Make the following assumption: In a pluralistic polity, the other institutions that form the external environment of agency rulemaking respond to constituent claims in something like the same way that the judiciary responds to litigants. In short, the institution analyzed, whether the OMB, the House, the Senate, or some legislative committee or subcommittee, is presumed to act to attempt to influence the rulemaking process only at the behest of some other person, firm, or interest group. From this perspective, the political institutions are passive until called upon by others, just as we generally view the courts as passive institutions for dispute resolution.

This assumption is, of course, to some degree — sometimes to a considerable degree — false. But it is equally false to imagine that the judiciary is entirely passive with respect to the claims of outside litigants. Judicial doctrine frames the conditions under which litigants may appeal to it, and the judiciary exercises considerable discretion in hearing or not hearing cases. Moreover, it is clear that the judiciary always has institutional interests at stake — at the very least its own legitimacy as a lawgiver. Its actions respond in part to incentives built into our constitutional conception of the judicial role. Hence, viewing litigation as litigant-instigated and uninfluenced by the courts, and the outcome of litigation as either a chance probability or a probability influenced solely by the existence or nonexistence of pertinent information, is also somewhat unrealistic.

After first looking at the institutions that control the political environment of rulemaking in this active-constituent passive-institutions framework, we will reconstruct the game to take account of the strategic reality of institutional competition between the executive and legislative branches. For it is surely also the case that the agencies' nonjudicial, political controllers must be looked at as active participants in policymaking in ways that courts seek to avoid. That analysis, while featuring a discussion of legislative versus executive power in molding rulemaking, will also show us something about the crucial importance of the way in which bicameralism, existing states of the world, judicial decisions, and prior agency decisions determine the outcomes of the rulemaking process.

ACTIVE CONSTITUENTS — PASSIVE INSTITUTIONS

We need not here engage in any further formal constructions in order to say something about the important policy parameters that result from either what we might call the "executive coordination game" or "the legislative oversight game." We know from looking at the judicial review game that there are three important factors bearing on whether claimants or constituents have sufficiently powerful incentives to try to control agency action by appealing to an agency's political principals: benefits (usually the avoidance of compliance costs or the achievement of competitive advantage), costs (in the judicial review game, the out-of-pocket costs of litigation, the possibilities of paying penalties, and some subtler costs of achieving or losing future agency cooperation), and the probability of success on appeal.

One of the principal implications of this prior analysis was that the current structure of preenforcement review skews the incentives of participants fairly strongly in the direction of litigation rather than compliance. One's intuitions are likely to be that the same would be true for appeals to an executive superagency like the OMB or to some part of the Congress. Most such appeals would be made prior to the adoption of a rule, much less its implementation. Moreover, since these sorts of petitions for political intervention might easily result in delay (if not derailment) of the agency's rulemaking process, benefits from delayed payment of compliance costs or the continuation of some competitive advantage from existing regulation (or its absence) should almost always be available. As a former EPA general counsel is reported to have said, "Anybody representing a client who did not use [the OMB] route would be damn negligent."[10]

On the other hand, there are clear costs involved in appealing to either the executive or legislative branches that do not obtain when seeking judicial review. The first is that there are some political constraints on making these sorts of individualized appeals. Claimants before courts are presumably seeking their "rights." Persons seeking intervention by the OMB or by a representative may well appear to be (or be portrayed by their opponents or the press to be) seeking quasicorrupt political favors, even if they avoid arguing anything save the merits of their position. Our political culture has become somewhat cynical, but cynicism is the posture of disappointed idealists. Individuals and organizations have not stopped caring about their reputations for responsible civic behavior.

That the process is political rather than legal also entails a second form of cost. The firm that seeks intervention from the Executive Office of the president, or from the home-state representative on OSHA's appropriations committee, incurs a political obligation. If a firm (or individual) is hesitant about owing an uncertain (and certainly undefined) political debt, it may be dissuaded from making the appeal. There are also direct costs to pursuing the legislative or executive option, just as there are litigation costs associated with appealing to the judiciary. Indeed, given the modern tendency to make such appeals through lawyers, the direct costs may be very nearly the same.

There are opportunity costs to making political appeals as well. The constituent who constantly begs for favors may believe, and quite rightly, that it will soon be perceived as a pest. Hence, what is asked for now may limit what could be asked for in the future. This sense of the opportunity costs of appeal will have some dampening effect on the willingness to use legislative or executive levers, a consideration that may well not obtain at all with respect to litigation. The litigant is generally going before different courts, or at least different judges and different panels seeking its "rights," not favors. And a reputation for being willing to litigate may actually be a negotiating advantage.

Finally, the likelihood of a successful political appeal may be rather limited. Scandal-mongering to the contrary notwithstanding, reports on the actual effects of OMB review of agency regulations suggest that the overloaded Office of Information and Regulatory Affairs can pay scant attention to most rules, even major ones. That someone outside the OMB is importuning it to take a particularly close look at a regulation may help, but influencing OIRA's agenda may be extremely difficult.

As I noted earlier, however, a targeted approach with respect to particular agencies and important rules can have an impact. Analysts who have concentrated on the OMB's relationship with the EPA find substantial intervention, considerable substantive effect, and constant problems of delay.[11] Moreover, experienced participants in the rulemaking processes of agencies that have little or no fear of judicial reversal report that executive branch oversight aided and abetted by congressional analytic requirements has been sufficient to cause the virtual abandonment of rulemaking.

The extent to which OMB involvement is predicated on appeals from privileged constituencies is unclear. One does not have to look far in the environmentalist community to find those who suspect that much of the OMB's interest in the EPA's regulations is stimulated by potentially or already regulated industry. That the OMB and other parts of the Executive Office of the president or the White House establishment act as "conduits" for ex parte representations or lobbying in informal rulemaking also shows up in litigation and is vividly portrayed by the press.[12] Whatever the difficulties of using executive branch contacts to influence rulemaking, a skillful lobbyist can bring a large number of pieces of the executive establishment to bear on a particular rulemaking proposal and can make the life of the proposing agency very complicated indeed.

Playing the "political card" to delay or derail rulemaking activity is surely common on the Hill, but it too faces obstacles. The individual congressperson may often be able to do little beyond passing on the constituent's complaint to the relevant agency. Powerful committee and subcommittee chairs are, of course, differently situated and may importune the agency with greater effect.[13] Nevertheless, we have virtually no data on the degree to which congressional intervention has delayed, derailed, or substantially altered agency rulemaking. The political science literature is in sharp disagreement concerning the influence of congressional oversight on agency action.[14] The legislative veto threat is gone, and while there are numerous appropriations riders sprinkled about in the Statutes at Large,[15] many seem symbolic rather than instrumental. Congress's power to hassle administrators and to claim credit with constituents for intervening with the bureaucracy is legendary, but there is virtually no hard data on the degree to which this external political force is a major impediment to effective rulemaking.[16]

That Congress passes vague and overambitious statutes gives agencies too little resources with which to implement them and constantly revels in the suggestion of bureaucratic laziness and scullduggery is well known. By common consent, the general politics of congressional policymaking is an amorphous drag on the rulemaking process. But that substantial congressional lobbying about agency regulatory activity persists could be attributed to multiple causes: the ignorance of constituents, the credit-claiming/blame-avoiding craftiness of congresspeople, and the public relations skills of Washington lobbyists. Those who keep a rationally calculating gaze on the benefits of seeking congressional assistance, discounted by the probability of success, and compared with the inevitable costs, may be skeptical that the game is often worth the candle.

Even if the intense lobbying of the executive and legislative branches that surrounds major rulemakings is instrumentally irrational, there surely seems to be a lot of it. The executive coordination and legislative oversight games attract hordes of players. For most "behaviorist" analysts, that in itself would be sufficient to prove that the participants were adopting rational strategies, and for them to conclude as well that these games, like the judicial review game, were providing major incentives for adversary political warfare. Further, if this sort of ubiquitous struggle is, as some commentators argue, undermining the timeliness and rationality of rulemaking, then the incentive structures of these games are also ripe for reform.

Indeed, even if all this political pulling and hauling is really much sound and fury signifying nothing of rulemaking substance, it may nevertheless signify much concerning the perceived fairness and rationality of the rulemaking process. After all, a widespread belief in the body politic that the process of agency rulemaking is "just politics," and subterranean politics at that, will undermine the legitimacy of agency policy directives and simultaneously erode administrators' will to resist political blandishments that diminish rather than enhance the quality of the rulemaking product.

Once again, one should not press this argument too far. The notion that agencies are "in politics" is necessary to the belief that agencies are politically accountable. Hence, the rulemaking design issue is how to integrate agencies into the political structure in a fashion that promotes *appropriate* political accountability without detracting too substantially from the perception or the reality of fairness and rationality.

Many commentators seem to believe that the most important reform in this direction is to increase the transparency of political contacts in the rulemaking process.[17] Agencies could bind themselves by rule to include all outside communications, whether written or oral, in their rulemaking dockets. Indeed, with the exceptions of communications from the president, who can claim executive privilege, courts may require "docketing" of this sort in any case.

Suspicions concerning the OMB might also be dissipated by further opening up the OIRA review process. The OMB might itself request that its transmission of communications be included in the rulemaking record;[18] it could avoid the appearance of substantive bias by refusing to waive the necessity for review only because proposals are "deregulatory" in nature; and it could better coordinate its demand that agency regulatory impact analysis (RIA) documents contain sufficient relevant information by coordinating that demand with its regulation of agencies' capacities to require information from regulated parties. An OMB that refuses to allow the gathering of cost and compliance data that it then faults the agency for ignoring in its RIA hardly inspires confidence that it is attempting to improve, not just impede, rulemaking. The Clinton administration has, indeed, instituted many of these reforms.

All of these movements towards transparency raise the costs of inappropriate political importuning of the regulatory process without necessarily impeding legitimate policy oversight and argument. They also provide incentives for the executive and legislative branches to explain why particular appeals for agency changes of policy are either technically appropriate or politically sensible from the wider perspective that necessarily adheres in the Congress and the office of the chief executive.

Further "strategic thinking" about the political oversight game suggests, however, that we should be wary of claims that transparency within the rulemaking process will have major effects on special interest pleading or on the ponderousness of the administrative regulatory process. Indeed, the requirement that everything be "on the record" tends to multiply both record keeping and explanatory tasks. When a lobbyist or congressperson suggests a bad idea off the record, a bureaucrat can respond quickly and pungently or obfuscate ("We'll sure consider that, Congressman"), without later having to write a rationale, perhaps backed by factual investigation, in the agency's "concise statement of basis and purpose" justifying the rule. If the comment is on the record, detailed explanation of its rejection may be thought essential to avoid prickly questions on judicial review of the rule.

In addition, if interest group theory works even somewhat similarly to what the public choice fraternity believes, transparency is a double-edged sword. A quarter-century ago (before 1969), when the Ways and Means Committee marked up tax legislation in executive session, lobbyists were easily told by committee members, "I did the best I could, but the chairman (or majority, or whatever) wouldn't go along." Now that mark-ups are open to the "public," guess who the public turns out to be? Mostly the same old special interests who can now *see* whether their congressperson really did his or her best for them. The same thing might be true of a complete and transparent agency record. It would help special interests monitor their erstwhile spokesperson.

Translated into public choice lingo, "Transparency lowers the 'agency costs' to organized interests."

Do not misunderstand me. I am not jumping on the McNollgast band-wagon and yelling, "See, procedural reform is just another way of 'stacking the deck' for favored interests." Encouraging procedural transparency may be the best that we can do to limit political importuning and shore up administrative legitimacy, if not efficacy. But thinking through the ways that rational actors in a pluralist bargaining game can turn transparency to advantage should at least induce more realistic assessment of what can be accomplished. "Transparency" thus becomes a strategic institutional design tool, not an end in itself. Justice Brandeis reportedly said that "sunlight is the best disinfectant" for a susceptible political process. A public choice perspective helps us at least to see that this rallying cry for decades of idealistic reformers should not go unexamined. Bandages are opaque, but they keep out a lot of bacteria.

The Legislative-Executive Separation of Powers Game

As I noted earlier, the "political oversight game" is not just one in which outside claimants or constituents appeal to different political institutions for help in their adversary battles for the hearts and minds of federal agencies. These political institutions also have constitutional roles that structure their two-century-long competition for control over the policy process. If Madison was right, in performing those roles political actors support normative considerations of constitutional design concerning separated powers in a liberal democracy. The separation of powers thus harnesses their desire to please constituents and reward supporters to broader conceptions of the public good. Looking at the problem in this way suggests some quite different insights about (1) the relative power of different institutions to control agency policymaking, and (2) why over time Congress and the courts have "proceduralized" and "legalized" the forms of internecine warfare that now surround the administrative rulemaking process. This institutional analysis also throws into sharp relief the differing directions down which reformers might proceed in improving the environment of agency rulemaking.

The spatial model that describes this game is a somewhat more elaborate version of the simple linear model discussed in Chapter 4. It imagines that policy is defined by a two-dimensional space in which the president, the House, and the Senate each have preferred points.[19] These are represented on figure 8.1 by the dots labeled P, H, and S. Q is the status quo or the present state of the world. Q obviously does not conform to the preferred position of any of the three institutions. It lies, however, at the intersection of an indifference

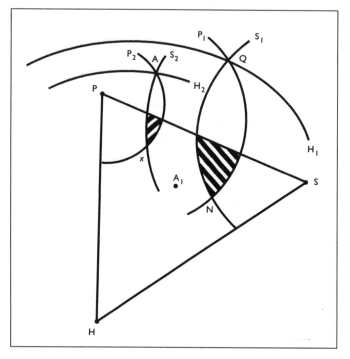

Fig. 8.1. The Legislative-Executive Separation of Powers Game

curve for each body. (An indifference curve is simply a curve connecting all the points that are equidistant from the institution's most preferred point. It is called an indifference curve because it is presumed that an institution or actor is indifferent with respect to points that are equidistant from that institution or actor's most preferred point.)

Because the House, Senate, and president each in effect have a "veto" over any legislative proposal, they must bargain about policy. The possible bargains that will make them all better off are defined by the lens QN. All the points within that lens are closer to the preferred positions of *all* of the actors than is Q. Hence, it is rational for them to make an agreement to enact legislation that defines a policy somewhere within that lens. Indeed, because the House (whose indifference curve is labeled H_1 as it runs through Q) can always propose some policy within the half-lens that is inside the triangle, and that makes it better off and neither the president nor the Senate worse off, there is no reason for the House ever to agree to a bargain that lies outside of the line PS. The relevant policy space within which a bargain should be struck is therefore the half-lens inside the triangle. Any legislation agreeable to all the parties will define a point somewhere within that half-lens. Given that all legislation is vague to some degree, it might be more realistic to imagine statutes as defining the half-lens as the jurisdiction of agencies which can then choose policies within that space.

From a normative perspective, the external environment of rulemaking should be structured to force administrative policy choice within the half lens. That is the democratically approved bargain embodied in the legislation. Ideally, we should want the House, the Senate, and the president to nudge the agency toward policy choice within this domain and to press it back into the area defined by the presidential-legislative bargain whenever an agency's policies, for our present purposes embodied in rules, stray from the half-lens of approved policy. Judicial review, not yet represented in the model, should have the same purpose. So far so good, but a little further analysis reveals that it is not so easy to make this system work well.

Assume, for example, that the administrative agency chooses a policy that lies at A. A lies closer to the president's preferences than any policy within the half-lens defined by the legislation, and further from the House and Senate's. If the Congress had a legislative veto, it could quash the agency's choice and presumably any other choice that lay outside the half-lens. But the Supreme Court has ruled the legislative veto unconstitutional, whether by one house or by both acting together. Without the legislative veto, Congress, or either house of it, must use other techniques to try to force an agency to live with the original statutory bargain, or rely on the judiciary to invalidate the agency's action at the behest of some adversely affected person. But, as our continuous experience with administrative governance has demonstrated, it may be quite difficult for the Congress to enact legislation that will not leave a broad range of discretion to an agency — discretion broad enough to make judicial policing for legality a problematic device for assuring the integrity of legislative-presidential bargains.

In the absence of effective judicial review to maintain the original bargain, or some other technique for putting pressure on the agency not to choose A, the House and the Senate can legislate to revoke the agency's policy choice and adopt a policy more pleasing to the Senate and the House. Note, however, that the new legislation will prescribe a policy somewhere in the half-lens defined by x and the intersection of the lens with the line PS. Any legislation seeking to move policy back into the lens defined by QN will be vetoed by the president. And, as the history of attempts to override presidential vetoes reveals, Congress is seldom successful in that enterprise.

The stakes involved in the constitutionality of the legislative veto may thus have been somewhat higher than they appeared at first blush, even to those who, like Justice Byron White, believed Congress needed that weapon to maintain parity with the president in the modern administrative state.[20] It is not just that without the legislative veto Congress will have to act by legislation (and perhaps by a supermajority) to overturn a policy with which it is displeased. Because policy choice in a bargaining situation is a function of both the preferences of the actors and the status quo point, in the face of presidential opposition Congress literally cannot get back to the policy space that it thought it and the president had defined in the preexisting statute. This may help to explain why Congress has developed a multitude of other techniques to try to regain the political control that it had with the legislative veto threat, notwithstanding its extremely sparing use of the veto when it was available.[21]

Another interesting aspect of looking at policy choice in this fashion is that it reveals something more about the power of an administrative agency under different assumptions about the efficacy of judicial review. Thus, for example, if the agency were to choose a policy like the one indicated at the dot labeled A_1 in figure 8.1, there would be nothing that any of the political actors could do about it through legislation, and only a modest prospect for correction on judicial review. The political actors are disabled from changing the policy by legislation because a policy anywhere within the triangle defines a point from which it is not possible to move without making one of the three actors worse off. The disadvantaged institution will thus veto that move and preserve the policy. (Were we to draw indifference curves for P, H, and S that run through A_1, it would be clear, for example, that any move back toward the lens defined by N and the line PS would make both the president and the House worse off and only the Senate better off.) Any policy inside the triangle is stable.

We might imagine that judicial review could be invoked to move agency policy back within the lens. But if we think for a minute about the task of discerning exactly where the original legislative-presidential bargain came to rest, we may be doubtful about any court's capacity in this regard. Looking at the terms of the statute and the initial statements (or bills favored) by the House, the Senate, and the president might well define a general space like the triangle PHS. Hence the choice of A, outside the triangle, might well be invalidated. But it seems quite optimistic to imagine that the much smaller policy space defined by the lens will appear with clarity to a reviewing court. Therein lies part of the wisdom of judicial deference to administrative judgments. For if the court mistakes legislative intent, then *it* will, through its interpretation, define a new status quo point which either will also be stable (if within the triangle) or will lead to a wholly new policy (if outside the triangle) that was not the intent of the legislative-presidential bargain in the first instance.

The likelihood, then, is that agencies will have significant power to make policy choices within the broad boundaries of the political space defined by the preferred positions of the three political institutions to which they are accountable. The separation or "balance" of powers stakes in rulemaking are thus high, even if we assume that each institution is acting out of its own sense of good public policy, not as a simple conduit for private interests. From this "institutional" perspective, it is hardly surprising that agency rulemaking is a major constitutional battleground. What we need now to address is why this political-institutional competition has resulted in a rulemaking process that provides a major example of what Robert Kagan has called "adversarial legalism."[22] Put another way, why has the "legislative-executive separation of powers game" produced the "judicial review game" and all its attendant political checks and balances (the executive coordination and legislative oversight games) that empower rulemaking opponents and ossify the rulemaking process?

From Games to Institutional Design

The legislative separation of powers game and adversarial legalism leveraged by ubiquitous preenforcement judicial review are closely connected. It is not mere coincidence that the examples of agency choice modeled in figure 8.1 were all tilted toward presidential preferences. Appointment and removal powers, OMB review, and the simple fact of agencies generally being a part of the administrative "team" all tend to give presidents an advantage in molding agency behavior.[23] Without an easily exercisable veto over agency rules, the Congress must fight back either directly (with much more specific legislation) or indirectly (through oversight, jawboning, or the empowerment of surrogates), even if all of these techniques may do more to clutter the landscape of rulemaking with legal obstacles than to improve its fairness, rationality, or conformity to legislative-presidential policy compromises.

In particular, the McNollgast thesis — that much of the procedural complexity and legal control that Congress now builds into rulemaking statutes has its origin in a congressional need to empower its constituents to police legislative bargains that it cannot monitor or enforce on its own — could be seen to be motivated not just by self-interest, but by a real problem in maintaining the balance of separated powers in an administrative state.[24] While I argued earlier that this analysis is somewhat overdrawn, if taken as an attempt to explain the overall structure of administrative procedure, there is surely some power to the argument as well. Arbitrary time limits, "hammers," procedural complexity, analytic requirements, heightened evidentiary demands, and instantaneous access to judicial review all give legislative constituents (and others) levers with which to press agency policies in the direction of the original legislative-presidential bargain. (Whether they are well designed for this task is, of course, a different question.)

Thus, however much administrative law responds to deeper currents in our constitutional culture, the political scientists' story surely suggests that Congress has powerful incentives to institute or continue potentially debilitating and delegitimating "legal rights" for various constituencies to challenge agency policy choice. Other means of policy control at its disposal are either weak (oversight) or have all too obvious risks of political or policy disaster (specific legislative commands adopted under enormous uncertainty about their consequences).

Although the public choice literature has tended to ignore the presidential role in creating legal checks and balances on agency rulemaking, we seldom find the president vetoing legislation because it provides too much in the way of judicial review or rulemaking procedure. And even though the president or the Executive Office of the president seems generally to attempt to influence the rulemaking process through administrative or political means, proceduralized rationality review may well leverage the positions of both executive departments and their constituencies. While the analytic requirements embodied in various executive orders concerning major rulemakings explicitly exclude judicial review of the quality of those analyses, the analyses nevertheless become a part of the rulemaking record. So do analyses provided by other executive departments. Judicial review of agency rulemaking on "the whole record" thus reinforces the necessity for agencies to respond cogently to the positions put forward by executive department agencies and superagencies.

In this sense, then, the courts' struggles to "relegalize" the legislative-executive political warfare surrounding rulemaking — to make it fit the judicial role by creating the contemporary technique of review for "process rationality" — leverage the weight that political warfare between legislative and executive institutions adds to the inertia of the whole rulemaking system. For if the story that we have been recounting is true, there is a mismatch between political motivations and constitutional purposes, on the one hand, and legal technique on the other. Legal control is being employed to leverage political-institutional warfare about administrative policy in ways that disempower the policy process.

The American administrative state replicates the more general tensions built into a liberal democratic legal order. The majority rules, but individuals have rights; and majoritarian preferences are not always consistent with the protection of individual liberties. Similarly, the normative project of administrative law has been to reinforce the political and legal accountability of administrative agencies. But just as reinforcing political accountability supports democracy, so legal accountability features the protection of individual rights. Control through judicial review thus replicates in a legal form the continuous conflict between political preferences and individual rights. The judicial response to this competition has not been, indeed could not be, to resolve it but to manage it through the construction of "fair procedure" and the oversight of "process rationality."

Political controllers also often favor proceduralized forms of oversight. And because administrative agencies have multiple principals who compete for control over administrative policymaking by creating their own multiplicitous devices for monitoring and sanctioning errant administrators, administrative processes grow more and more cumbersome.

The resulting position of administrative governance in the United States is thus surely peculiar. Given vague statutes and competition for primacy by multiple principals, administrators seem to have significant policy discretion. On the other hand, critics see them as consistently underperforming in relation to their statutory mandates. Administrators seem to have vast political discretion but modest ability to use it. And that inability seems to be a direct product of the "adversarial legalism" generated by pluralist politics and interinstitutional competition dressed up in the forms of legal rights. The administrative leviathan is like Gulliver among the Lilliputians: He could crush them if he could just stand up.

Public choice scholars are, of course, not the first to have noticed that American administrators manage to appear both tyrannical and ineffectual at the same time. To use James Freedman's terminology, this is the "crisis of legitimacy"[25] that American administrative law has been attempting to address at least since the New Deal. Nevertheless, looking at these problems through the lens of public choice ideas helps us to understand just how intractable these issues are given our form of governance. Principal-agent analysis helps to sharpen our understanding of the problems of administrative accountability in a constitutional system based on separated powers and hence multiple principals. And a game-theoretic approach, which includes the judiciary and judicial review in the mix of competing claims on administrators' attention, helps to explain how we can appear to have such massive amounts of governmental activity while producing modest policy outputs.

Looking at these problems in this way also helps to explain why parliamentary systems have consistent allure for American governmental reformers. For as long as we have a government of separated powers with a strong commitment to rights enforcement through judicial review, it is unlikely that we will also have a strong sense that administrators can be both effective and accountable. Parliamentary systems, by contrast, radically reorganize the electoral game in ways that tie the fate of elected politicians to the efficacy of administrations. Heads of ministries are expected to combine energy with accountability. Professional bureaucrats can remain accountable to the party in power because although governments change, it is always possible to know who the government is.

Moreover, because administrators in parliamentary regimes have one political principal, who can be held accountable for administrative policy at the polls, judicial excursions into general administrative policymaking are as infrequent as into the control of legislative action. Where political accountability is clear, courts may protect individual rights without being called upon to review the good sense of administrative policies.

Of course, on closer inspection parliamentary systems have their own dysfunctional attributes. My point is not to argue for major constitutional revision in the direction of the British parliamentary system. My point instead is that looking at administrative action and its control from the public choice standpoint of struggles among competing interests and institutions is a sobering enterprise. The nested set of politico-legal games that characterize the American administrative state strongly shapes what administration and administrative legality can and will be. There surely are ways to restructure the game in order to make it serve us better. But a principal-agent\game-theoretic perspective makes clear just how much careful analysis is required before useful reform is likely to be revealed. At the very least, when coming at these problems from a public choice perspective, one is unlikely to think that ideal arrangements are just around the corner. Or that slogans like "transparency," "access," and "legal control" do much to advance our understanding of how reform should proceed.

9

Public Choice Pragmatics

Although the precise issues change from decade to decade—indeed, from year to year or week to week—American public law is continuously preoccupied with the general issues that have been canvased in the preceding pages: How actively should judges review statutes for constitutionality or administrative judgments for arbitrariness? What is the best way to interpret statutes? How does the separation of powers really work? What should be the role of administrative action in a liberal democratic constitutional regime? My purpose has been to rethink these issues in the light of public choice ideas: voting theory, interest group theory, and game theory (including agency theory). The time has come to review these discussions briefly to see what we have learned. Is public choice a useful way to think about the perennial problems of American public law? If so, how? And to what degree?

A Pox on Public Choice

For some, the answer to these questions seems straightforward: To its detractors, public choice theory is not only useless, it is pernicious. It fails to do a good job of either prediction or explanation; it reinforces a cynical view of public life that tends to eliminate the possibility of public-spiritedness; and to the extent that it tells us anything, it tells us things that we already knew.

As we have seen, these critics clearly have a point. Public choice theorists, at least some of them, have some very bad habits. They tend to overclaim, oversimplify, and reinvent wheels that have been better engineered elsewhere. Yet, I am uncomfortable with the suggestion that we would be better off to forget about public choice ideas and get on with the business of improving public law and public institutions.

It is true that public choice theorists have committed high crimes against social science methodology. But so have most practitioners in most domains of social inquiry. "Controlled tests" of social science hypotheses are generally unavailable. Empiricists are left then with oversimplified laboratory experiments or heroic regressions that may or may not have accounted for the relevant variables. Empirical social science, public choice included, varies enormously in quality. It must all be handled with care if one's purpose is to translate "findings" into public policy. Here, it seems to me, James Buchanan has got the matter essentially right. The issue is not whether public choice has elegant and persuasive explanations for the workings of public law processes. The important question, instead, is whether the public choice approach can assist in institutional design.

"No" is not a plausible general answer to that question. The most basic premises of social choice analyses merely remind us that people will pursue their own or institutional interests, at least some of the time, and that those attempts to realize private or institutional benefits are structured in different ways by different decision rules. Were we to forget those general propositions, we would surely be poor institutional designers, however laudable our goals and however sophisticated we were about the normative ideals of liberal democratic constitutionalism.

The harder question is whether public choice scholarship tells us anything in particular about institutional design that is not already known by sophisticated public law scholars or practitioners. Those who would respond "no" to that question are difficult to answer because it is not clear what evidence would refute their claim. They seem to be saying that they have sufficiently well developed intuitions about these matters that they are never surprised by public choice findings — save, perhaps, where the public choice results turn out to be wrong. There may indeed be such people. And there certainly may be a good many for whom useful public choice findings are modest in relation to the effort that is expended in producing them.

Nevertheless, I think that the discussions in the preceding pages suggest that there is a good bit of use here for most students and practitioners of public law. In part, the utility lies precisely in refining our intuitions or making us more sensitive to the types of institutional dynamics and potential institutional failures that preoccupy public choice analysts. More particularly, the public choice analyses that we have canvased often *contradict* the intuition-based analyses that populate major fields of public law. In the paragraphs that follow, let me draw out a few of these lessons both to summarize and to reinforce the prior discussion.

The Lessons of Voting Theory

Some commentators have misused voting theory to create grotesque cartoons of collective action and to engage in rampant "democracy bashing." Yet, properly understood, Arrovian voting theory does not demonstrate that collective choice processes are necessarily chaotic or that their outputs are uninterpretable. Nor does it delegitimate the democratic pedigree of representative elections or public assembly action. Indeed, sensibly applied, voting theory can lead us to think more carefully about some cherished images of "democracy" and to see them in a different and more revealing light.

The first useful lesson of voting theory is a debunking of naive populism. Americans seem to have a nostalgia for a lost Eden of popular sovereignty, whether represented by a vision of an eighteenth-century New England town meeting or by Ross Perot's late twentieth-century electronic plebiscites. Voting theory teaches us that, whatever this yearning for direct democracy, it is likely to disappoint our expectations if put into practice. If the political process allows anybody to put anything on the table to be voted up or down against any number of alternative proposals, the outcome is likely to be chaotic. Decision processes must be structured by rules that exclude possibilities and that order the consideration of proposals.

That such processes and institutional constraints divorce "majority rule" from the "direct will of the people" is a fact. But voting theory teaches us that this is not a fact that is or should be taken to be a criticism of mediated democracy. Direct democracy is not just expensive and time-consuming to organize; the outcomes of direct democratic processes have no particular claim to be the "will of the people." We can therefore set about the business of designing good institutional structures for collective decisionmaking freed from the potentially delegitimating image of a lost populist-majoritarian ideal. Representative democracy with highly structured institutions for assembly choice is not a pale shadow of "true democracy." True democracy, if by that we mean voting processes that accurately reflect the aggregate preferences of all of the populace over all issues for collective action, has never been an available option.

Perhaps nowhere has this idea of the popular will been so pernicious as in the constitutional lawyer's repetitive mantra of the "countermajoritarian difficulty." This catchphrase has structured decades of theorizing about the appropriate role of judicial review. But a moment's reflection on the teachings of voting theory makes clear that whatever the difficulty with judicial review, countermajoritarianism is an odd way to put the problem. If the suggestion is that courts reviewing statues confront the true will of the people, then the image is surely false. Not only do we not have popular democracy in the sense that this vision of the "countermajoritarian difficulty" suggests, we could not have it. On the other hand, if all that is meant is that a majority of elected representatives voted for this bill, then "countermajoritarianism" loses a good bit of its punch.

The real issue in structuring judicial review has to do with different modes of accountability for different branches of our government and how those differing modes of accountability should structure their respective competencies. To put the question in this way does not make the question of judicial review easier. But so phrased, it does not prejudge the potential sources and limits of the legitimacy of judicial "second guessing" of legislative judgment, as does the "countermajoritarian difficulty" mantra. To be sure, not all constitutional lawyers or constitutional law scholars forget this all of the time. But enough of them do enough of the time to make one wish that they were forced to take a course in at least the voting theory aspects of public choice.

A second perception about legislative processes follows quite readily from the first. Voting theory helps us to appreciate just how crucially important procedural structures are to collective outcomes. Moreover, because legislative policy decisions are highly structured, chaos is not the likely result of collective decisionmaking. Procedural structures are designed to permit purposive action, as well as purposive obstruction.

This "institutionalist" perspective on legislation suggests that crucial actors can be identified whose utterances and actions have high salience for understanding the meaning that was intended to be given to statutory terms. As McNollgast plausibly argue, when combined with a game-theoretic understanding of when actions or utterances "count" in the legislative process, attention to structure and process can guide an intelligent utilization of legislative history in the interpretation of statutes.

This may be an insight that merely reinforces the intuition of many judges and lawyers. Most lawyers and judges act as if what legislators say in the legislative process is probative on questions of statutory interpretation — and that some expressions are more probative than others. Nevertheless, it is a reinforcement that seems needed in the face of a relentless "textualist" critique that seeks to delegitimize all (or most) uses of legislative history.

The Lessons of Interest Group Analysis

Interest group explanations of legislative, bureaucratic and, even judicial outcomes have often been little more than examples of post hoc, ergo propter hoc ("after that, therefore because of that") logical fallacies. This is the arena of public choice theory in which most felonies against social science have been committed. Nevertheless, there is much good sense in thinking about organizational influences on public policy, while avoiding simpleminded approaches that, like Judge Easterbrook's approach to statutory interpretation, translate the possibility of interest group influence into algorithmic prescriptions for cramped statutory interpretation.

For example, the taxonomy of statutory types that William Eskridge has constructed using public choice ideas can provide a useful checklist of positive and negative signals about the "public-spiritedness" of legislation. Employed as a prod to serious thought, rather than as a conclusion about underlying processes, Eskridge's taxonomy becomes a set of useful reminders and suggestive rules of thumb. In a similar vein, Bruce Ackerman analyzes the *Carolene Products* footnote from an interest group perspective and finds it a naive guide to the full range of danger signals that should have some influence on judicial review for constitutionality. Judges would surely be better instructed to consider the problem of diffuse and unorganized majorities as well as the difficulties of discrete and insular minorities in the legislative process. In both cases, systematic thinking about the potential effects of interest group formation and activity takes us well beyond conventional intuitions.

The Lessons of Game Theory

Broadly considered, a game-theoretic perspective, including agency theory ideas, seems to have much to teach us. The critical insights of game theory are those having to do with the way in which decision processes may create perverse incentives or sharply constrain possible outcomes.

The perverse-incentives problem was much in evidence in my discussion of the "judicial review game" that characterizes preenforcement review of administrative rulemaking. While lawyers have seen this technique for legal control as an important bulwark against administrative arbitrariness, preenforcement judicial review seems increasingly to be a formula for adversary legalism and regulatory, or deregulatory, gridlock. Investigating the dynamics of judicial review from a game-theoretical perspective helps make sense of why a plausibly praiseworthy institution may turn out to produce unhappy results. It also suggested a focus on the timing of judicial review that has heretofore been thought to be of modest relevance to the "ossification" of the administrative rulemaking process.

A game-theoretic perspective also had some sobering news concerning the dynamics of policy change should the legislative branch feel that either the judiciary or the executive has failed to implement statutory norms appropriately. While there is much conventional wisdom about the difficulty of mobilizing legislative majorities to undo the mistaken activities of either agencies or the judiciary, the conventional wisdom significantly understates the difficulties that the legislature encounters. Structuring this problem either in the way that Eskridge and Ferejohn articulate the Article I, Section 7 game, or as I later portrayed the separation of powers game, causes certain salient features of legislative bargaining, to appear in sharp relief. In particular, it demonstrates both the crucial importance of status quo points in decisionmaking and the degree to which legislative systems may be stable in the face of implementing actions that clearly violate the original understanding of the statute.

These results are sufficiently powerful that a couple of caveats might be useful at this juncture. Although not much was made of it in the prior discussion, the judicial review game, for example, is highly sensitive to the hypothesized numerical parameters in the examples. Changes in the costs of compliance, the likelihood of judicial reversal, the size of penalties, or the dimensions of competitive disadvantage, all would produce different net costs and benefits from pursuing judicial review. Every attempt was made to choose values that were plausible in the light of recent experience, but that is not the same as saying that the "game" describes reality.

Second, game-theoretic models are "static" in the sense that they view the preferences of actors as stable. Hence, when I illustrated deviance from an agreed legislative outcome by placing a judicial interpretation or administrative action at some point different from the original "legislative bargain," there was at least the suggestion that the judiciary or the administrator had the power to undermine legislative preferences. This is true so far as it goes. However, to the extent that implementing action or interpretive decisionmaking influences the way that legislative participants understand their own actions, preferences may shift. Once taken and explained, implementing action that deviates from the original legislative compromise may seem preferable to all participants when compared with their original "bargain." Seen in this light, interpretation or implementation can be understood as a power to participate actively in an ongoing process of constructing legislative meaning, rather than as a power to subvert legislative preferences in favor of those of either the judiciary or the executive branch.

Indeed, if the public choice perspective has one overarching defect, it is the static images of public life that inhabit its stories and puzzles. Political actors generally have fixed preferences and interests; decisions emerge as fully specified contracts or "deals"; implementors should be, but constantly threaten not to be, "faithful agents," committed to realizing predetermined results. Public choice practitioners and consumers make their most serious errors when they forget that those stylized assumptions are not necessarily true or desirable.

Delegation of Authority to Administrators: A Synthetic Example

One way of solidifying ideas about the utility of public choice analysis of public law problems is to apply all of the perspectives that make up the public choice tool kit to a particular issue. Examining the good sense and likely effects of delegating policy authority to administrators provides an instructive example of how public choice analysis can illuminate the pros and cons of particular institutional choices.

During the vast expansion of administrative capacities at the federal level in the New Deal era, the American Bar Association issued a statement describing administrative agencies as that institution "beloved of tyrants and abhorred by free men." However hyperbolic this statement may have been, the ABA was surely on to something. Administrators implementing vague statutory language have substantial discretion and very important "first mover" advantages. As the separation of powers game illustrates, administrative action may be impervious to legislative change, provided the administrator stays within the general bounds of the preferences of the House, the Senate, and the president. The question is whether this is a good thing from the standpoint of either democratic governance or the general welfare.

Some in the public choice fraternity clearly believe the answer is no. But I was critical of their response because it seems premised primarily on the notion that vague delegations facilitate legislation. Delegation of authority to administrators may well lower the cost to legislators of reaching agreement. But that has no determinate implications for whether such delegations support or subvert democracy or the general welfare.

Others have developed elaborate theories of why administrators will consistently escape effective control by the legislative branch because of administrators' substantial monopoly on information. Not only will this allow administrators to pursue the policy they prefer, it will empower them to extract greater and greater budgets from legislative committees engaged in monopsonistic bargaining concerning the agency's future budget. Yet, further public choice perspectives suggest that these concerns may be overdrawn and that there are democratic advantages to the delegation of authority to administrators.

From a game-theoretic perspective, for example, it seems clear that monopsonistic bargaining with legislative committees is not the only "game in town" when it comes to constraining administrative discretion. Judicial review obviously has a major, potentially disabling, impact on administrative policy-making. This may result in part from the dynamic that McNollgast described: congressional attempts to monitor agency action through procedural devices backed by judicial review. Moreover, it seems clear that the president has very substantial power with respect to administrative policymaking through the simple devices of appointments, removals, and "administrative leadership." Even if direct congressional control is limited, other legal and political controls may make administrative action both perilous and protracted. Whether administrators are the tyrants of midcentury ABA imagining or the "wimps of Washington" depends upon the highly complex analysis of the particular position of particular agencies with respect to particular issues. Public choice analysis illuminates these issues without by any means speaking with one voice.

Thus, for example, the presidential power to influence agency action has ambiguous democratic consequences. It clearly detracts from *assembly* control of administration. An agent with two principals, moreover, may effectively have none. On the other hand, "democratic control" and "assembly control" are not synonymous. Because presidential politics are more ideological and party-based than interest group–based, presidential control of administration may help to reconnect agency action to the general political process and to avoid some of the worst forms of agency capture through interest group persistence. The requirements of open processes and rationalized decision-making embodied in administrative law may push in the same direction.

Finally, the delegation of authority to administrative agencies may provide assistance in avoiding some pathologies of majoritarian voting. For example, a proposal to grant broad authority to an agency under general criteria poses a particular sort of legislative question. At its most general, it asks whether the legislature favors an attempt to solve this problem over maintaining the status quo. It thus puts the choice in a binary form that removes considerable scope for intransitivity or inconsistent legislation were the legislature to attempt to arrive at specific remedies itself. Moreover, delegation to an agency bound by administrative law's procedural and substantive constraints may help insulate particular issues from interest group trading in the future. The delegation of particular issues to particular agencies therefore tends to dampen the pernicious effects of logrolling.

In short, properly understood and applied, public choice approaches can refract issues of institutional design through multiple lenses. The gloomy prognostication that greed and chaos are the major explanatory determinants of governance in the United States is not the necessary finding of public choice analysis. Stripped of ideological special pleading, simplistic application, and disciplinary hubris, public choice analyses have useful lessons for public lawyers who keep their wits about them. As with any cross-disciplinary borrowing, careful attention must be paid to both the strengths and weaknesses of the discipline borrowed and the differences between its ambitions and those of legal theory. Yet if public law lawyers are to continue to discharge their most fundamental task — the design of normatively appropriate institutions that also work — they will ignore the teachings of public choice at their peril. While lawyers often rightly pride themselves on their institutional intuition, those intuitions can be both challenged and refined by public choice analyses.

Public Choice and Reform in the Public Interest

As we have seen, certain public choice analysts, and those who translate their work into policy prescriptions, have a truly radical reform agenda. They would reinvigorate pre–New Deal constitutional doctrines to sharply constrain governmental action, interpret statutes like bond indentures, and eliminate most administrative agencies. For them, governmental action is indeed the product of either greed or chaos. And in such a world the public interest must be sought by attempting to reduce collective choices to a bare minimum.

In the foregoing pages, I have argued that this reform program is unsupported by substantial empirical investigation or normative argument. It is plausible to argue on public choice grounds that delegations of authority to administrative agencies enhance both democratic accountability and public welfare. And neither voting theory nor interest group theory gives us any substantial reason to construe all statutes narrowly or to retreat to a formalistic textualism that avoids all talk of collective purposes legislatively pursued.

But I have also argued that beyond these libertarian enthusiasms lies a public choice scholarship that raises fruitful and interesting issues concerning conventional legal understandings and the design of public institutions. In the two general areas that we have investigated, public choice approaches suggest some major issues for further investigation and reform.

The first, broadly speaking, has to do with the relationship between judicial action and majority rule. This is a conventional concern of public law, but from a public choice perspective some old questions come into a different, and sometimes sharper, focus: Is it really majority rule that is at stake in the exercise of the judicial power to review statutes for arbitrariness? Do the dynamics of pluralist politics present special threats primarily to the interests of discrete and insular minorities or to diffuse and unorganized majorities? Should judicial interpretation attempt to take account of the differing under- lying political dynamics of categories of legislation that have radically dif- ferent distributive consequences? Given the interaction of status quo points and institutional competition in a regime of separated powers, is judicial re- view a greater or lesser threat to democratic governance than judicial inter- pretation? Can a more strategic understanding of the procedural history of legislation make the use of legislative history a more reliable guide to statutory interpretation?

To each of these questions a public choice analysis provides a plausible and unconventional answer. On reflection, these answers may or may not be sound. But they are surely worth serious consideration.

The second general area concerns the political and legal accountability of administrative agencies. Here I found much to criticize in some public choice accounts, but once again valuable insights emerged. While agency policy dis- cretion has generally been viewed as a constitutionally problematic form of delegated legislative judgment, it can also be understood as solving certain pathologies in the legislative process (preeminently logrolling) and as rein- forcing an issue-oriented presidential politics. "Proceduralization" of agency action seems to have explanations both in conventional "rule of law" or "fair- ness" terms and as a part of strategic political action to monitor agency perfor- mance. Thus understood, administrative process overkill may be an all too predictable result.

In this context, "proceduralized rationality review" by the judiciary takes on a potentially ominous cast. Rather than a restrained form of legal control, essential to preserving the rule of law, judicial review may be the catalyst that transforms regulatory warfare into regulatory gridlock. When these consider- ations are combined with the political control possibilities inherent in the "separation of powers game," the basic problem for American administrative law may be transformed. Rather than the conventional goal of assuring that agency action is "according to law," the contemporary challenge may be to structure a decision process that has a reasonable capacity for authoritative action.

My argument is not that without a public choice perspective these concerns are invisible. Nor do I believe that public choice analyses often lead to a crisp resolution of what to do to make public institutions perform better. Indeed, as public choice analysts and their critics refine their perspectives, issues may appear to become more rather than less complex, and less rather than more tractable. My claim instead is that public choice consumers, critics, and analysts are together shaping a reform agenda — as well as an intellectual tool kit for addressing that agenda — that is both energizing and reconfiguring conventional debates about how collective decisionmaking is and should be conducted. In that process, we are constrained to pursue the public interest by attempting to learn from those who sometimes seem to suggest that it could not possibly exist.

Notes

1. Alexander Hamilton, James Madison, and John Jay, *The Federalist,* ed. Benjamin Fletcher Wright (Cambridge, Mass.: Harvard University Press, 1961).

2. Woodrow Wilson, *Constitutional Government in the United States* (New York: Columbia University Press, 1911), 56.

3. Ibid., 5–6.

4. Kenneth Joseph Arrow, *Social Choice and Individual Values,* 2d ed. (New Haven: Yale University Press, 1963); James M. Buchanan and Gordon Tullock, *The Calculus of Consent: Logical Foundations of Constitutional Democracy* (Ann Arbor: University of Michigan Press, 1962); George Joseph Stigler, *The Citizen and the State: Essays on Regulation* (Chicago: University of Chicago Press, 1975); William A. Niskanen, Jr., *Bureaucracy and Representative Government* (Chicago: Aldine, Atherton, 1971); Mancur Olson, *The Logic of Collective Action: Public Goods and the Theory of Groups* (Cambridge, Mass.: Harvard University Press, 1965).

5. For a generally accessible overview of the field, see Dennis C. Mueller, *Public Choice II* (Cambridge: Cambridge University Press, 1989).

6. See generally Richard B. Stewart, "The Reformation of American Administrative Law," *Harv. L. Rev.* 88 (1975): 1669–813; and R. Shep Melnick, *Regulation and the Courts: The Case of the Clean Air Act* (Washington, D.C.: Brookings Institution, 1983), 5–9.

7. Some prominent examples include Ann P. Bartel and Lacy Glenn Thomas, "Direct and Indirect Effects of Regulation: A New Look at OSHA's Impact," *J. L. & Econ.* 28

(1985): 1–25; Peter Linneman, "The Effects of Consumer Safety Standards: The 1973 Mattress Flammability Standard," *J. L. & Econ.* 23 (1980): 461–79; Sam Peltzman, "The Effects of Automobile Safety Regulation," *J. Pol. Econ.* 83 (1975): 677–725; W. Kip Viscusi, "Consumer Behavior and the Safety Effects of Product Safety Regulations," *J. L. & Econ.* 28 (1985): 527–53.

8. Bruce A. Ackerman and William T. Hassler, *Clean Coal/Dirty Air* (New Haven: Yale University Press, 1981).

9. Steven Kelman, "Public Choice and Public Spirit," *Pub. Int.* 87 (1987): 70, 93–94.

10. Geoffrey Brennan and James M. Buchanan, "Is Public Choice Immoral? The Case for the 'Nobel' Lie," *Va. L. Rev.* 74 (1988): 179, 187.

11. Ibid., 188.

12. For a discussion of these issues, see Jon Elster, *Sour Grapes: Studies in the Subversion of Rationality* (Cambridge: Cambridge University Press, 1983), 37–42.

Chapter 2

1. Michael E. Levine, "Revisionism Revised? Airline Deregulation and the Public Interest," *L. & Contemp. Probs.* 44 (1981): 179–95.

2. See E. Donald Elliott, Bruce Ackerman, and John C. Millian, "Toward a Theory of Statutory Evolution: The Federalization of Environmental Law," *J. L. Econ. & Org.* 1 (1985): 313–40.

3. See Jerry L. Mashaw and David L. Harfst, *The Struggle for Auto Safety* (Cambridge, Mass.: Harvard University Press, 1990).

4. Compare Morris P. Fiorina, "Legislative Choice in Regulatory Forms: Legal Process or Administrative Process?" *Pub. Choice* 39 (1982): 33ff., with Richard L. Doernberg and Fred S. McChesney, "On the Accelerating Rate and Decreasing Durability of Tax Reform," *Minn. L. Rev.* 71 (1987): 913–62.

5. Compare George J. Stigler, "The Theory of Economic Regulation," *Bell J. Econ. and Management Science* 2 (1971): 3–21, with Gary S. Becker, "A Theory of Competition Among Pressure Groups for Political Influence," *Q. J. Econ.* 98 (1983): 371ff.

6. See, e.g., Joseph P. Kalt and Mark A. Zupan, "Capture and Ideology in the Economic Theory of Politics," *Amer. Econ. Rev.* 74 (1984): 279–300.

7. See Daniel A. Farber, "Democracy and Disgust: Reflections on Public Choice," *Chi. Kent L. Rev.* 65 (1989): 161, 163–64.

8. Gerald H. Kramer, "The Ecological Fallacy Revisited: Aggregate-versus Individual-Level Findings on Economics and Elections, and Sociotropic Voting," *Amer. Pol. Sci. Rev.* 77 (1983): 92–111.

9. William H. Riker, *Liberalism Against Populism: A Confrontation Between the Theory of Democracy and the Theory of Social Choice* (San Francisco: Freeman, 1982).

10. See the discussion in Daniel A. Farber and Philip P. Frickey, *Law and Public Choice: A Critical Introduction* (Chicago: University of Chicago Press, 1991).

11. See generally Donald P. Green and Ian Shapiro, *Pathologies of Rational Choice Theory: A Critique of Applications in Political Science* (New Haven: Yale University Press, 1994).

12. David Schoenbrod, *Power Without Responsibility: How Congress Abuses the People through Delegation* (New Haven: Yale University Press, 1993).

Chapter 3

1. 439 U.S. 96 (1978).

2. 372 U.S. 726, 730 (1963).

3. Having abandoned "economic rationality" as a constitutional doctrine in the 1930s, the Court perhaps missed one of the major developments in economic theory since that time — developments that earned Herbert Simon the Nobel Prize. See, e.g., Herbert Alexander Simon, *Models of Man: Social and Rational* (New York: Wiley, 1957). Economic theory now recognizes that rationality is "bounded," that economic actors make decisions based on the special and often nontransferable knowledge they have. Thus, when some line of progression based on experience and knowledge is foreclosed, the worker or entreeeneur is often unable to make a lateral transfer into some larger field. Taking the "next-best alternative" may involve larger rather than marginal losses, particularly where, as may be true generally, productive intelligence is very specifically related to work experience. See generally Lester C. Thurow, *Generating Inequality: Mechanisms of Distribution in the U.S. Economy* (New York: Basic Books, 1975).

4. 198 U.S. 45 (1905).

5. Ibid. at 75 (Holmes, J., dissenting).

6. See, e.g., Gordon S. Wood, *The Creation of the American Republic, 1776–1787* (New York: Norton, 1969), 273–82.

7. See, e.g., Robert Alan Dahl, *A Preface to Democratic Theory* (Chicago: University of Chicago Press, 1956).

8. See generally James M. Buchanan and Gordon Tullock, *The Calculus of Consent: Logical Foundations of Constitutional Democracy* (Ann Arbor: University of Michigan Press, 1962).

9. Perhaps the most comprehensive catalogue of the structural and organizational deficiencies of state legislatures is to be found in Citizens Conference on State Legislatures, *State Legislatures: An Evaluation of Their Effectiveness* (New York: Praeger, 1971). For a less structural, more "political" approach to the evaluation of state legislative performance, see, e.g., *State Legislatures in American Politics,* ed. Alexander Heard (Englewood Cliffs, N.J.: Prentice Hall, 1966).

10. See, e.g., John Hart Ely, "The Wages of Crying Wolf: A Comment on *Roe v. Wade,*" *Yale L. J.* 82 (1973): 920–49.

11. See *Brown v. Board of Education,* 347 U.S. 483 (1954); *Griswold v. Connecticut,* 381 U.S. 479 (1965); *Virginia State Board of Pharmacy v. Virginia Citizens Consumer Council, Inc.,* 425 U.S. 748 (1976).

12. 425 U.S. 748 (1976).

13. *Friedman v. Rogers,* 440 U.S. 1 (1979).

14. *Bell,* 402 U.S. 535 (1971); *Stanley,* 405 U.S. 645 (1972).

15. *Vlandis v. Kline,* 412 U.S. 441, 452 (1973).

16. The basic cases are *FPC v. Texaco, Inc.*, 377 U.S. 33, 39–41 (1964), and *United States v. Storer Broadcasting Co.*, 351 U.S. 192, 204–05 (1956).

17. See Note, "The Irrebuttable Presumption Doctrine in the Supreme Court," *Harv. L. Rev.* 87 (1974): 1534, 1548–49.

18. Compare Bell v. Burson, 402 U.S. 535 (1971), and Stanley v. Illinois, 405 U.S. 645 (1972), with Mourning v. Family Publications Serv., Inc., 411 U.S. 356 (1973).

19. *Gibson*, 411 U.S. 564 (1973); *Williamson*, 348 U.S. 483 (1955).

20. 411 U.S. at 579.

21. Note, "Legislative Purpose, Rationality, and Equal Protection," *Yale L. J.* 82 (1972): 123, 135–37.

 22. Cass Sunstein has been the most vocal proponent of this view and has elaborated it in slightly different terms in a series of articles: "Naked Preferences and the Constitution," *Colum. L. Rev.* 84 (1984): 1689–732; "Constitutionalism After the New Deal," *Harv. L. Rev.* 101 (1987): 421–510; and "Interest Groups in American Public Law," *Stan. L. Rev.* 38 (1985): 29–87.

23. See generally John Hart Ely, "Legislative and Administrative Motivation in Constitutional Law," *Yale L. J.* 79 (1970): 1205–341; Paul Brest, "*Palmer v. Thompson*: An Approach to the Problem of Unconstitutional Legislative Motive," *Sup. Ct. Rev.* (1971): 95–146.

24. This seems to be the posture, for example, in *United States v. O'Brien*, 391 U.S. 367 (1968).

25. 304 U.S. 144, 152 n.4 (1938).

26. Bruce A. Ackerman, "Beyond Carolene Products," *Harv. L. Rev.* 98 (1985): 713–46.

27. See, e.g., Richard A. Epstein, "The Mistakes of 1937," *Geo. Mason Univ. L. Rev.* 11 (1988): 5–20; "An Outline of Takings," *U. Miami L. Rev.* 41 (1986): 3–19; "Toward a Revitalization of the Contract Clause," *U. Chi. L. Rev.* 51 (1984): 703–51.

28. William H. Riker, *Liberalism Against Populism: A Confrontation Between the Theory of Democracy and the Theory of Social Choice* (San Francisco: Freeman, 1982); William H. Riker and Barry R. Weingast, "Constitutional Regulation of Legislative Choice: The Political Consequences of Judicial Deference to Legislators," *Va. L. Rev.* 74 (1988): 373–401.

29. Frank H. Easterbrook, "The Supreme Court, 1983 Term-Forward: The Court and the Economic System," *Harv. L. Rev.* 98 (1984): 4–60; "Statutes' Domains," *U. Chi. L. Rev.* 50 (1983): 533–52.

30. Hans A. Linde, "Due Process of Lawmaking," *Neb. L. Rev.* 55 (1976): 197–225.

31. Kay Schlozman and John T. Tierney, *Organized Interests and American Democracy* (New York: Harper & Row, 1986).

32. See, e.g., Daniel A. Farber and Philip P. Frickey, "The Jurisprudence of Public Choice," *Tex. L. Rev.* 65 (1987): 873, 908–911; and Einer R. Elhauge, "Does Interest Group Theory Justify More Intrusive Judicial Review?" *Yale L. J.* 101 (1991): 31–110.

33. In procedural due process cases the Court has perhaps most explicitly enunciated criteria that take this form. See, e.g., Jerry L. Mashaw, "The Supreme Court's Due Process Calculus for Administrative Adjudication in *Mathews v. Eldridge*: Three Factors in Search of a Theory of Value," *U. Chi. L. Rev.* 44 (1976): 28–59.

34. For example, Note, "Specifying the Procedures Required by Due Process: Toward Limits on the Use of Interest Balancing," *Harv. L. Rev.* 88 (1975): 1510–43. See generally Ronald M. Dworkin, *Taking Rights Seriously* (Cambridge, Mass.: Harvard University Press, 1977); Charles Fried, *Right and Wrong* (Cambridge, Mass.: Harvard University Press, 1978).

35. The basic rationale for regulatory limitations of entry is "ruinous competition," that is, a situation in which all competitors will fail because continuously declining marginal costs press competitive prices relentlessly below average costs, thereby precluding profitability. For a general discussion see, for example, James C. Bonbright, *Public Utilities and the National Power Policies* (New York: Columbia University Press, 1972). This situation afflicts only a few industries requiring very large fixed investments to begin operation in relation to their incremental costs of operation. Automobile dealerships are very unlikely "natural monopolies."

36. See generally Oliver E. Williamson, "Transaction-Cost Economics: The Governance of Contractual Relations," *J. L. & Econ.* 22 (1979): 233–61.

37. Madison was both alive to the problem (Federalist 10, [J. Madison]) and too sanguine concerning the power of factions in a heterogeneous political space. See Dahl, *Preface,* 15–17.

38. 304 U.S. 144, 152 n.4 (1938).

39. When "exhuming" substantive due process three decades ago, Robert McCloskey convincingly demonstrated the similarity of that review to other areas of constitutional adjudication. "Economic Due Process and the Supreme Court: An Exhumation and Reburial," *Sup. Ct. Rev.* (1962): 34–62. He "reburied" substantive due process review only on the ground that the Court, perhaps, had too much other business. Yet one almost doubts that McCloskey himself, having so thoroughly demolished the idea that review in this area was different from other areas, could have been persuaded by that argument to cast a spadeful of earth back into the open grave.

40. *Brown,* 347 U.S. 483 (1954); *Bakke,* 438 U.S. 265 (1978).

41. See *Gaffney v. Cummings,* 412 U.S. 735 (1973) (discussing result of one-man-one-vote). Compare Lillian R. BeVier, "The First Amendment and Political Speech: An Inquiry into the Substance and Limits of Principle," *Stan. L. Rev.* 20 (1978): 299–358 (uncertainty and disorder permeates concept of freedom of speech); Robert H. Bork, "Neutral Principles and Some First Amendment Problems," *Ind. L. J.* 47 (1971): 1–35 (lack of consistent theory of scope of constitutional guarantee of freedom of speech).

42. See, e.g., Andrew S. MacFarland, *Public Interest Lobbies: Decision-Making on Energy* (Washington: American Enterprise Institute for Public Policy Research, 1976); Gary Orfield, *Congressional Power: Congress and Social Change* (New York: Harcourt Brace Jovanovich, 1975).

43. 467 U.S. 340 (1984).

44. Ibid. at 348.

Chapter 4

1. See the general discussion in Daniel A. Farber and Philip P. Frickey, "Legislative Intent and Public Choice," *Va. L. Rev.* 74 (1988): 423–69.

2. See, e.g., Jerry L. Mashaw, *Due Process in the Administrative State* (New Haven: Yale University Press, 1985), 104–08; Stephen L. Carter, "From Sick Chicken to Synar: The Evolution and Subsequent Deevolution of the Separation of Powers," *B. Y. U. L. Rev.* (1987): 719–813; E. Donald Elliott, "Regulating the Deficit After *Bowsher v. Synar,*" *Yale J. on Reg.* 4 (1987): 317–62; Geoffrey P. Miller, "Independent Agencies," *Sup. Ct. Rev.* (1986): 41–97.

3. See, e.g., *Allen v. Wright,* 468 U.S. 737 (1984) (standing); *Block v. Community Nutrition Institute,* 467 U.S. 340 (1984) (same); *Lujan v. Defenders of Wildlife,* 504 U.S. 555 (1992) (same); *Touche Ross & Co. v. Redington,* 442 U.S. 560 (1979) (implied rights of action); *Thompson v. Thompson,* 484 U.S. 174 (1988) (same).

4. See, e.g., *Middlesex County Sewerage Authority v. National Sea Clammers Association,* 453 U.S. 1 (1981); *Smith v. Robinson,* 468 U.S. 992 (1984); *Jett v. Dallas Independent School District,* 491 U.S. 701 (1989).

5. See Frank H. Easterbrook, "Statutes' Domains," *U. Chi. L. Rev.* 50 (1983): 533–52; "The Supreme Court, 1983 Term-Forward: The Court and the Economic System," *Harv. L. Rev.* 98 (1984): 4–60.

6. Gary S. Becker, "A Theory of Competition Among Pressure Groups for Political Influence," *Q. J. Econ.* 98 (1983): 371–87.

7. Jonathan R. Macey, "Promoting Public-Regarding Legislation through Statutory Interpretation: An Interest Group Model," *Colum. L. Rev.* 86 (1986): 223–68.

8. 464 U.S. 238 (1984).

9. Macey, "Promoting Public-Regarding Legislation," 252.

10. Compare Richard A. Posner, "Economics, Politics, and the Reading of Statutes and the Constitution," *U. Chi. L. Rev.* 49 (1982): 263–91, with Richard A. Posner, *The Federal Courts: Crisis and Reform* (Cambridge, Mass.: Harvard University Press, 1985), 265–93.

11. Guido Calabresi, *A Common Law for the Age of Statutes* (Cambridge, Mass.: Harvard University Press, 1980).

12. William N. Eskridge, Jr., "Politics Without Romance: Implications of Public Choice Theory for Statutory Interpretation," *Va. L. Rev.* 74 (1988): 275–338; Michael T. Hayes, *Lobbyists and Legislators: A Theory of Political Markets* (New Brunswick, N.J.: Rutgers University Press, 1981); James Q. Wilson, *Political Organizations* (New York: Basic Books, 1973).

13. The only positive theories about judging that have surfaced to date are hopelessly inconclusive. See the discussion in Robert C. Ellickson, "Bringing Culture and Human Frailty to Rational Actors: A Critique of Classical Law and Economics," *Chi. Kent L. Rev.* 65 (1989): 23–55.

14. Justice Scalia's first published attack on the use of legislative history seems to have been his opinion as a circuit judge in *Hirschey v. FERC,* 777 F.2d 1 (D.C. Cir. 1985). For further references to Justice Scalia's views, see Daniel A. Farber and Philip P. Frickey, *Law and Public Choice: A Critical Introduction* (Chicago: University of Chicago Press, 1991), 89, n. 3.

15. For a more elaborate discussion, see William N. Eskridge, Jr., "The New Textualism," *U.C.L.A. L. Rev.* 37 (1990): 621–91.

16. Kenneth A. Shepsle, "Congress Is a 'They,' Not an 'It': Legislative Intent as an Oxymoron," *Int'l. Rev. L. and Econ.* 12 (1992): 239–56.

17. Matthew D. McCubbins, Roger G. Noll, and Barry R. Weingast, "Legislative Intent: The Use of Positive Theory in Statutory Interpretation," *L. and Contemp. Probs.* 57 (1994): 3–37.

18. Barry R. Weingast and William J. Marshall, "The Industrial Organization of the Congress; or Why Legislatures, Like Firms, Are Not Organized as Markets," *J. of Pol. Econ.* 96 (1988): 132–61.

19. See, e.g., Keith Krehbiel, *Information and Legislative Organization* (Ann Arbor: University of Michigan Press, 1991).

20. William N. Eskridge, Jr. and John Ferejohn, "The Article I, Section 7 Game," *Geo. L. J.* 80 (1992): 523–64.

Chapter 5

1. Richard B. Stewart, "The Reformation of American Administrative Law," *Harv. L. Rev.* 88 (1975): 1667–813; Cass R. Sunstein, "Factions, Self-Interest, and the APA: Four Lessons since 1946," *Va. L. Rev.* 72 (1986): 271–96.

2. Murray Edelman, *The Symbolic Uses of Politics* (Urbana: University of Illinois Press, 1964).

3. Gerald E. Frug, "The Ideology of Bureaucracy in American Law," *Harv. L. Rev.* 97 (1984): 1276–1388.

4. Ibid. at 1278.

5. Matthew D. McCubbins, Roger G. Noll, and Barry R. Weingast, "Administrative Procedures as Instruments of Political Control," *J. of L. Econ. & Org.* 3 (1987): 243; and "Structure and Process, Politics and Policy: Administrative Arrangements and the Political Control of Agencies," *Va. L. Rev.* 75 (1989): 431–82.

6. Stephen G. Breyer, *Regulation and Its Reform* (Cambridge, Mass.: Harvard University Press, 1982).

7. See "Report of the Special Committee on Supreme Court Proposal," *ABA J.* 23 (1937): 882–85; and Roscoe Pound, "The Future of Law," *Yale L. J.* 47 (1937): 1–13. For the response, see James M. Landis, "Crucial Issues in Administrative Law," *Harv. L. Rev.* 53 (1940): 1077–1102; Louis L. Jaffe, "Invective and Investigation in Administrative Law," *Harv. L. Rev.* 52 (1939): 1201–45; and particularly Charles Woltz, ed., *Administrative Procedure in Government Agencies* (Charlottesville: University of Virginia Press, 1967).

8. As is generally well known, the Supreme Court has invalidated a delegation of authority as too broad in only two cases in its history. See *Panama Refining Co. v. Ryan*, 293 U.S. 388 (1935); and *A. L. A. Schechter Poultry Corp. v. United States*, 295 U.S. 495 (1935). Although the Court's statements concerning the vitality of the nondelegation principle both before and since 1935 suggest a vigorous constitutional restraint (see, e.g., *Field v. Clark*, 143 U.S. 649 [1892]), the doctrine is in fact very nearly an empty formalism. See, e.g., *Yakus v. United States*, 321 U.S. 414 (1944); *Arizona v. California*, 377 U.S. 546 (1963).

9. See *Humphrey's Executor v. United States*, 295 U.S. 602 (1935).

10. James T. Patterson, *Congressional Conservatism and the New Deal: The Growth of the Conservative Coalition in Congress, 1933–1939* (Lexington: University of Kentucky Press, 1967); Elihu Root, "Address of the President," *ABA J.* 2 (1916): 736–55; Frank J. Goodnow, "Private Rights and Administrative Discretion," *ABA J.* 2 (1916): 789–804.

11. Arnold M. Paul, *Conservative Crisis and the Rule of Law: Attitudes of Bar and Bench, 1887–1895* (Gloucester, Mass.: Peter Smith, 1976); William C. Chase, *The American Law School and the Rise of Administrative Government* (Madison: University of Wisconsin Press, 1982); Baron Gordon Hewart, *The New Despotism* (London: E. Benn, 1929); and James M. Beck, *Our Wonderland of Bureaucracy: A Study of the Growth of Bureaucracy in the Federal Government, and Its Destructive Effect Upon the Constitution* (New York: Macmillan, 1932).

12. *Joint Anti-Fascist Refuge Committee v. McGrath,* 341 U.S. 123 (1951) (decisions affecting rights in accordance with due process); *American School of Magnetic Healing v. McAnnulty,* 187 U.S. 94 (1902) (judicial testing of legality of altering rights).

13. Louis L. Jaffe, "Invective and Investigation in Administrative Law," *Harv. L. Rev.* 52 (1939): 1201–45.

14. Sanford H. Kadish, "Methodology and Criteria in Due Process Adjudication — A Survey and Criticism," *Yale L. J.* 66 (1957): 319–63; Jerry L. Mashaw, *Due Process in the Administrative State* (New Haven: Yale University Press, 1985); and G. Edward White, "Allocating Power Between Agencies and Courts: The Legacy of Justice Brandeis," *Duke L. J.* (1974): 195–244.

15. *NLRB v. Hearst Publications,* 322 U.S. 111 (1944).

16. Theodore J. Lowi, *The End of Liberalism: Ideology, Policy, and the Crisis of Public Authority* (New York: Norton, 1969).

17. Kenneth Culp Davis, *Administrative Law Treatise,* 2d ed. (San Diego: K. C. Davis, 1978), §3:15; Henry J. Friendly, *The Federal Administrative Agencies: The Need for Better Definition of Standards* (Cambridge, Mass.: Harvard University Press, 1962) (discussing standards for prior administrative adjudications).

18. Charles A. Reich, "Individual Rights and Social Welfare: The Emerging Legal Issues," *Yale L. J.* 74 (1965): 1245–57; and "The New Property," *Yale L. J.* 73 (1964): 733–87.

19. Henry J. Friendly, " 'Some Kind of Hearing,' " *U. of Pa. L. Rev.* 123 (1975): 1267–1317; and Doug Rendelman, "The New Due Process: Rights and Remedies," *Kentucky L. J.* 63 (1975): 531–674.

20. *Association of Data Processing Service Organizations, Inc. v. Camp,* 397 U.S. 150 (1970) (standing); *Abbott Laboratories v. Gardner,* 387 U.S. 136 (1967) (ripeness); *Citizens to Preserve Overton Park, Inc. v. Volpe,* 401 U.S. 402 (1971) (reviewability).

21. Stephen F. Williams, " 'Hybrid Rulemaking' Under the Administrative Procedure Act: A Legal and Empirical Analysis," *U. of Chi. L. Rev.* 42 (1975): 401–56.

22. Jerry L. Mashaw and David L. Harfst, "Regulation and Legal Culture," *Yale J. on Reg.* 4 (1987): 257–316.

23. Jerry L. Mashaw and Richard A. Merrill, *Administrative Law: The American Public Law System,* 2d ed. (St. Paul: West, 1985).

24. John Hart Ely, *Democracy and Distrust: A Theory of Judicial Review* (Cambridge, Mass.: Harvard University Press, 1980).

25. Jerry L. Mashaw, "Administrative Due Process as Social-Cost Accounting," *Hofstra L. Rev.* 9 (1981): 1423–52; and "The Supreme Court's Due Process Calculus for Administrative Adjudication in *Matthews v. Eldridge*: Three Factors in Search of a Theory of Value," *U. of Chi. L. Rev.* 44 (1976): 28–59.

26. See, e.g., *Heckler v. Campbell,* 461 U.S. 458 (1983).

27. For a discussion of the "due process revolution," see Jerry L. Mashaw, *Due Process in the Administrative State* (New Haven: Yale University Press, 1985). For a discussion of the "rational process" paradigm for administrative rulemaking, see Colin S. Diver, "Policymaking Paradigms in Administrative Law," *Harv. L. Rev.* 95 (1981): 393–434; and James V. DeLong, "Informal Rulemaking and the Integration of Law and Policy," *Va. L. Rev.* 65 (1979): 257–356.

28. Joseph Vining, *Legal Identity: The Coming of Age of Public Law* (New Haven: Yale University Press, 1978).

29. Daniel A. Farber and Philip P. Frickey, "The Jurisprudence of Public Choice," *Tex. L. Rev.* 65 (1987): 873–927; William H. Panning, "Formal Models of Legislative Processes," in *Handbook of Legislative Research,* ed. Gerhard Loewenbert, Samuel C. Patterson, and Malcolm E. Jewell (Cambridge, Mass.: Harvard University Press, 1985), 669–97; Mark Kelman, *A Guide to Critical Legal Studies* (Cambridge, Mass.: Harvard University Press, 1989); and Herbert Hovenkamp, "Legislation, Well-Being, and Public Choice," *U. of Chi. L. Rev.* 57 (1990): 63–116.

30. Mathew D. McCubbins, Roger G. Noll, and Barry R. Weingast, "Administrative Procedures as Instruments of Political Control," *J. of L. Econ. & Org.* 3 (1987): 243–77; and "Structure and Process, Politics and Policy: Administrative Arrangements and the Political Control of Agencies," *Va. L. Rev.* 75 (1989): 431–82.

31. McCubbins et al., *Va. L. Rev.* 75 (1989): 431, 435–40.

32. See *Block v. Community Nutrition Institute,* 467 U.S. 340 (1984).

33. *Bowsher v. Synar,* 478 U.S. 714 (1986); *Northern Pipeline Construction Co. v. Marathon Pipe Line Co.,* 458 U.S. 50 (1982).

34. James A. Gross, *The Making of the National Labor Relations Board: A Study in Economics, Politics and the Law* (Albany: State University of New York Press, 1974).

35. Jerry L. Mashaw, "Disability Insurance in an Age of Retrenchment: The Politics of Implementing Rights," in *Social Security: Beyond the Rhetoric of Crisis,* ed. Theodore R. Marmor and Jerry L. Mashaw (Princeton, N.J.: Princeton University Press, 1988), 151–75.

36. Charles C. Ames and Steven C. McCracken, "Framing Regulatory Standards to Avoid Formal Adjudication: The FDA as a Case Study," *Cal. L. Rev.* 64 (1976): 14–73.

37. *United States v. Storer Broadcasting Co.,* 351 U.S. 192 (1956); *Federal Power Commission v. Texaco,* 377 U.S. 33 (1964); *Heckler v. Campbell,* 461 U.S. 458 (1983).

38. *Executive Order No. 12,498,* 50 Fed. Reg. 1036 (1985).

39. Frederick R. Anderson, *NEPA in the Courts: A Legal Analysis of the National Environmental Policy Act* (Baltimore: Johns Hopkins University Press, 1973).

40. Eugene Bardach and Lucian Pugliaresi, "The Environmental Impact Statement vs. the Real World," *Pub. Int.* 49 (1977): 22–38; Glen O. Robinson, "Access to Government Information: The American Experience," *Fed. L. Rev.* 14 (1983): 35–66.

41. Indeed, the process did not really begin until about 1970 in *Automotive Parts &*

Accessories Association v. Boyd, 407 F.2d 330 (D.C. Cir. 1968). For further developments, see James V. DeLong, "Informal Rulemaking and the Integration of Law and Policy," *Va. L. Rev.* 65 (1979): 257–356.

42. *Sierra Club v. Costle,* 657 F.2d 298 (D.C. Cir. 1981).

43. *Motor Vehicle Manufacturers Association v. State Farm Mutual Insurance Co.,* 463 U.S. 29 (1983).

44. James Q. Wilson, ed., *The Politics of Regulation* (New York: Basic Books, 1980).

Chapter 6

1. 143 U.S. 649, 692 (1892).

2. Ibid., at 693.

3. E.g., The Brig Aurora, 11 U.S. (7 Cranch) 382 (1813).

4. E.g., *United States v. Grimaud,* 220 U.S. 506 (1911).

5. 276 U.S. 394 (1928).

6. Ibid. at 409 (emphasis added).

7. Louis L. Jaffee, *Judicial Control of Administrative Action* (Boston: Little, Brown, 1965), 51–62.

8. 293 U.S. 388 (1935).

9. Ibid., at 430.

10. 295 U.S. 495 (1935).

11. Ibid. at 550 (Cardozo, J., concurring).

12. 321 U.S. 414, 423 (1944).

13. See, e.g., *Arizona v. California,* 373 U.S. 546 (1963).

14. Theodore J. Lowi, *The End of Liberalism: Ideology, Policy, and the Crisis of Public Authority* (New York: Norton, 1969).

15. Ibid. at 125–26.

16. Ibid. at 148–55.

17. John Hart Ely, *Democracy and Distrust: A Theory of Judicial Review* (Cambridge, Mass.: Harvard University Press, 1980).

18. Ibid., at 133–34.

19. *Industrial Union Department,* 448 U.S. 607, 671 (1980); *Donovan,* 452 U.S. 490, 543 (1981).

20. 448 U.S. at 685 (Rehnquist, J., concurring in judgment).

21. 452 U.S. at 546 (Rehnquist, J., dissenting).

22. Morris P. Fiorina, "Legislative Choice of Regulatory Forms: Legal Process or Administrative Process?" *Pub. Choice* 39 (1982): 33–50; and *Congress: Keystone of the Washington Establishment,* 2d ed. (New Haven: Yale University Press, 1989); Peter H. Aranson, Ernest Gellhorn, and Glen O. Robinson, "A Theory of Legislative Delegation," *Cornell L. Rev.* 68 (1983): 1–67.

23. William H. Riker and Steven J. Brams, "The Paradox of Vote Trading," *Amer. Pol. Sci. Rev.* 67 (1973): 1235–47.

24. David Schoenbrod, *Power Without Responsibility: How Congress Abuses the People through Delegation* (New Haven: Yale University Press, 1993), 103.

25. See, generally, Isaac Ehrlich and Richard A. Posner, "An Economic Analysis of Legal Rulemaking," *J. of Leg. Studies* 3 (1974): 257–86.

26. See, generally, Michael C. Jensen and William H. Meckling, "Theory of the Firm: Managerial Behavior, Agency Costs and Ownership Structure," *J. of Financial Economics* 3 (1976): 305–60.

27. 467 U.S. 837 (1984).

28. Ibid., at 865.

29. Ibid., at 865–66.

30. See, e.g., Eugene Bardach and Robert A. Kagan, *Going by the Book: The Problem of Regulatory Unreasonableness* (Philadelphia: Temple University Press, 1982).

31. Kenneth A. Shepsle and Barry R. Weingast, "Structure-induced Equilibrium and Legislative Choice," *Pub. Choice* 37 (1981): 503–19.

32. Pierre Hansen and Jacques-François Thissen, "Outcomes of Voting and Planning: Condorcet, Weber, and Rawls Location," *J. of Pub. Econ.* 16 (1981): 1–51.

33. Richard Zeckhauser, "Majority Rule with Lotteries on Alternatives," *Quart. J. of Econ.* 83 (1969): 696–703; and Alan Gibbard, "Manipulation of Voting Schemes: A General Result," *Econometrica* 41 (1973): 587–601.

Chapter 7

1. Thus, when Judge Henry J. Friendly gave his influential Holmes Lectures, *The Federal Administrative Agencies: The Need for Better Definition of Standards* (Cambridge, Mass.: Harvard University Press, 1962), his title defined a problem to which his answer was a clearer enunciation of agency policy in the course of rendering adjudicatory decisions.

2. Here again Judge Friendly provides an instructive example. Eleven years after his exhortation to agencies to enunciate standards in adjudication, he reversed a decision of the National Labor Relations Board doing just that on the ground that the rulemaking process was a superior vehicle for policy development and that it was, therefore, an abuse of discretion for the board to announce new policies via adjudication. *Bell Aerospace Co. v. NLRB*, 475 F.2d 485 (2nd Cir. 1973), reversed *NLRB v. Bell Aerospace Co.*, 416 U.S. 267 (1974).

3. Kenneth Culp Davis, *Administrative Law Treatise*, 1st ed., Supp. (San Diego: K. C. Davis, 1970), §6.15.

4. Perhaps the most famous of these critiques was Murray Weidenbaum's estimate that the yearly costs of federal regulation were more than one hundred billion dollars. Murray L. Weidenbaum, "On Estimating Regulatory Costs," *Regulation* May/June 1978: 14–17. The estimate was hardly noncontroversial. *See* Mark J. Green and Norman Waitzman, *Business War on the Law*, rev. ed. (Washington, D.C.: Corporate Accountability Research Group, 1981), 33–40 (detailing the empirical flaws of Weidenbaum's calculation).

5. See, e.g., Antonin Scalia, "Back to Basics: Making Law Without Making Rules," *Regulation* July/August 1981: 25.

6. See Merrick B. Garland, "Deregulation and Judicial Review," *Harv. L. Rev.* 98 (1985): 505–91.

7. See, generally, Thomas O. McGarity, "Some Thoughts on 'Deossifying' the Rulemaking Process," *Duke L. J.* 41 (1992): 1385–1462.

8. Jerry L. Mashaw and David L. Harfst, *The Struggle for Auto Safety* (Cambridge, Mass.: Harvard University Press, 1990), 10–11.

9. Terrence M. Scanlon and Richard A. Rogowsky, "Back-Door Rulemaking: A View from the CPSC," *Regulation* July/August 1984: 8–27.

10. Sidney A. Shapiro and Thomas O. McGarity, "Reorienting OSHA: Regulatory Alternatives and Legislative Reform," *Yale J. on Reg.* 6 (1989): 1–63.

11. Richard J. Pierce, Jr., "The Unintended Effects of Judicial Review of Agency Rules: How Federal Courts Have Contributed to the Electricity Crisis of the 1990s," *Admin. L. Rev.* 43 (1991): 7–29.

12. Barry B. Boyer, "The Federal Trade Commission and Consumer Protection Policy: A Postmortem Examination," in Keith Hawkins and John M. Thomas, eds., *Making Regulatory Policy* (Pittsburgh: University of Pittsburgh Press, 1989), 93–132.

13. "Symposium: Assessing the Environmental Protection Agency After Twenty Years: Law, Politics, and Economics," *L. & Contemp. Probs.* 54 (1991): 1–374.

14. Fred Emery, "Rulemaking as an Organizational Process" (report prepared for the ACUS, 1982).

15. See Stephen G. Breyer, "Judicial Review of Questions of Law and Policy," *Admin. L. Rev.* 38 (1986) 363, 393n93.

16. For an accessible introduction, see Eric Rasmusen, *Games and Information: An Introduction to Game Theory*, 2d ed. (Cambridge, Mass.: Blackwell, 1990).

17. Here the basic arguments parallel Mancur Olson, *The Logic of Collective Action* (Cambridge, Mass.: Harvard University Press, 1971), 53–65.

18. Let G = probability that G.M. sues and C = probability that Chrysler sues. If G.M. is to be willing to mix in equilibrium, it must find the two alternatives over which it is mixing (randomizing) equally desirable; that is, its expected profit from suing, 2.0C, must equal its expected profit from not suing, $3.0 + 0 (1 - C)$. Solving this equation yields C = .67. By a symmetrical argument, G = .67 as well. Hence the probability of at least one suit is .91 $(1 - .33^2)$.

19. The recent outpouring of articles concerning the *Chevron* case is illustrative. The loss of forests necessary to make the paper to print all of the articles written on the proper standard of review in interpreting statutes following this case might well have justified requiring the Supreme Court to issue an environmental impact statement along with the opinion. See, e.g., Thomas W. Merrill, "Judicial Deference to Executive Precedent," *Yale L. J.* 101 (1992): 969–1034; Maureen B. Callahan, "Must Federal Courts Defer to Agency Interpretations of Statutes? A New Doctrinal Basis for *Chevron U.S.A. v. Natural Resources Defense Council*," *Wis. L. Rev.* 1991: 1275–99; Gary J. Edles, "Has *Steelworkers* Burst *Chevron*'s Bubble? Some Practical Implications of Judicial Deference," *Rev. Litig.* 10 (1991): 695–712; Cass A. Sunstein, "Law and Administration After *Chevron*," *Colum. L. Rev.* 90 (1990): 2071–2120; Laurence H. Silberman, "*Chevron*—The Intersection of Law and Policy," *Geo. Wash. L. Rev.* 58 (1990): 821–28; Richard J. Pierce, Jr., "*Chevron* and Its Aftermath: Judicial Review of Agency Interpretations of Statutory Provisions," *Vand. L. Rev.* 41 (1988): 301–14; Eric M. Braun, Note, "Coring the Seedless Grape: A Reinterpretation of *Chevron U.S.A. Inc. v. NRDC*," *Colum. L.*

Rev. 87 (1987): 986–1008; Kenneth W. Starr, "Judicial Review in the Post-*Chevron* Era," *Yale J. on Reg.* 3 (1986): 283–312.

20. The Occupational Safety and Health Act, 29 U.S.C. §651 et seq., and the Consumer Product Safety Act, 15 U.S.C. §2051 et seq., are prominent examples. It is hardly clear what Congress had in mind in applying the substantial evidence rule to informal proceedings. It was perhaps merely a compromise between those who supported the bills, along with their logical corollary of informal rulemaking subject only to review for "arbitrariness", and those who opposed the legislation and wanted at least to hamper its effectiveness through the use of formal procedures for rulemaking that would actuate the "substantial evidence" rule under the APA. The judges who had to deal with this compromise were not pleased. See *Industrial Union Department AFL-CIO v. Hodgson*, 499 F.2d 467, 469 (D.C. Cir. 1974), where Judge McGowan lamented that "[t]he federal courts . . . surely have some claim to be spared additional burdens deriving from the illogic of legislative compromise."

21. Veterans' Judicial Review Act, Pub. L. No. 100–687, 102 Stat. 4105, Div. A (1988).

22. *Universal Camera Corp. v. NLRB*, 340 U.S. 474 (1951).

23. Antonin Scalia and Frank Goodman, "Procedural Aspects of the Consumer Product Safety Act," *U.C.L.A. Rev.* 20 (1973): 899–934.

24. Here one is reminded of Judge Harold Leventhal's suggestion in *Greater Boston Television Corp. v. FCC*, 444 F.2d 841, 851–52 (D.C. Cir. 1970), cert. denied 403 U.S. 923 (1971), that courts reviewing agency actions are looking for some "combination of danger signals" that might justify close scrutiny and perhaps a reversal or a remand. In his view, the review function "combines judicial supervision with a salutary principal of judicial restraint," an awareness that agencies and courts together constitute a "partnership" in the furtherance of the public interest and are "collaborative instrumentalities of justice." These sentiments are echoed in the Attorney General's Committee on Administrative Procedure, Administrative Procedure in Government Agencies, Senate Doc. No. 8, 77 Cong., 1st Sess. 75–76 (1941).

The difficulty of combining deference and skepticism in the proportions that Congress intended through some verbal formulation of the scope of judicial review was put in rather exasperated form by Judge Brown in *American Petroleum Institute v. EPA*, 661 F.2d 340, 349 (5th Cir. 1981): "In summary, we must accord the agency considerable, but not too much deference; it is entitled to exercise its discretion, but only so far and no further; and its discretion need not be ideal or even, perhaps, correct so long as not 'arbitrary' or 'capricious.' "

25. John M. Mendeloff, *The Dilemma of Toxic Substance Regulation: How Overregulation Causes Underregulation at OSHA* (Cambridge, Mass.: MIT Press, 1988), 115–16.

26. George L. Priest, "Private Litigants and the Court Congestion Problem," *B.U. L. Rev.* 69 (1989): 527–59; George L. Priest and Benjamin Klein, "The Selection of Disputes for Litigation," *J. Legal Stud.* 13 (1984): 1–55.

27. And surrender may not work, as the recent reversal of OSHA's very watered-down toxic exposures rule demonstrates. 29 C.F.R. §1910 (1989). See also my critique of Mendeloff: Jerry L. Mashaw, Book Review, "The Dilemma of Toxic Substance Regula-

tion," *Rand J. of Econ.* 19 (1988): 486–94. See also Sidney A. Shapiro and Thomas O. McGarity, "Not So Paradoxical: The Rationale for Technology-Based Regulation," *Duke L. J.* 1991: 729–52.

28. Bruce M. Owen and Ronald Braeutigam, *The Regulation Game: Strategic Use of the Administrative Process* (Cambridge, Mass.: Ballinger, 1978).

29. See, e.g., *Board of Governors of the Federal Reserve System v. Investment Company Institute,* 450 U.S. 46 (1981); *Investment Company Institute v. SEC,* 401 U.S. 617 (1971); *Investment Company Institute v. FDIC,* 815 F.2d 1540 (D.C. Cir.), cert. denied, 484 U.S. 847 (1987); *Investment Company Institute v. C. T. Conover,* 790 F.2d 925 (D.C. Cir.), cert. denied, 479 U.S. 939 (1986).

30. See, generally, Henry H. Perritt, "Negotiated Rulemaking Before Federal Agencies: Evaluation of Recommendations by the Administrative Conference of the United States," *Geo. L. J.* 74 (1986): 1625–1717; Frederick R. Anderson, "Negotiation and Informal Agency Action: The Case of Superfund," *Duke L. J.* 1985: 261–380; Neil Eisner, "Regulatory Negotiation: A Real World Experience," *Fed. Bar News & J.* 31 (1984): 371–76; Philip J. Harter, "Negotiating Regulations: A Cure for Malaise?" *Geo. L. J.* 71 (1982): 1–118.

31. Paul Verkuil, "Judicial Review of Informal Rulemaking," *Va. L. Rev.* 60 (1974): 185, 205.

32. See, e.g., *United States v. Nova Scotia Food Prod. Corp.,* 568 F.2d 240 (2nd Cir. 1977) (remanding FDA smoked fish regulation for failure to reveal scientific methodology underlying its proposals in notice of proposed rulemakings).

33. The Supreme Court attempted to deal with this general class of problem in *Chevron, U.S.A. v. Natural Resources Defense Council, Inc.,* 467 U.S. 837 (1984), but a voluminous literature on *Chevron* seems unified in the conclusion that the attempt has failed.

34. An impressive catalogue of legislative preenforcement review provisions was provided over a decade ago in Frederick Davis, "Judicial Review of Rulemaking: New Patterns and New Problems," *Duke L. J.* 1981: 279–96. The Davis catalogue was incomplete at the time and numerous preenforcement review provisions have been passed or amended since.

35. The 1972 Amendments to the Federal Water Pollution Prevention Control Act are typical. 86 Stat. 891, §§509(b)(1) and (2), codified at 33 U.S.C. §§1369(b)(1) and (2) (1982 and Supp. 1991). They set a short deadline (120 days) from promulgation within which a rule may be challenged. Further challenge may be based only on grounds which arose after the prescriptive period, and review in any civil or criminal proceeding for enforcement is explicitly prohibited.

Chapter 8

1. For a review of the literature and the controversy, see Robert V. Percival, "Checks Without Balance: Executive Office Oversight of the Environmental Protection Agency," *L. & Contemp. Probs.* 54 (1991): 127–204.

2. See George C. Eads and Michael Fix, *Relief or Reform?: Reagan's Regulatory Dilemma* (Washington, D.C.: Urban Institute Press, 1984).

3. For the conclusion that OMB review exerts substantial influence over the content of agency regulations by a scholar who agrees in principle with the need for presidential review, see Thomas O. McGarity, "Presidential Control of Regulatory Agency Decision-making," *Am. U. L. Rev.* 36 (1987): 443–89.

4. John S. Applegate, "Worst Things First: Risk, Information, and Regulatory Structure in Toxic Substances Control," *Yale J. on Reg.* 9 (1992): 277–353; John P. Dwyer, "The Pathology of Symbolic Legislation," *Ecology L. Q.* 17 (1990): 233–316; Howard Latin, "Ideal Versus Real Regulatory Efficiency: Implementation of Uniform Standards and 'Fine-Tuning' Regulatory Reforms," *Stan. L. Rev.* 37 (1985): 1267–332; David Schoenbrod, "Goals Statutes or Rules Statutes: The Case of the Clean Air Act," *U.C.L.A. L. Rev.* 30 (1983): 740–828.

5. See, generally, Jonathan R. Macey, "Separated Powers and Positive Political Theory: The Tug of War Over Administrative Agencies," *Geo. L. J.* 80 (1992): 671–703.

6. See Neal E. Devins, "Regulation of Government Agencies through Limitation Riders," *Duke L. J.* 1987: 456–500. All agencies must comply with the requirements of the National Environmental Policy Act, 42 U.S.C. §4321 et seq. (1982), and the Regulatory Flexibility Act, 5 U.S.C. §601 et seq. (1982). Compliance with the former only is subject to judicial enforcement, but routine compliance with the latter is also expected. These general analytic requirements in broad framework statutes are added to the specific, and sometimes highly technical analytic, requirements built into particular agency statutes.

7. See, generally, Richard J. Lazarus, "The Neglected Question of Congressional Oversight of EPA: Quis Custodiet Ipsos Custodes (Who Shall Watch the Watchers Themselves)?" *L. & Contemp. Probs.* 54 (1991): 205–39.

8. See, e.g., Matthew D. McCubbins, Roger G. Noll, and Barry R. Weingast, "Structure and Process, Politics and Policy: Administrative Arrangements and the Political Control of Agencies," *Va. L. Rev.* 75 (1989): 431–82.

9. Michael Asimow, "Nonlegislative Rulemaking and Regulatory Reform," *Duke L. J.* (1985): 381, 424. The Consumer Product Safety Commission is perhaps the best example of congressional mandating of innovative procedural requirements that ultimately proved disabling. Apparently hoping to infuse the new CPSC both with the zeal of outsiders for safety regulation and with the expertise of those have long experience with particular products, the Congress gave the CPSC unique procedures by which members of the public could petition for the promulgation of rules and through which outside "offerors" could develop the substance of those rules. Both the petition and the offeror processes turned into procedural nightmares (for a description, see Teresa M. Schwartz, "The Consumer Product Safety Commission: A Flawed Product of the Consumer Decade," *Geo. Wash. L. Rev.* 51 [1982]: 32–95), and both were ultimately repealed by a Congress dissatisfied with the pace of CPSC regulation. But that same Congress then substituted new and additional procedures and analytic requirements.

10. Thomas O. McGarity, *Reinventing Rationality: The Role of Regulatory Analysis in the Federal Bureaucracy* (Cambridge: Cambridge University Press, 1991), 289.

11. See Erik D. Olson, "The Quiet Shift of Power: Office of Management and Budget Supervision of Environmental Protection Agency Rulemaking Under Executive Order 12,291," *Va. J. of Nat. Res. L.* 4 (Fall 1984): 1–80b. See also Thomas O. McGarity,

"Presidential Control of Regulatory Agency Decisionmaking," *Am. U. L. Rev.* 36 (1987): 443–89.

12. See, e.g., *Sierra Club v. Costle,* 657 F.2d 298 (D.C. Cir. 1981); Bob Davis, "What Price Safety? Risk Analysis Measures Needed for Regulation, but It's No Science," *Wall Street Journal,* Aug. 6, 1992: A1, col. 6.

13. Bruce A. Ackerman and William T. Hassler, *Clean Coal/Dirty Air* (New Haven: Yale University Press, 1983), argue that a fair amount of the delay and incoherence of the EPA's wet-scrubber rule resulted from political influence exerted by two powerful senators.

14. Compare Bernard Rosen, *Holding Government Bureaucracies Accountable* (New York: Praeger, 1982), 21; and Kenneth W. Clarkson and Timothy J. Muris, *The Federal Trade Commission since 1970: Economic Regulation and Bureaucratic Behavior* (Cambridge: Cambridge University Press, 1981), 34, with Barry R. Weingast and Mark Moran, "Bureaucratic Discretion or Congressional Control? Regulatory Policymaking by the Federal Trade Commission," *J. of Pol. Econ.* 91 (1983): 765–800.

15. See Neal E. Devins, "Regulation of Government Agencies through Limitation Riders," *Duke. L. J.* 1987: 456–500.

16. It is, however, clear that agencies are better able to protect themselves from congressional intervention if they shift policymaking into a formal adjudicatory format. See, e.g., *Pillsbury Co. v. FTC,* 354 F.2d 952, 963–65 (5th Cir. 1966). Only in the extreme case in which congressional intervention forces an agency to decide on grounds not authorized by its governing statute is congressional political interference likely to be considered legally illegitimate. See, e.g., *D.C. Federation of Civic Associations v. Volpe,* 459 F.2d 1231, 1245–49 (D.C. Cir. 1971), *cert. denied,* 405 U.S. 1016 (1972).

17. See Margaret Gilhooley, "Executive Oversight of Administrative Rulemaking: Disclosing the Impact," *Ind. L. Rev.* 25 (1991): 299–350; Thomas O. McGarity, "Presidential Control of Regulatory Agency Decisionmaking," *Am. U. L. Rev.* 36 (1987): 443–89; Paul R. Verkuil, "Jawboning Administrative Agencies: Ex Parte Contacts by the White House," *Colum. L. Rev.* 80 (198): 943–89.

18. The OMB had made considerable strides in regularizing its own processes and eliminating opportunities for undisclosed "conduit" communications by the mid-1980s. The breakdown in presidential congressional relations and the activist posture of the (Quayle) Council on Competitiveness, however, rekindled suspicion and internecine warfare. See Deborah R. Hensler, "Taking Aim at the American Legal System: The Council on Competitiveness's Agenda for Legal Reform," *Judicature* 75 (1992): 244–50; Vice President Danforth Quayle, "Agenda for Civil Justice Reform in America," Address Before the American Bar Association (Aug. 13, 1991), in *N.J. L. J.* (Aug. 29, 1991); Kenneth Victor, "Quayle's Quiet Coup," *Nat'l J.* (July 6, 1991), 1676; "Quayle Council Recommends Killing Recycling Provision in Incinerator Rule," *Env't Rep. (BNA)* 21 (1990): 1595–96.

19. The basic model is borrowed from McCubbins et al., "Structure and Process."

20. *INS v. Chadha,* 462 U.S. 919, 967–1003 (1983) (White J., dissenting).

21. See, generally, Jonathan R. Macey, "Separated Powers and Positive Political Theory: The Tug of War Over Administrative Agencies," *Geo. L. J.* 80 (1992): 671–703; Harold Hongju Koh, "Why the President (Almost) Always Wins in Foreign Affairs:

Lessons of the Iran-Contra Affair," *Yale L. J.* 97 (1988): 1255–342; Stephen Breyer, "Reforming Regulation," *Tul. L. Rev.* 59 (1984): 4–23.

22. Robert A. Kagan, "Adversarial Legalism and American Government," *J. Pol'y Analysis & Management* 10 (1991): 369–406.

23. Using a different game-theoretic model, Eskridge and Ferejohn reach similar conclusions. William N. Eskridge, Jr., and John Ferejohn, "Making the Deal Stick: Enforcing the Original Structure of Lawmaking in the Modern Regulatory State," *J. L. Econ. & Org.* 8 (1992): 165–89.

24. See, e.g., Jonathan R. Macey, "Organizational Design and Political Control of Administrative Agencies," *J. L. Econ. & Org.* 8 (1992): 93–110, and the authorities therein cited.

25. James O. Freedman, *Crisis and Legitimacy: The Administrative Process and American Government* (Cambridge: Cambridge University Press, 1978).

Index